STARTING YOUR CAREER
AS A FREELANCE
ILLUSTRATOR OR
GRAPHIC DESIGNER

BY MICHAEL FLEISHMAN

ALLWORTH PRESS
NEW YORK

© 2001 Michael Fleishman

05   04   03   02   01   5   4   3   2   1

Published by Allworth Press
An imprint of Allworth Communications
10 East 23rd Street, New York, NY 10010

Copublished with the Graphic Artists Guild

Cover and interior design by Jennifer Moore, James Victore Inc, New York, NY
Cover and interior illustrations © 2001 Michael Fleishman
Page composition/typography by Sharp Des!gns, Inc., Lansing, MI

ISBN: 1-58115-199-3

LIBRARY OF CONGRESS CATALOGING-IN-PUBLICATION DATA
Fleishman, Michael, 1951–
Starting your career as a freelance illustrator or graphic designer /
by Michael Fleishman
p.   cm.
ISBN 1-58115-199-3
1. Commercial art—Vocational guidance. 2. Graphic arts—Vocational guidance. I. Title
NC1001 .F58 2001
741.6'023'73—dc21
2001005296

Printed in Canada

For Joanne, for our boys, for me

TABLE OF CONTENTS

20 | MARKETING ON THE WEB 239

ACKNOWLEDGEMENTS

Thanks to all the folks who added their unique insights and seasoned comentary—your valuable input was most appreciated. I am indebted to the following friends, family, and colleagues for their generous help, expert advice, and words of wisdom: Roger Brucker, Norton Gusky, Larissa Kisielewska, Robert Saunders, Randy Glasbergen, Matt McElligott, Marti McGinnis, Mark Monlux, Jay Montgomery, Ilene Winn-Lederer, Todd M. Williams and Kevin R. Horner, Peter Zale, Robert Zimmerman, Dan Johnson, Ryan Osborne, MaryAnn Nichols and Juda Kallus, Ward Schumaker, Elwood Smith.

Here's to Stephanie Norris, Julie Robinson, and all the Keystroke Kops: Amanda Allmandinger, Ty Cooper, Bridget Crimeans, Valerie Lawson, Jason McCauley, Corina St. Martin, Micah Sitzman, Casey Telger, Mark Wells.

My great thanks to Tad Crawford and Nicole Potter at Allworth Press, to Jennifer Moore, to Susan Conner and all the folks who contributed to the first editions of this book.

If this book had a bibliography, at the top of the list would be *Starting an Online Business for Dummies* (IDG Books Worldwide Inc.) by Greg Holden. This was a great resource and cross reference for chapter 19, and I highly recommend it.

And finally, to my wife Joanne Caputo, and my sons Cooper and Max; because family is what counts when you absolutely, positively have to get your book written overnight.

➡ INTRODUCTION

There have been many changes in the profession since this book first appeared as two separate volumes for another publisher. There have also been big changes for me personally, but you'll have to wait for my epic masterpiece *Starting Your Career As a Full-Time Husband and Parent* to hear these tales.

Professionally, the biggest shockwaves have been ushered in by the computer and the Internet: digital illustration and design, the advent of online portfolio sites, the proliferation of stock art and royalty-free image banks. We have not developed the vaccine to successfully beat spec work, all-rights contracts, and work-for-hire yet, but the fight continues. Another point of note: Let's not forget sophisticated, efficient—and reliable—communications and delivery systems that have dumped the global market right in your own backyard.

So a brave new world is here, but I remember my first professional efforts very clearly. Not long out of grad school, it occurred to me that freelance illustration would be a fun way to put my art to work. I bought the biggest portfolio I could find and loaded it with the best of my graduate material. Setting my sights high, I traveled halfway across the country, and dropped my "book" off at a most prestigious greeting card company (which shall remain nameless, but call me and I'll spill the beans). At the time, my pen-and-ink drawings were hardly greeting-card friendly, but I figured—hey, they'll be able to see I can draw, right?

Not only was my portfolio rejected, but it was returned with bits of somebody's lunch and manicure statically charged to the acetate. Talk about dejection! Nevertheless, I believed in that portfolio. With some evaluation and a bit of regrouping, my next stop brought me two immediate assignments for a local newspaper. It was a great kick, opening the Sunday edition at the laundromat and seeing my illustrations in print. I was freelancing, and I was hooked.

I'm still hooked. And if you're reading this, you must be fishing, at least. *Starting Your Career As a Freelance Illustrator or Graphic Designer* addresses the common problems facing those who want to open up their own shop. You may be a beginning illustrator—long on talent but short on experience—or perhaps you're a designer just getting out of school. You could be on staff and interested in branching off or you just might be a gallery artist wanting to explore a new arena.

Wherever you are on the ladder, I wanted to keep the new *Starting Your Career* realistic, honest, relevant, and up-to-date. There have been the sea of changes mentioned above, but as illustrator Ward Schumaker commented in a recent correspondence, "Those who have moved with the changes are doing quite well."

Schumaker went on to remark that there is no such thing as thinking locally, and I agree. I live in a lovely village of 4,000 people in rural Ohio but I work nationally, even internationally. The technology that has made this possible was only hinted at in the first editions of this book.

What else have I learned over the years? It matters more than ever who you know and where you stand, and in our current business climate, networking and activism just make sense. To deal with that reality, I took a bigger role in the Graphic Artists Guild (initially as a chapter rep and serving on our grievance committee; I next co-chaired the Guild's Campaign for Illustration and am now President of the At-Large chapter). For, as Schumaker says, "We must use each other to compare techniques, talk business and finances, join in solidarity, fight unfair contracts, and devise new marketing paradigms. And, of course, we must be there for our colleagues—who but a fellow illustrator (or designer) could ever understand?"

Another lesson, as designer (and master marketer) Roger Brucker will tell you: diversify, diversify, diversify. My illustration career opened the gates to a variety of new arenas for me. I work both digitally and traditionally and relish both disciplines. As you can see, I am also a writer about illustration and the arts with numerous book and magazine credits on my résumé. Since 1995, I've been teaching illustration, and administered a degree program at a local design school. I also have a regular roster of private students and teach group classes in cartooning, drawing, and computer illustration.

Illustrator Elwood Smith puts it another way. Changes in the industry, says Smith, "Have marked the beginning of a whole new opportunity for creative growth." In fact, he says, "The Creative Muse is already guiding me into areas I never dreamed of. I've been inspired to move into other areas of commercial creativity that I've been meaning to investigate (but was previously too busy to do)."

Generously salted with studio-smart tips and nuts-and-bolts information from both "young Turks" and "big guns," *Starting Your Career As a Freelance Illustrator or Graphic Designer* answers some basic questions about:

- ◘ How to find the jobs and analyze what market is right for you
- ◘ Ways to stay ahead of the competition and pick up new business
- ◘ How to get noticed
- ◘ What art directors want to see
- ◘ How to network, get referrals—and much more!

This update, like the earlier editions of the book, offers a well-rounded, personal perspective from men and women who've been there (and seen that and done that, too). The new *Starting Your Career* still presents a positive yet honest look at freelancing—both process and product. But hey, enough schmoozing already—let's get you hooked.

chapter 1

WHY SHOULD YOU FREELANCE?

Freelancing is like Christmas. Will Santa bring me a shiny new assignment today? Will one of Santa's helpers call me on the phone with a special surprise? What will I find when I unwrap the goodies in the mailbox today? Santa doesn't come every day, but each day has the potential, and that's usually enough to keep me excited until the next visit!

– Randy Glasbergen, Cartoonist and Illustrator

What is a freelancer? Defined simply, freelancers are self-employed subcontractors who market their art by the job to several buyers. That's very short and sounds just as sweet. But in the real world beyond the dictionary, a freelancer is also the office manager, secretarial pool, sales staff, marketing department, maintenance, and mail room rolled into one. The ever-growing stack labeled "Important Things That Must Be Done Right Now" lies immediately under the bowling ball, cleaver, and cream pie you'll swear you're juggling as a one-person shop.

Common to all freelancers (in fact, their primary motivation) is a dedicated passion for their chosen vocation; it's more than a mere job, it's a calling. Freelancers are entrepreneurs with an independent spirit, a sense of adventure, and their own bold vision of success. Come April 15th, freelancers benefit from the same tax breaks any small business enjoys. And, like small business owners, freelancers don't want to work for somebody else (indeed, there is a certain pride one only gets from working for yourself). A freelance business is the vehicle to exercise your particular talents as your own boss, in your environment of choice, at the hours you choose.

WHAT ARE THE PLUSES AND MINUSES OF FREELANCING?

Freelancing is a demanding vocation. You're going to hustle. You'll work extended hours, and the buzzword here is "more." More hours, yes, but you can do a wider variety of more creative assignments, do more of the type of work you want to do, with the potential to earn more money in the process.

Freedom, at last. There's no time clock to punch, and it's your schedule. Providing you meet your deadlines, you decide when you go to work and for how long. No toiling "nine-to-five," unless you want it that way. The flip side to this is that the steady paycheck is history. Your money will come in dribbles, drabs, spurts, and bursts. You will finally understand the true meaning of the terms "accounts receivable" and "accounts payable." Boys and girls, can you say "cash flow"? What you knew as professional security at your full-time position is not applicable here, as freelancing can be a bit of an emotional and fiscal roller coaster ride. Jobs may not be steady; you may miss a meal or two. You won't land every exciting assignment you pursue, and you'll have to take some mundane jobs simply to pay the bills.

A freelancer must have great reserves of self-discipline; if you don't, you won't be working this time next year. Say a fond "good-bye" to that grumpy manager staring over your shoulder. Look in the mirror and meet a tough new employer. And that salesman's gig your dad was always telling you about? Congratulations, you got the job! Marketing and self-promotion will become very important to you. Like it or not, we should emphasize right now that this is a business! However, the worlds of art and commerce can be quite compatible— how else are there so many successful illustrators out there?

Many people actually believe that because you freelance from home, you're not really working. As your business takes off, you'll be working alone, without the feedback and camaraderie of coworkers, weathering the peaks and valleys minus the support system of an office or staff. Outside your door, the competition is awesome—in numbers and ability. But you're up to the challenge, right? Your new boss thinks so.

Good organizational skills will be crucial. While it is the art that'll be your bread and butter, realize early that an artist's beret is only one hat you'll be wearing. Remember your coworkers at Chaingang, Slavemine, and Sweatshop? All those people, doing all those things. Working all day. Getting it all done. Those are all your responsibilities now.

Drawing must be your love—something enjoyed with all your heart, something you need to do, something you would do purely for yourself without pay. When you come right down to it, how many folks can say they truly love their work? As a freelance illustrator, you can—and that's the biggest plus of all.

HOW DO I FIND OUT IF I HAVE THE RIGHT STUFF FOR FREELANCING?

If you bought this book, you have more than a vague curiosity about going out on your own. That's a good sign right there. You won't be required to break the sound barrier every workday, but ask yourself these questions and think about the following points:

What are you getting out of this? Why are you doing it? Question your motives and answer honestly. You can make a nice hunk of change freelancing, but you could also win the lottery before you create the next *Simpsons*. If you want to freelance just for some easy "big bucks," you're in for a rude surprise. And do you have the special skills that translate into that moneymaking opportunity? Your business exists only to profitably practice your craft. Without talent, even a superbly structured framework won't take you very far.

Do you have the drive and ambition to turn that skill into a success? Talent without drive and motivation does not generate income. A dream without desire cannot be fulfilled. Freelancing should be what you *have* to do—for your soul and your checkbook.

How's your business acumen? If you have little or no sense of how to run a business, it's time to learn. On-the-job training will teach you the hard way; better to read, research, and study before you become the one-minute manager.

Are you self-disciplined? It's easy to be excited about getting the cover of *Time* magazine. The great assignments spark an energy that feeds itself. But behind the glitter of those "important" jobs lies your everyday world. As a freelancer you must diligently face the small daily drudgeries with the same aplomb shown those "bigger" responsibilities. A poor attitude will cripple your workday. Lackadaisical habits will get you into trouble very quickly.

There will be mundane tasks and tiresome chores, and your commitment lies here as well. You may be bored by those simple jobs that cover the rent, but you must have the determination to see them through, to make sure they're done right. You should attend to all the "little" tasks with a healthy, positive spirit. There may come a day when you can pick and choose only the select commissions while delegating lesser responsibilities to your assistants. Until then, can you do grunt work and think in the long term?

Are you decisive? As the Lord High Everything, you'll be making all of many decisions and taking responsibility for the consequences. Remember, you are the boss. And, hey, boss—does taking a risk scare you? If you can't even chance a response, you've answered the question already! Without being cute, freelancing is risky business. After all, it is your time, your energy, and your money being poured into this venture. Professionally, no one else goes down the tubes with you if you fail; personally, you and your family have much to lose. Outside your studio, it's not a controlled experiment. You may well ask how much luck figures into the equation. I'm one of those who believe that luck is that moment when preparation meets opportunity. You minimize the gamble with sweat and organization, but there are no guarantees and lots of variables. You have to be willing to wager a bet to reap the reward.

Can you tolerate a fair amount of rejection? Unfortunately, this is a fact of life for every freelancer up and down the ladder. You will get rejected for many reasons, those misjudgments regarding your abilities probably being the least of your worries. In simplistic terms, the creative director looks at your work and says, "Can I sell my product with this art? Will I make my point by using this illustration?" If the answer is no, your work will be rejected.

When all is said and done, it is the portfolio that counts. Remember that rejection is the downside of an isolated opinion, a particular preference. It's not the gospel. I won't kid you, rejection hurts. But if you have faith in yourself and your ability, it will never kill. Create an inner strength from your substantial talent, and draw from it. Rejection is simply part and parcel to freelancing. Can you handle it?

The decision to assign any illustration usually comes down to the best (read: most appropriate) illustrator to meet that job's particular needs. Serendipity—being in the right place at the right time—is your good fortune, but beyond your control. It's nothing to brood over, nothing you can fine tune. Knowing somebody within the organization can help, but doesn't always. Your politics don't often enter into the scenario (unless your politics are synonymous with your work).

It's not that they won't like your tie—unless you give new meaning to bad grooming or dress like you just lost a bet. You shouldn't lose work because of casual (but tasteful) attire. Assuming you haven't provoked an international incident or insulted anyone's sainted mother, you won't lose an assignment because "they hate you" (always for some vague, undetermined reason).

At some point an artist's personality can certainly influence the art buyer's decision, and that winning smile is to your definite benefit. Obviously, the two parties must interact, so personalities can't be avoided. However, if you don't have the style and skills the task requires, you won't get an assignment on pure congeniality.

Attitude and reputation will be factored into the equation, too. Art directors are looking for skilled individuals who can deliver the goods on time. Your samples may sizzle and glow, but if you're an argumentative prima donna who can't meet a deadline, you're not a viable commodity. Be down to earth, be yourself. Be dependable, be on time, be flexible. No matter how small the assignment or business, always do your best job.

Can you thrive on competition? They're out there. They're good. They're waiting for you. While this may sound like the promo to a bad slasher flick, it's really not hype or horror. The small army of your skilled peers is tremendously talented, hard-working, and organized. In general, I've found the competition to be a rather loose and friendly fraternity. We do play the same game, in the same ball-park. But your comrades-at-arms won't all act like your bosom buddies, nor is that a requirement in their job description.

Competition in free enterprise is the American way. Use it as your motivation, and you'll have an edge. Have a keen and healthy esteem for your competition. Respect their work, and keep your eyes open: Know what your associates are doing by researching the trade magazines, creative directories, and annuals. Don't be a rubber stamp of the hot new style, but do know what's current. A key to real success is to offer something that's original and fresh—something the buyer can't get just anywhere, from just anybody. And as Matt McElligott says, "It's vitally important to be true to yourself." Combine this with good service, strengthen it all with determination and forethought, and your competition will not be so scary after all.

How do you handle stress? Keep the following buzzwords in mind when pondering the considerable tensions of freelancing: grace under pressure . . . flexibility . . . rolling with the punches . . . shooting from the hip . . . adaptability . . . creativity . . . thinking on your feet. I could go on, but you get the picture.

If you rattle like nuts in a jar when the pressure builds, you're going to be in trouble. The landlord is banging on your studio door; you're certain there'll be a horse's head in your bed the next morning if you don't pay the rent. A once-generous deadline screams at you from the calendar, while that simple watercolor wash becomes a life-or-death situation. Panicky?

How's your bankbook? In times of low pay, slow pay, or (heaven forbid) no pay, can you—should you—support yourself and your business with personal savings? Realistically, how long should you do this if your business is new, not up to speed, or in a lull?

My accountant tells me to have a reserve of at least three months in the bank just in case, but everyone's situation is slightly different; your safety net might be a year or six months. The numbers will vary, but a hard fact of economics remains constant: Can you launch and sustain your business if you're not generating income?

Initially, it may be wiser for you to freelance as a sideline, with outside employment (full- or part-time) smoothing the rough financial edges. It's no crime to build towards independence, rather then leaping romantically, albeit imprudently, into the fray.

Do you mind working alone? Hopefully you have a stunning relationship with the only one sharing your work space—you. Art school is a pleasant memory now—the halls buzzing with kindred spirits spilling into the comfortably familiar studios, a common ground, awaiting the arrival of teachers and students with a singular purpose and shared excitement. That glorious phase of your life's education is over.

At first you'll laugh, as if at a dumb joke, but you'll discover that it's really true: You'll need to get out and practice those "real world" skills! Life away from the studio, with friends and acquaintances who make actual conversation (and not necessarily shop talk) helps balance the isolation. Outside interests temper the hours spent hunched over the drawing table keeping your own company. Seek activities and nurture a support system outside the studio. You may very well be your own best friend, but don't go at it alone.

How do you feel about selling yourself? Aside from your artistic responsibilities, this is a salesperson's job. It's a fairly simple situation (at least on paper): You must bring in the work to sustain the business that satisfies your creative impulse.

WOULD A STAFF POSITION BE MORE HELPFUL AT FIRST?

Working on staff always provides invaluable training and experience, and a "hardcore" design student with good illustration skills has no problem. But these days (at least outside of the major metropolitan areas), staff illustration jobs may not exist anymore.

"I run into this trying to recommend a career path for my students who don't want to leave the area," says illustrator and educator Matt McElligott. And this author agrees; as an instructor at a Dayton, Ohio–area design school, I always have students who lean more towards illustration than design. I advise those more-provincial students to take a designer's position and actively campaign within the ranks for every illustration assignment they can. Once working, you can freelance outside the job and evaluate your true ambitions from this position of security and strength.

A staff job is a perfect atmosphere to hone your skills and perfect your art, and I strongly suggest it. Likewise, you'll need an economic cushion when initiating your freelance venture, so a staff job is a sensible first step.

Benton Mahan, an Ohio illustrator with years of staff and freelance experience, states unequivocally, "I think it's almost impossible to freelance right out of school—or start cold—and make a good income without doing something else. It's helpful to have the stability, that regular income [of a staff position] when you first start out."

Where better to learn and grow, to discover who you are and where your direction lies? However, development is directly proportionate to a nurturing and challenging environment. You must interview with your eyes open and a look to the future.

A staff position can be the perfect place to meet and make contacts (but not beg, borrow, or steal clients). But a staff job won't necessarily teach you about the business of freelancing. Unless you interact with those freelancers contracting with your company, you may have no idea about how these independents actually operate.

If you're a staffer and wish to prepare for freelancing, work yourself into assignments that involve freelancers—and don't balk at added responsibilities; seek them out.

You can gain valuable negotiating skills by sitting at the other side of the table as the art buyer. Relating to clients takes on a new perspective when you are the client yourself.

By getting a job into print, you'll balance brainstorm and budget, guide the bright idea into actual camera-ready art, and deal with the printer to get the desired results on the page. Keeping that aesthetic dream from becoming a lithographer's nightmare garners you technical expertise and practical information about printing costs and pricing.

A staff position can definitely work to your advantage as a freelancer; it's a smart choice. If you're inclined to go this route, you'll be in good company.

MAKING THE BREAK TO FREELANCING

First discuss it with your boss. As long as there are no conflicts of interest with house accounts and your freelancing doesn't interfere with your staff work, there shouldn't be any problem.

But perhaps it's a house rule that staff may not freelance. When you signed your contract, you agreed to abide by company regulations, so honor those terms. Don't believe a discreet, covert operation will remain your little secret for long. The artistic community is smaller than you might think; I guarantee that it'll catch up to you.

It's been said that it's better to look for a new position while you still have your old job. It makes a lot of sense, and only you can decide when (and if) you're ready to make a complete break.

If freelancing is okay with your employer, test the water first. *Don't* leave on impulse or in anger. Instead, take a few outside assignments and, hopefully, maintain at least one substantial account. Over a period of time, get a taste of the freelance life. When you're mentally prepared, with your financial safety net in place, simply hold your nose and jump!

IS ART SCHOOL NECESSARY?

Luck may be a small factor where job opportunities are concerned, but not when we're discussing ability. To compete in this field, art education is essential. Learn the basics, pick up the tools, and gain the skills necessary to play the game well. Unless your father was Andrew Wyeth, the best place I know to learn all this (in the shortest time period, as painlessly as possible) is art school.

Is a two-year commercial art school better than a four-year art program at a university? The answer depends on your needs and attitudes, your goals and personal timetable. A two-year commercial program is designed to be focused and intense. The four-year university curriculum will be rounded and diverse.

Many university art departments sponsor a year (usually the junior year) at an affiliated commercial school. This is the best of both worlds for many students. Neither form of training is inferior to the other, so the choice of an eclectic university process versus a concentrated commercial approach must be an individual one.

DO INTERNSHIPS HELP?

They can. Of course, internships aren't for everyone. Most likely, this will be your first real taste of that particular work experience, but long hours at no pay are not universally appealing. If you're willing to invest your time and energy in some professional training, an internship can be invaluable, just the catalyst to change the course of your life and career. When available and practical to your situation, the internship can be a smart beginning move.

SELLING IT

Perhaps you dread the thought of selling your work, but feel you're best suited temperamentally to freelancing. Illustrator Ben Mahan says you are not alone: "It's just something that you have to do. Most artists can really sell themselves better than anyone else, and you must get out and sell yourself a bit. If you don't like dealing one-to-one, work through the mail. However, you'll need that personal contact, if you can make the connection."

Some artists feel that marketing their work is akin to putting their children up for sale. But first, recognize that someone is paying you to produce images for a purpose. Next, know that you are selling yourself as a problem-solver first and a person second. And if you remember that you are selling usage of the art rather than the product itself, this anxiety is easily suppressed.

Dallas illustrator Mary Grace Eubank cautions you to "realize that you're selling your work, not your soul. Read books on self-projection and confidence building. Possibly attend motivational seminars on sales techniques. Hire a rep, and stay in the background until you can develop a more positive persona."

HUSTLE AND BUSTLE

Your time schedule will hardly be regular; you'll be a slave to other people's deadlines. There will be moments so quiet you can hear a pen drip and hectic periods when twenty-four-hour days are not enough—hustling is all relative for the freelancer.

Happiness and security? It's my experience that happiness and security in freelancing are achieved by hustling. Perhaps we have given this word a bad connotation. Hustling, as I define it, is nothing more than honest, hard effort. It is aggressively and energetically plying your trade, an assertive attitude combined with a robust work ethic and a good product.

THE TEN COMMANDMENTS OF FREELANCING

1. Thou shalt learn when to say "no." If you don't like the suggestion, work it out amicably. Learn the art of compromise. Compromise is not capitulation; it leaves both parties feeling that they work well as a team. However, accept the fact that there are actually some art directors who just won't meet you halfway. These folks are not worth the headaches or heartaches. At this point, you just need to safely get out of Dodge with some style and grace.

2. Thou shalt be polite, persistent, and positive. Always communicate in a professional manner. Listen to your client. Educate your client.

3. Thou shalt strive to constantly increase your skill level and expertise. Grow and learn; get it better than the day before.

4. Thou shalt relax and have confidence in yourself. Nobody's shooting at you, and you're not doing brain surgery on your mom. Believe in yourself, and others will, too.

5. Thou shalt make it a point to have fun. Love your profession. Do what you want, work where and when you want, and work with nice people only.

6. Thou shalt have a personal life. Never feel guilty about making (and taking) time for yourself and loved ones—it's important.

7. Thou shalt always be honest and ethical. Never promise something you can't deliver, and remember: You are selling a product, not your soul.

8. Thou shalt be a good businessperson. With stars in our eyes, we key on those first four letters in the word "freelancer." The financial (and physical) costs of running and maintaining your business will quickly alert you to the realities behind the lofty conceptions. Be an informed freelancer: Protect your rights by keeping abreast of the ethical standards, laws, and tax reforms. Stay current with pricing guidelines. Learn effective negotiation skills. Maintain excellent records. Don't start a project without paperwork.

9. Thou shalt not take rejection personally.

10. Thou shalt never miss a deadline! Be late with a job, and chances are, that particular art director will never call you again.

➡

PROFESSIONAL ⬇ VIEWPOINTS

The best thing about freelancing is that every day has the potential to be exciting and rewarding. The opportunity of a lifetime could be waiting for you in the next e-mail or phone call. It may take a few years to get rolling, but once your career is established, a freelance career can be exhilarating. If you find a receptive market for your work, there's no limit to what you can earn. —Randy Glasbergen, Illustrator

I love working for myself. I earn more now than I ever thought possible (I also work harder), and best of all—there are no corporate politics. —Alyn Shannon, Designer

If you're an outgoing person who thrives on social interaction and water-cooler chat, the lonely life of a self-employed freelancer may not be right for you.
—Randy Glasbergen, Illustrator

A lot of designers decide they want to go out on their own to have "freedom." It rarely works out that way. There's always someone you have to answer to—the client who's paying the bill.
—Don Sibley, Designer

The bad news may be that we're never sure how the bills get paid, but the good news is that life is an adventure. The Taoist philosopher Lao Tsu was the first to come up with the concept of "going with the flow," meaning, don't dwell on the negative—turn your disappointments into lessons. While you're forging your path, you'll meet interesting people, you'll learn some neat stuff, and you will eventually become financially secure.
—Jennifer Berman, Illustrator

EVERYTHING THESE DAYS IS DOT-COM THIS AND DOT-NET THAT! I JUST CAN'T STAND IT ANYMORE!!!

I KNOW A WEB SITE THAT CAN HELP YOU...

© 2000 Randy Glasbergen

GLASBERGEN

"You have the right to remain silent. Anything you say may be used against you until death do you part...."

I am a solo agent at heart—I enjoy the freedoms of freelancing. It's risky going out on one's own; there is a lot of work other than the creative process to be done. But the rewards are all yours. It is the freedom to work when and where you wish, the self-determination of being able to work with only those you want to work with, driving your job in the direction that you want, the self-satisfaction of nurturing a business and watching it grow and mature. —Peg Esposito, Designer

You never know from day to day who you'll be working for, what you're going to be creating next. But a freelance illustration career is also extremely rewarding, satisfying, and exciting. It's a delicate balance, but you're never bored. That's the hook of it. It's just totally captivating. I think the positives outweigh the negatives. —Chris Spollen, Illustrator

The whole reason for my being in communications, as opposed to fine arts, was because I liked the idea of being paid for what I did. The economics fascinated me. —Kim Youngblood, Designer

chapter 2

FREELANCE ILLUSTRATION:
WHERE DO YOU START?

This is a business; no matter how artsy-shmartsy illustrators are going to be. It's called "commercial art," and it's a real name for something. But success in this business is relative. There are a lot of artists who work in a small market who may never be Mr. or Ms. Famous Illustrator, but they make a nice living. They breathe decent air, have a family and a good life, do all the things that are important to people.

— Elwood Smith, Illustrator

This is a business of people.

— Simms Taback, Illustrator, Designer, and Art Director

What is an illustrator? Steven Heller and Lita Talarico, in their book *Design Career*, succinctly define illustration as "the painting, drawing, collaging, or sculpting of an image that decorates, complements, or interprets a text or brief." Illustrator Fred Carlson broadens that definition a step further by citing illustration as "the act of creating artistic images for use in advertising, promotion, industry, manufacturing, media, or specialty publishing."

Illustration is the bridge between the mind's eye and the camera lens; the illustrator builds that bridge when an idea challenges the camera beyond its capacities. An illustrator acts as a conduit of emotion and mood that photography finds elusive. When a concept dictates looking beyond the real, illustration jumpstarts the intellectual process to capture the fantastic, to create a world where reality is only regulated by the imagination of the person pushing the media.

A graphic designer orchestrates type and visuals to communicate, sell, provoke a response, inform, or educate a mass audience. Bob Bingenheimer, former president and owner of his own design studio in Yellow Springs, Ohio, defines it this way: "Graphic designers are professionals trained in communications problem-solving through the use of typography and images. They are schooled in printing and communications technologies. Design means 'organization' and arose out of the need for an interface between aesthetics and the industrial age. The designer develops communications materials based on knowledge of communication, symbols, and communications technologies."

SHOULD YOU DO IT ALL?

"I have a concern," says Matt McElligott, "that we imply that graphic design is something easily added to an illustrator's skill set. We might not put enough emphasis on the idea that successful graphic design requires a separate and equally robust amount of training."

Illustration may be only one of your skills. Being a jack-of-all-trades—if you can cut it—would be to your distinct advantage in the beginning, when you may have to do everything to make a living. As your business takes off, you'll eventually concentrate on what you do best.

If you are an illustrator/designer, you can promote yourself as such, or simply market your illustration to some companies and design work to others. It will be easier—and smarter—to do this on a local level. Granted, it is good for an illustrator to have as much understanding of design as possible, but if you're serious about doing both, you may find it more convenient to market and advertise yourself as a designer.

As part of the team, an illustrator will do only one end of a job—the illustrations, obviously—but a designer may wear many hats on a project (including snagging the juiciest illustrations). The designer controls the creative flow, while an illustrator may not enjoy the same perks.

Of course, along with any perks come added responsibilities. Jobs can become so design-intensive, you may not do any drawing for days or weeks at a time. If you want to be an illustrator, this will present real problems, so seriously consider how you're going to sell yourself.

FINDING THE RIGHT MARKETS

How do you analyze what market is right for you? First, consider and understand what you like to do best. Then, take a walk to the local library, followed by a trip to the newsstand. Look at everything—this is serious browsing now! Study printed material to see who's doing what and how they're doing it. Research who's publishing and what's being published. Evaluate your work in light of the marketplace's current needs and trends, and take some notes.

Freelancers with strong political convictions and the passionate need to express those views will find numerous magazines—both regional and national—covering current affairs. These periodicals, plus the newspaper's op-ed section, are ideal vehicles for your art.

If you have the eye of a storyteller, look to magazine and book illustration (and to the newspaper again) to challenge that sharp sense of visual narrative.

Perhaps pictorial commentary is not your thing. A light, whimsical, or just downright funny drawing style will keep you in great demand at greeting card companies. You'll also sell to book publishers, magazines, newspapers, plus advertising agencies and design studios.

Every market mentioned above has an enormous need for a wide variety of styles and sensibilities. Look to your head and heart to tell you where your direction lies, then explore what markets fit your criteria.

THE GREAT ART-VERSUS-ILLUSTRATION DEBATE

The late N. C. Wyeth, a true virtuoso of illustration, lamented that he was—by his own estimation—"merely" an illustrator. Today, we recognize him simply as a master painter, and his oils are considered not only milestones of book illustration, but great works of art as well. I'm not saying you'll be the next Wyeth (his grandson, Jamie, already has that honor), but I think you can be both artist and illustrator. While there are those who split hairs regarding this terminology, I find the titles interchangeable.

Humorous illustrator (and *Mad Magazine* art director) Sam Viviano dislikes the label "fine" art. Viviano says, "It's as if the commercial arts are not particularly fine—in the sense of meaning good—and that the fine arts are not particularly commercial. Unfortunately, the public in general, and too many artists, buy into this." Instead, Viviano uses the terms "graphic" and "gallery" arts. "What's really different is whether one's art hangs on a wall or is intended for reproduction."

LOCAL VERSUS NATIONAL

What are the best markets for a beginner to try? Start locally and small, but with an eye on the national (yes, even international) markets and the big time. Learn to conduct business at home, and then use this training to branch out beyond your own turf.

You shouldn't limit yourself to local clients. Digital technology and modern postal/courier service have made it just as easy to get a job around the world as it is across town. But there are good markets waiting for you, and literally right down the street. Local businesses, with needs ranging from advertising or promotional material to signage and stationery, are excellent markets for the beginner. Case in point:

- ➡ The public television station may need you to energize the mailers for its current fund drive.
- ➡ Local magazines are always on the lookout for images.
- ➡ Professors at the university could use an artist to pump life into those classroom handouts for next semester.
- ➡ Your neighborhood newsletter would jump at the chance for some snappy drawings.
- ➡ Advertising agencies all over town need art on a continual basis; call them!
- ➡ The corner deli is looking for a new graphic identity.
- ➡ A dentist, interested in stationery and letterheads, also needs a catchy cartoon on the front of her check-up reminders.
- ➡ An insurance company wants to soften payment notices and complement other mailed material with humorous illustration. Their in-house magazine regularly uses visuals, too.

It's easy to see that good assignments are where you find them. Keeping that in mind, I'd look to your own backyard for those first jobs. With this invaluable experience, moving to larger markets will be that much easier.

NEW KID IN TOWN

If you're new in town, getting started again locally, or expanding your horizons regionally, publicity is the name of the game right now.

Advertise in the local newspaper. You might even consider an announcement on your cable channel's community calendar or a late-late-night television spot (when ad rates are dirt cheap). Organize that mailing program. Tell your new neighbors to spread the word around. Join the local art organizations and schmooze. Stuff mailboxes, send e-mails, or stick flyers on windshields. Check in at the chamber of commerce; maybe members can refer you to potential clients who need your work. Let your fingers do the walking and make cold calls. Get a listing in the yellow pages. The idea is to tell the business community who you are, what you do, and where to find your services.

At this point, it's a relatively short hop to go regional, but I wouldn't until you've established a home base—professionally and personally. The markets aren't going away; they'll be there when you're comfortably situated and in position to solicit their business.

LOCATION, LOCATION, LOCATION

Do freelancers who live in a big city really have a better chance at success than those who live in small towns? Regardless of location, your shot at success will not be the proverbial "piece of cake," and not too many years ago, the answer to the question would have been a resounding "yes!"

Today, the answer is still "yes." But with the rise of the Internet, modern computer/telephone technology and systems, the proliferation of phone answering services, express mail couriers (local, national, and international), an out-of-town freelancer has all the tools to effectively set up shop in any city, just about anywhere. Success can be elusive wherever you operate. Living in New York City, considered the hub of the industry, doesn't guarantee a cushy career. It's a bit like peeling the layers of an onion, and defining what qualifies you as "a success" is relative and rather subjective. The busy freelancer getting $40 to $60 an hour may be tickled to earn this money, until he talks to an illustrator making $75,000+ a year. That fellow discovers a colleague who casually drops the bomb that she earned even more while working half the assignments (and with a month's vacation to boot)! The big name illustrator she encountered who netted at least $300,000 last year awes this woman. She vows that she, too, will be "just as successful."

Your numbers may vary, but you get the picture. Your chances for success may be better by living in the big city. Without a doubt, there is more work in the right New York City block than in all of my village of Yellow Springs, Ohio. But the relaxed quality of life in this friendly, tranquil spot cannot be found anywhere in New York. It's a trade-off the artists living and working here have made without a second thought.

It's definitely easier to market your services on the spot, as opposed to marketing from a remote location. Realistically, small-town freelancers wanting to market illustration in the big city will meet challenges of time and distance their metropolitan brothers and sisters don't face. But it can be done. How? With talent, of course; but talent alone is no guarantee of success. Rather, the key is your ability plus lots of elbow grease, coupled with intensive customer service and energetic marketing and self-promotion.

WORKING WITH NEW BUSINESSES

Freelancers just starting out may look at new businesses as kindred spirits, but some words of caution here: Be careful when taking an assignment with a new business, as new businesses frequently fail and don't pay. Do your homework prior to working for any company, regardless of track record. Chances are very good that that pioneering enterprise or established organization will treat you right, but reputation—or bright promise, for that matter—is no guarantee that this firm will be a dream client.

The best offense is always a strong defense. Take good notes over the phone (if you're a terrible note-taker, buy an answering machine with two-way record). Ask incisive questions at the meeting. Be prepared to discuss your rates and evaluate how the client's needs compare with yours. It's best to clarify terms right at the start.

BIDS AND ESTIMATES

Whether you are working with new or established businesses, you will need to deal with bids and estimates. Don't be pressured into talking money or cutting the deal on the spot; when you need the time, take it. Excuse yourself for ten minutes, saying, "I'll call you back in an hour." Tell the client you'll have the figure for them on Wednesday or whatever. Just take the time to work out a realistic bid. Of course, as illustrator Robert Saunders advises, "Make sure you're not too casual, though. The reality is, it can cost you the job if a client's pressed for time."

Don't be afraid to ask for what you really need to do the assignment. Be prepared to say no and maybe lose the job. Approach all negotiations with open eyes and mind. Remember that negotiation is a bit of a game, and it's all a learning process. Nobody's shooting at you. Actually, life is one long negotiation, so you're fairly seasoned already.

Drawing up a purchase order, or written documentation of some sort, at the beginning of a job is wise. "I use an unthreatening 'order-form' style of confirmation accompanied by a faxed cover letter informally stating any remaining details," says Saunders. "I ask the client to check it over for errors and then sign if everything looks okay. This gives clients input while requiring them to take some responsibility. It's all designed to be a comfortable, routine procedure."

If for some reason you don't get a contract on the outset of an assignment (or the client is simply slow with the paperwork), do it from your end. Send a letter of confirmation yourself. This can even be a short thank-you note outlining the terms of the agreement and job specifications. You'll simply describe what you expect to furnish, how much you expect to be paid, and when—no legalese, just plain, polite talk spelling out the arrangement made between the illustrator and art buyer.

Let's say the client looks shaky for some reason and you still take the job (brave soul). You can minimize your risk by asking for payments at various points of completion. This could be half on signing and half on delivery of the finished work, or ⅓ at the beginning, ⅓ on acceptance of roughs, and ⅓ upon delivery of the final.

True, you can always build a "pain-in-the-butt" factor into your bid, raising your prices accordingly to compensate for the inevitable conflict you're about to endure. But why bother? If your experience, radar, or research tells you that a buyer is dubious, you don't really need the aggravation or the bucks. There is no adequate compensation for time spent in hell, despite the invaluable lesson learned. Better to politely decline and move on. If the potential payoff proves too alluring, know what you're getting into and strap on your seatbelt—it's going to be a long, interesting ride before you see that money.

NETWORKING

Networking is a low-key, direct means of communication that pays handsome dividends, because there is much to learn from other freelancers. The one thing everybody has (and almost always loves to give away) is advice. Yes, it's okay to seek advice; don't shy away or sniff your nose at this informal information gathering.

Your fellows are veritable storehouses of information. Frankly, it can be downright fun to compare notes with someone sharing the same experience. Most contacts enjoy talking shop and are easy to find. Start with the Internet, of course, and the proliferation of chat boards, news and discussion groups—go immediately to places like the Graphic Artists Guild Web site (*www.gag.org*) and the ispot (*www.theispot.com*). Obviously, check out your local art and design community sites as well.

If you're a traditionalist, start with the local yellow pages under "Artists" (commercial and fine arts) or "Graphic Designers." If you go national, research the creative annuals, like *American Illustration* or *The Society of Illustrators*, and talent directories, such as *American Illustration Showcase*, *Creative Black Book*, *The Graphic Artist's Guild Directory Of Illustration*, and *The Alternative Pick*. These volumes are invaluable references highlighting the best of the best. They're a wonderful source of inspiration and will supply addresses, phone numbers, Web sites, and e-mail addresses.

How to network? Regardless of method or scope, the formula is simple: Introduce yourself, make friendly conversation while asking pertinent questions, acquire other names and numbers, and then repeat the process. Keep in touch with everybody.

The results? Stimulating ideas and information, new colleagues, and fresh contacts. Dallas, Texas, illustrator Mary Grace Eubank reminds us, "I'm a firm believer in what goes around, comes around. Keep track of whom you contact, and be aware of how they can help you. Don't feel guilty about using these connections. Most artists are receptive and helpful; you must do the same."

Why network only with other illustrators? If a knowledgeable source is willing and available, talk to an editor, art/design director, copywriter, or production coordinator (even when you're not involved on a job). Don't forget typesetters or layout artists. How about the pressman at the printers? Approach the sales manager, too. If you really want some insider information, talk to any secretary, assistant, or clerk! It's medieval to believe that the illustrator is the center of the design universe when so much is accomplished by collective process. Most folks are complimented to be considered experts. If you have specific questions, why not go right to a particular source?

It should also be said that there could be a flip side to networking. Some folks simply lack interpersonal skills. Others are just plain busy; too busy to talk at length. I've also found that, while just about everybody is willing to contribute a certain amount of information regarding the business of freelancing, there are many artists unwilling to share the mechanics behind an innovative technique or unique approach.

This is justified and perfectly legitimate; it's not to their advantage to simply give this information away. Don't ask other artists to analyze or dissect their methodology for you. Don't call to promote a free drawing lesson. I have sometimes discussed materials (common window shopping) when networking, but I'll usually draw the line at an artist's technical process.

While most of your conferees will be happy to chat or will politely decline, you'll inevitably run into those who virtually accuse you of stealing state secrets. Remember that tough competition and the drive to succeed may create surprising attitudes. Credit that person for his interesting perspective, thank him for his fascinating advice, and say "good-bye."

VOLUNTEERING

Volunteering your time and/or your art services (pro bono work) to good causes is definitely a win/win situation.

Let's discuss pro bono work a bit, shall we? Some may see pro bono as merely freebies, but look at the big picture. As a volunteer, you'll gain confidence at the drawing board doing actual assignments. You'll have creative freedom without any pressures to cut the best deal, and you can design according to your vision. You will learn about deadlines and working with a client.

You acquire a printed piece for your portfolio, work experience for your résumé, and achieve name recognition. You get profitable leads, make new contacts, and establish a reputation as someone willing to go the extra mile. In addition, volunteers have the happy and satisfying experience of completing a job well done for a worthwhile purpose.

You'll find established artists donating their services, so don't look at volunteering as a simple giveaway or merely paying your dues. Far from it, it's a healthy investment of time, energy, and spirit for any artist, regardless of stature.

REFERRALS

If you do your best work, meet your deadlines, and are dependable, the referrals will take care of themselves.

Referrals come in two varieties: as leads and as references. To get a reference, you'll need a few jobs under your belt first. These referrals usually are the result of a rewarding and positive performance. The client likes your illustration and passes the word on: "This is the person to see to get the assignment done right. Call her!"

Leads often accompany references. The satisfied client above not only refers you to one compatriot, she also supplies you the name and address of yet another businessperson needing your services. A graphic designer gives you a hot tip that the design studio across town is looking for an artist of your caliber right away. You make the phone call, mention your contact, and arrange a portfolio review. You call the art director on your last job and network a little: "Do you know anybody who knows anybody who needs anybody?" This art director, more than happy to help, gives you a list of five new contacts. It's now up to you.

ORGANIZATIONS

Professional organizations you might join are: the Graphic Artists Guild, the Society of Publication Designers, the American Institute of Graphic Arts (AIGA), the Society of Illustrators, and the Illustrators' Partnership of America (IPA). Consult the City and Regional Magazine Association (CRMA), the Society of Photographers and Artist Representatives Inc. (SPAR), the Society of Typographic Arts (STA), and your local art directors club.

FIFTEEN QUICK AND EASY WAYS TO LOSE CLIENTS

➡ Be a pest. "Drop by" without an appointment or "pop in" unexpectedly.

➡ Don't return phone calls or answer your mail. Don't follow up. Delay sending requested samples. In that same spirit, arrive late for meetings.

➡ Push your wares too fast or so hard that you are insensitive to the client's needs and wants (while remaining overly sensitive to your own).

➡ Be overconfident; better yet—be arrogant or rude. Always project a negative attitude and unpleasant demeanor.

➡ Act intimidated or lack confidence.

➡ Give a slipshod, unprofessional presentation. If you still get the job after this, do sloppy work.

➡ Copy someone else's art, or present work that is not your own.

➡ Don't listen to the client; don't ask questions; then, don't follow directions.

➡ Overprice. Then, turn in a bill that's larger than the quote.

➡ Whine, whimper, or balk at suggestions.

➡ Require the client to do more work than is their responsibility.

➡ Fluster easily, panic consistently.

➡ Promise more than you can deliver; give less then what was asked.

➡ Miss a deadline.

➡ Do bad work.

➡

PROFESSIONAL ⬇ VIEWPOINTS

Graphic design has gone through some extreme changes since I graduated from college three decades ago. At that time, it was essential to be located in large cities where support services were available. Now, you can locate anywhere; no longer needing these services, we are able to do it ourselves. The "computer age" helped us reinvent the role of the designer. Now, we may wear many hats: retoucher, illustrator, typesetter, and prepress expert. With the support of new technology, faxes, overnight delivery services, phones, and the Internet, we are free to move to remote locations in search of a better quality-of-life. This works best if you have built a strong client base before you move. —Mary Ann Nichols, Designer

Illustration is everywhere. I discovered that anything—fine art, beautiful oil paintings, lithography, or woodcuts—could be considered illustration.

—Laura Cornell, Illustrator

© Joe Ciardiello 2001

It's always a little difficult when you start out. I phased into it, which I think is the best way to do it.　　—Ben Mahan, Illustrator

Starting out was a difficult, but positive experience, because I was very excited about my future as an illustrator. The excitement overpowered everything else. That motivated me to keep trying.

—Joe Ciardiello, Illustrator

The bottom line is: If you really want to do this, you'll jump any obstacles. If you want to just think of illustration as a "nice little career"—reconsider. In the beginning, there's virtually no return, just a lot of sweat equity and the idea that, at the end of the road, you're going to have this "nice little career" and enjoy it. This can pull you through, but if you were looking for an immediate, steady income, I'd say illustration is a tough gig.

—Chris Spollen, Illustrator

I'm reminded of a bit of advice we always joke about at [Graphic Artists Guild] illustration meetings: It seems like, for many of us, we owe our starts to a spouse with a steady job and great patience. When a newcomer asks about how to get started, we tell them to get married.

—Matt McElligott, Illustrator

The second best friend you can have (the first being someone who can give you a good job) is another designer or illustrator.

—Ward Schumaker, Illustrator

There is a lot of joy in trying other things, and if you are gifted enough to be successful in design and illustration—and have a huge energy level—I would say go for it. Most people have a difficult time doing so much in both areas. Possibly, there are people who do more than two areas, but I'd like to know what type of vitamins they are on and where I can get them.　　—Mike Quon, Designer, Illustrator

My goals have not changed, but my courage has increased. I set out to do good work and earn a living; it wasn't ever about getting rich (although I would be delighted if that comes along), but about having a stimulating and comfortable life. It's great if you can get it all.

—Jilly Simons, Designer

23

chapter 3

OFF ON THE RIGHT FOOT

Good design is good business.

— Overworked to death over the last decade or two. Many have claimed authorship and almost everyone has quoted it, but it's still true (maybe now more than ever).

I am not just an illustrator, not just a designer—I am involved in much more.

— Mike Quon, Designer and Illustrator

What do you need to succeed in your own design business? It's a good question, and one we will explore in depth in this chapter.

For clarity's sake, let's define the basic term *design studio*. A design studio is an entity with a definite name and identity (something as straightforward as "Sue Jones, Freelancer" would qualify, as well as the more esoteric "Chicken Soup Graphics"). These concerns would be owned by graphic designers who work primarily out of their own place of business (at home or in the studio) and do not work primarily in someone else's studio, agency, or graphic design department. The primary business would be total design, from concept to completion, rather than single aspects of production.

Regardless of whether you call yourself "Sue Jones, Freelancer" or "Chicken Soup Graphics," you are engaged in running a design studio—an endeavor fraught with many complexities. To make a go of it, you'll need to be a qualified professional and businessperson.

DO YOU HAVE WHAT IT TAKES?

The beginning of your career—before you invest your time, energy, and capital—is the best time to objectively assess your design and business skills (plus personal qualities). I assure you, this is not as silly as it may sound at first reading. During a crisis, bad year, or crunch time, too many designers question their abilities (or worse yet, realize they don't quite have what it takes) and throw in the towel. Answer this question by breaking it down into parts:

Evaluate Yourself and Your Experience

Be honest about who you are, what you can do, and how well you do it. This won't necessarily prevent headaches, heartbreak, or disasters, but it will give you a strong foundation to weather the storm. Begin with this self-evaluation:

- Design is communication. Are you an effective communicator?
- Can you market your work and promote yourself, personally sell your vision to the client, and translate your client's needs into dynamic printed materials?
- One goes to a specialist for something special—not pedestrian or cookie-cutter graphics, but striking, thought-provoking, quality work. Are you a designer capable of leading the band rather than jumping on the bandwagon?
- Do you understand (and not fear or loathe) the world of business and finance?
- Experience makes a difference. Do you have enough? There is an advantage to starting up with some experience versus diving in right out of school. There is foresight in building business gradually as a moonlighter, while working full time for someone else (some designers get work from their employer's overload or turn-downs).
- Why are you going into business for yourself? You shouldn't be doing it if you are motivated entirely by ego. Don't do it if you're after fame, fortune, or respect. And, last but not least, don't do it out of anger.

Evaluate Your Design and Production Skills

Knowing that you have the chops to do a job (and do it well) should be a given. You will need to be able to take a project from conceptualization to completion, bring in and supervise support personnel and services, and make sure that all aspects of a project are done right. Your portfolio should reflect this by showing a variety of printed samples.

If you have worked for two or more years in a graphic design studio, advertising agency, or even publishing house, chances are that you've had some experience managing projects through all phases of production. You've probably had experience dealing with vendors, suppliers, and freelancers and have acquired a lot of the know-how necessary to run your own studio. Chances are, especially if this was a small studio, you've been aware of, if not directly involved in, the firm's day-to-day operations.

To determine if you have the design and production skills necessary for going into business on your own, see if you agree with the following statements. Be honest—if you're lacking in any area, you can always work to develop additional skills or bring on a partner to supplement your abilities.

- ➡ I can render a concept and present it to a client through thumbnails, roughs, or comps.
- ➡ I know how to prepare print-ready design for a printer, color house, or service bureau.
- ➡ I can come up with dynamite visual concepts on my own.
- ➡ I can design just as well or better than my competition.
- ➡ I have good organizational abilities. I can juggle several projects at once and keep track of progress on them all.
- ➡ I can convince clients that my work can help in meeting their business objectives.
- ➡ I am quick and efficient in executing most design and production-related tasks.
- ➡ I know enough about production and printing to know when my client's request is not feasible to produce.
- ➡ I know when (and how) to suggest more cost-effective solutions to achieve a client's end goal.
- ➡ When necessary, I can design to the audience my client is trying to reach rather than just execute my own style (perhaps I even know how to identify my client's target audience).

Evaluate Your Business Skills

You will need to practice salesmanship, basic accounting, and business procedures—the kinds of things many college graduates know, but designers are less prepared for. In order to determine if you have the business and management aptitude necessary for going out on your own, see if you agree with the next statements. Again, if you're lacking in any area, you can always work to develop these skills—there are many courses and books on business management and marketing basics.

- ▶ I have good communication skills. I am familiar with business etiquette and procedures when making written and verbal contact.
- ▶ I can set reasonable goals and follow through on them.
- ▶ I am able to get along with just about anybody and can motivate others to help me with what I am involved in.
- ▶ I can sell an idea to a client.
- ▶ I make decisions quickly.
- ▶ I don't procrastinate. I work steadily instead of waiting until a few days before a project deadline.
- ▶ I can see and understand the whole picture. I don't concentrate on one thing, while ignoring other aspects of a situation.
- ▶ I have good organizational abilities. I can handle several projects at once and keep track of progress on each.
- ▶ I can juggle the projects on hand, while cultivating new business.
- ▶ I know when to turn down work.
- ▶ I can keep clients informed of the job's status and any glitches as they arise.
- ▶ I can keep track of escalating costs and inform clients when a project might exceed the budget before it actually does.
- ▶ I can work with disorganized clients.
- ▶ I can explain the design process to clients and teach them to be better clients, thus helping them be more time- and cost-efficient.

Evaluate Your Entrepreneurial Savvy

You will also have to develop strong personal skills. Juggling finance, design, and production is one thing, but you will also need to subjectively appraise your individual strengths and weaknesses. Take stock of your grit, determination, and discipline. In order to determine how you stack up, see if you agree with the statements below (and be honest—you know yourself best):

- ▶ I am confident about my design abilities. If my work is not appreciated, I can shrug it off and apply myself with confidence to other projects.
- ▶ I am a self-starter. Nobody has to tell me to get going.
- ▶ I am highly motivated. I can keep working on a project for as long as needed to complete it on time.
- ▶ I can concentrate on the task at hand. I'm not easily distracted from what needs to be done.
- ▶ I am persistent. Once I know what I want, or make up my mind to do something, almost nothing can stop me.
- ▶ I am in excellent health and have a lot of stamina and energy.
- ▶ I can put the needs of my business above my own personal needs when required.
- ▶ I can put the needs of my employees above my own needs when required.
- ▶ I can ask for help when I need more information or feel overwhelmed.

TALLY, HO!

Only you know the outcome of the above evaluations. And as you'll need these abilities to make the business work, you didn't kid yourself, right?

Tally the number of "yes" and "no" answers and see how they stack up against your potential for success. All the answers raise issues that are important to maintaining a business. If you answered "no" to only one item in each of the above sections, chances are good that you can go it alone without any help. But if you answered "no" to more than three questions or statements (or more than one in any single category), you may be taking on more than you can handle by yourself. Unless you feel you can cultivate these qualities on your own, consider finding a partner (or rep) to help in the weak areas.

IS THE OPPORTUNITY TO SUCCEED THERE?

You will need to evaluate your potential market. Is there a niche out there that you think you can fill? While it's not best to have all your eggs in one basket, it's good to have at least one major client to rely on—do you already have this client lined up? Do you have some idea of the kind of work you will be doing and the compensation you can expect?

Let's determine the size of your potential market. What type of work do you think you will be doing, and whom do you think will buy it? How many clients are out there? You need to get a realistic picture of what you do best and what you think you could be doing to get business. To help guide you in this process, ask yourself the following questions:

- What do you really like to do?
- What kind of design makes you happy?
- Are there any types of design that you dread or in which your skills are not up to par?
- What's your idea of a dream job, and what would you do gratis (just to have that type of work or client)?
- What's your design history—what were your biggest triumphs?
- What were your near-misses?
- What were biggest flops?
- Who is your competition? Think about your peers, and analyze their work.
- How many other designers are out there doing the same thing you want to do for the same kinds of clients? Realistically assess if you're able to provide better design or better service than your competition. You don't want to spend valuable time where there's little chance of gaining any business. Be a tough (but objective) critic: Who blows you out of the water? Who is the cream of the crop? Be mindful of what the competition is doing, and honestly evaluate yourself.
- Are you in a position to fill a void the competition is not filling?
- What's your current reputation? What do clients and vendors believe you have going for you? On the street, what might people hear about you, think of you and your work? Where has your work been seen? What work might they have seen?

As nebulous as it all may be, determining where you stand may make the difference between getting a job offer and getting a "try again next time, bud." You don't want to waste your time marketing stellar design capabilities to your local mechanic. However, if you have very little experience, you'll want to think twice about selling your services to the biggest corporations in town—you may not get beyond the receptionist. Until you've proven yourself, you're better off working as a freelancer with the design firms these corporations are currently employing.

WHERE ARE YOUR POTENTIAL CLIENTS?

After you've taken stock of what you want to do and where you stand relative to others doing similar work, you'll have a better idea of where to direct your marketing efforts. But you also need to ask yourself some more specific questions about your design and production capabilities. What aspects of a job do you do best? Are innovative design concepts your forte, or is meeting impossible deadlines your strongest capability?

Likewise, if there's a particular area of design that you're strongest in, you need to think about what kind of clients are in greatest need of that skill. If you're good at logo and identity work, you're better off looking into the private sector—particularly new businesses. If you're best at print advertising, you're obviously going to be knocking on the doors of all the local agencies.

Consider related areas to expand into as well. If you're a great book jacket designer, expanding into book and brochure design may not make as much sense as considering poster design—essentially a blown-up version of what you're already doing. But if you've been doing brochures, annual reports, and booklets, then magazine and book design would be a natural spin-off.

What's your design style? Is it flamboyant, or is it better suited to an attorney's office? Is your work likely to look dated in a few years, or does it have a classic feel? Or do you have a diversified style, adapting the look of your work to suit the project at hand? The look of your work, and how well you can adapt it to the image a client wants to project, has a great deal to do with where your work is best marketed. For example, your local fitness center isn't likely to be sold on portfolio samples with a decidedly sweet slant.

RESEARCH, RESEARCH, AND MORE RESEARCH

Study the creative directories and competition annuals, and note the clients of those designers whose work you admire. Scan the yellow pages. Talk to your friends to see what services other design firms market and how they price that work. Network with those other designers. Window shop downtown. Really look at who's out there doing what jobs and who is offering these plum assignments to whom. Where is woefully inadequate design being done; where is design expertise needed? Now evaluate—what clients and which assignments are in synch with your particular design vision?

YOUR CURRENT CLIENTS

If you're currently employed, but moonlighting freelance jobs, you have existing clients you can probably bank on, to some extent. Get a realistic picture of how much you can count on these clients in the future. Be frank—let them know you're considering going into business for yourself and want to know if they will continue to provide you with work.

Any client you have been working with under your current employer can be one of your clients, as long as you don't rob your employer of his existing business with this client. Can you perform a service for this client that your employer doesn't want to perform? Is this client looking to expand its business into an area in which your employer doesn't want to be involved? Let's say your employer specializes in designing annual reports and doesn't want to be bothered with the company newsletter a client is contemplating. There's no reason why you shouldn't have the opportunity to do this.

Ongoing projects like newsletters can be the mainstays for a new design studio. Check it out by gently probing for spin-offs from the projects you are currently involved in. If you have a good relationship with a client who likes your work, go for it! Of course, as designer Larissa Kisielewska cautions, "Check with your boss first, not only to be ethical and fair to your employer, but also in case the client mentions something to your design firm."

LOVE WHAT YOU DO

Once you get an idea of how to make money, it's also important to be sure that this is the type of work you really want to do and will find fulfilling. Finding your niche involves finding something that you can do well and make a living at, too. To stick with it through both lean and green times means you must truly love your work.

If you're cranking out schlock for the bucks when what really turns you on is coming up with innovative ad concepts, you won't be happy for long. You need to take care of your heart's desire as well as your livelihood if your business is going to thrive over the long haul. Look for the kind of clients who are willing to give you projects that will be personally fulfilling, as well as the ones that provide easy cash.

PROFESSIONAL ⬇ VIEWPOINTS

Most designers reach a point where they begin to feel they could do it just as well as the guy they're working for. There comes a time when maybe there's a disagreement in design philosophy or approach. And as those differences become more and more uncomfortable, you decide it's not worth it—it's definitely time to either make a move or start your own business. My partner Rex Peteet had already worked in all the best places in town, so moving to another studio wasn't an option. It was the appropriate time to go out and test the waters.

—Don Sibley, Designer

[Starting out, my goal was] to do high-visibility work and to do the best work I could—no matter what I was charging. Money wasn't a consideration. [At one time] I thought a three-figure income included the cents! My services were based on hourly rates, but mainly on the value of the work to that particular client and application. These goals haven't changed much over the years.

—Rick Tharp, Designer

I tried many times before making it—my goal for that first year was survival.

—Mike Salisbury, Designer

The biggest mistake I made was not having any clients when I started my graphic design business. From day one, I had rent, salaries, and other expenses, but no foreseeable clients. Although I finally realized what I had to do about that, I borrowed so much money while I figured it out that I spent years afterwards getting out of debt.   —Larissa Kisielewska, Designer

© Larissa Kisielewska 2001, Optimum Design & Consulting

My business developed slowly (which was fine at the time). Accommodating my clients and providing the service promised was my goal. Satisfied clients will recommend you to others, and this will help your business flourish. Happily, I still work with a number of my original clients. —Mary Ann Nichols, Designer

[The key to] making a graceful break is to avoid disrupting your former employer's business. It really comes down to just that—your employer doesn't take it personally that you chose to leave, and you shouldn't believe that "he won't like me anymore." You should do your best to look out for your former employer's business needs and interests. If you, in good faith, are trying to do that, you will have a graceful parting. —Tom Nicholson, Designer

It really does take an amazing amount of discipline and drive to make it. If you don't have that, or if you're just accustomed to working for somebody else and you're a nine-to-five kind of person, the chances of really making it are pretty slim. —Rex Peteet, Designer

chapter 4

CREATING
A PLAN FOR YOUR
BUSINESS

Work, study, learn, and learn. I think I have learned some valuable lessons: (1) Don't go into business without business, (2) you must promote if you want to eat, (3) don't spend more than it takes to get the job done . . . ever, (4) don't do things you're not qualified to do, and (5) don't burn any bridges—employers and employees can all turn out to be clients someday.

— Mike Salisbury, Designer

Now, it's time to develop a working plan detailing why you want to be in business, what you expect to achieve, and how you intend to make it all gel. We'll examine how you'll do what you do—whether it be working alone or forming a partnership or corporation—and how to handle the myriad responsibilities involved (sales, client service, design time, production management).

We'll also discuss services you'll need to buy regularly (such as printing, photography, copywriting, illustration, etc.) and look at your present vendors, contacts you'll need to make, plus the costs of these services.

Think of the next section as a combination wish list/mission statement. It will help you evaluate your goals plus gauge your commitment to, attitude toward, and satisfaction from your chosen venture. Why do this little exercise? Your new business must be fueled by perception and passion as well as profits, otherwise, it will certainly become a mere chore or, worse yet, a losing battle.

So, what do you *really* want and why? Get in touch with yourself and your values. What's your perception of a successful business? Simply making ends meet? Having the freedom to take time off and do your own thing as often as you wish? Or throwing yourself into a labor of love that will consume all of your time and energy?

DECIDE WHAT YOU'RE GOING TO DO

Set goals that reflect your personal and professional values. In order to determine what you want and will be most comfortable with, ask yourself some questions. Write down your answers, and try to be as specific as possible in defining what you want. Don't edit yourself at first; just get your ideas down. Then, review them for realism.

Why are you in this business, and what are your personal aims? Is it an extension of something you enjoy doing as a hobby? Do you want more creative freedom and control over your design projects than you had under your employer? Do you want public or peer recognition for your work? Do you expect to make more money? Do you want financial security?

What are you putting into this enterprise—just your wallet or your heart and soul? Are you making a wholehearted commitment or just looking to get by?

What are your business objectives? Do you want to break even after two years? Have twenty regular clients in three years? Increase billings a certain percentage each year? Win at least five design awards each year? Make enough to pay bills and eat? Manage a staff?

What do you want from your personal life? Owning your own business is often a delicate balancing act. Your obligations to your family can have profound bearing on your business and on whether that business will serve a local or national clientele. A workaholic slaving away long hours at the studio (or a jet-setter with a hectic travel schedule) will surely be missing in action on the home front.

It's important to be realistic about your personal expectations and abilities. If you're looking for security, starting a design business that is based solely on the talents of its owner is not the place to find it. Your business would immediately be in jeopardy if you became injured or ill and could not work.

SET GOALS

You've done some soul searching, and you're in touch with your personal and professional aspirations. Now, it's time to set goals that reflect those values.

Figure out what you need to earn. You'll want to figure on making enough to meet your current salary level at some point in the near future. If you're the sole breadwinner in your household, this is especially important. Project yourself into the future, and get an idea of what you want to be earning and when you need to attain this income level. If you've made a sizable investment in equipment and other start-up expenses, you'll also want to determine when the payback will be. In this chapter (and chapter 6), you'll find out how to draw up a financial plan to help do this, but for now, get an approximate figure and date in mind.

Decide how much time to put into your business. If you have very few personal obligations and are extremely ambitious, you may want to invest fifty to sixty hours a week. This would give you the opportunity to bill out a lot of your time and still spend a large portion of it cultivating additional business. But if you have parenting obligations, you probably have some limitations imposed on your time already. Be realistic about how much time you can allot per week before you figure on where your business efforts are best spent.

Now, determine what your image will be. Is it important to you to set a standard to which your peers will aspire? Do you want to do the kind of cutting-edge design featured in the awards annuals? Or is your business a spin-off from your hobby—something with which to make some extra bucks?

If maintaining a high profile in the design community is very important to you, you'll want to set goals based on that aspiration. If you want to do trendsetting work, you'll probably want the design freedom that comes with occasional pro bono work; paying clients frequently want what's safe and traditional, and they will pay only for getting the design they want, not the design you want to give them.

You'll have to determine what's most important. It's hard to do the kind of design jobs that allow you to do the most expressive work (possibly pro bono) when you're trying to pay off the studio equipment you're currently financing. It's just as hard to make a sizable salary if you only have thirty hours per week to devote to billable work.

DECIDE HOW YOU WILL MAKE IT WORK

Now, you'll want to consider the basic configuration of the studio. Can you go at it alone, should you take on a partner, or will you need to create a team? If you need additional people or services to supplement your design skills, how do you find them and where? You'll also be doing many administrative and marketing tasks beyond design and production. There's a lot to do, somebody has to do it, and it must be done with organization and efficiency.

One of the best ways to get a handle on how you're going to get started is to draft a work plan. Organize your time and prioritize the tasks that need to be done at the onset of the business. Divide your time into three basic areas:

- ◘ *Promotional:* This category includes all activities you engage in while trying to obtain business. These activities include researching potential clients; follow-up calls to past clients; time spent on self-promotional mailings, cold calling, and designing your logo and business materials.

- ➡ *Billable:* In this category is all time that can be billed to a client—every task and every aspect of completing a job that you know you will be paid for when a job is finished.
- ➡ *Administrative:* Ongoing tasks, including day-to-day and month-to-month things like paying bills, invoicing clients, ordering supplies, and running errands, are considered administrative tasks.

Now, come up with a yearly plan. Analyze where your time is needed and for how long. You'll want to factor in more time for acquiring business when you're just starting out—you won't be needing much time to complete projects if you don't have any clients, right? You'll also want to allow for more administrative time while you're setting up shop—for instance, looking for studio space, buying equipment, and setting up accounts.

Then, break your yearly plan into twelve monthly plans that include a realistic projection of where your efforts will be best spent and how much time you'll spend in each arena. You may want to also take into account seasonal ebbs in the industry and vacation time (will August typically be a slow month and a good time to take a two-week vacation?). The point is, organizing your priorities gives you a guide to where your time will be best spent and allows you to project a realistic goal for your gross income after a year of doing business.

To set up your monthly plan, start first with an idea of how you'll be spending your time on a weekly basis. As a start-up business, plan to spend 20 hours in promotion, 10 in administrative needs, and another 10 in billable hours within a 40-hour week. Multiply your weekly figure by four to get an idea of your monthly time allotment for each segment of your business. Continuing with the numbers above, out of those 160 hours in one month, 80 would be spent in promotion, 40 in administration, and the remaining 40 in billable time. (See chapter 7 for an example of a one-year projection.)

A chart like this will also give you an idea of where you may need help. Let's say that after six months your promotional efforts are yielding more business than you ever dreamed possible. You feel that you're spending so much time cranking out work that you're robbed of the hours you need to keep track of billing and other administrative responsibilities. You'll know then that it's time to consider hiring someone part-time to help in production or administration.

Charting time spent on billable hours will also give you an opportunity to set goals for your business income. If you spend 40 billable hours a month on your business at the onset and you intend to charge an average of $50 per hour for your time, you can expect your income before expenses to be $2,000. Perhaps you've set a goal for an average of 100 billable hours per month. By the end of your one-year plan, at $50 per hour, you can look forward to hauling in $5,000 per month. Sound good? You bet!

Don't just work up these figures during your start-up period and then throw them in a drawer. Keep reviewing and refining them. If your plans aren't working, why? What do you need to change?

CHOOSE A BUSINESS STRUCTURE

There are various legal and tax considerations involved in choosing a structure for your business. You may choose to establish a sole proprietorship, a partnership, a corporation, or a limited liability company.

If you're in business as a sole proprietor, the business is *you*. You personally garner all the profits, and you personally are responsible for any losses, legal liabilities, and business obligations. No formal papers need be drawn up when you begin operation. You'll file a Schedule C (Profit or Loss from Business or Profession) along with your 1040 come tax time, and your social security number will act as your business identification number. You can get a Federal ID number to protect the use of your social security number; it's free and obtained through a one-page faxed questionnaire.

In a partnership, profits, losses, legal liabilities, and business obligations are shared. You'll want to draw up a partnership agreement, and you'll need to obtain a federal ID number. Income or loss is reported on a form 1065 and schedule K-1. The K-1 schedule flows over into your 1040, and you pay taxes at your personal tax rate.

A corporation will safeguard you against personal liability. Legal action against Chicken Soup Graphics, Inc. is not an action against an individual of that studio. Personal assets can't be touched should the business go sour or if your partner gets the firm into hot water.

A corporation is much like a person in the eyes of the law—an entity separate from the owners. As a salaried shareholder, you are an employee of the corporation and must file legal papers and obtain a federal ID number.

The first stage of incorporation is known as a "C" corporation (and should you incorporate, you are automatically a C corporation). In general, C corporation tax rates are higher than personal tax rates. Estimate your income—it might be to your advantage to do business under one of the other designations (do consult an accountant here, as the process—and decision—can get complicated).

Once incorporated, a business can then elect to become an "S" corporation. The S corporation tax structure allows the corporation to be treated almost like a sole proprietorship or partnership, avoiding double taxation. Income from an S corporation is reported on the shareholder's tax return through form K-1.

An S corporation is taxed similarly to a partnership, in that you will pay taxes at your personal tax rate. However, you have better liability protection with an S corporation over a partnership.

The "limited liability company" (LLC) is a fairly new entity formed in the mid-nineties. Like a corporation, this tax structure offers 100 percent liability protection, but only sets you back $85 in fees (forming a corporation usually runs about $500). Reporting as an LLC is easy— you simply use a schedule C along with your 1040 (just like a sole proprietor).

Dayton, Ohio, accountant Todd M. Williams, a CPA at Hammerman, Graf, Hughes, and Co., strongly suggests all sole proprietors become an LLC. "A limited liability company can have one member or many," he says. "You have personal liability coverage and the same reporting requirements, all at a substantial cost savings. And there are no separate 1065 or 1120 tax forms, which mean lower tax fees paid to your accountant."

Examine the procedures involved in running a corporation. Study the tax laws, pension plans, and savings options available. Consider the legal pros and cons. The decision must be based on your specific situation, and as you do your homework, it will be readily apparent that expert legal and financial guidance will be needed.

Incorporation is a legal procedure, requiring an attorney—your accountant cannot incorporate you. But visit your accountant before you visit a lawyer. A lawyer is going to ask questions about taxes and accounting. Why do you want to incorporate? Do you have a federal ID number? Unless you see your accountant to secure those facts and figures, you may not have the answers for your attorney.

If you think that incorporation is the way to go, then double-check with your attorney to see if he agrees. In fact, if you are an illustrator or designer with minor assets, your lawyer may not recommend this—there simply may be no need for such protection. And yes, you can file papers of incorporation yourself, but you'll probably find the attorney's fee will be money well spent (usually in the general neighborhood of $500).

As a last thought, grow into a corporation, don't rush into it.

PARTNERSHIP PITFALLS

Do you need a partner? Do you want a partner? Let's discuss this by first offering a simple definition. A partnership is two or more people getting together and combining their assets and talents to form a business enterprise. Partners may offer numerous benefits, such as:

- Capital
- Business acumen or creative prowess
- An established clientele
- Moral support
- Fresh ideas
- In-house feedback
- Complementary skills
- The ability to run the studio when you're away

A partnership can be a simple form of business. All you need is a handshake—you don't even have to have a formal written arrangement—and you can be partners. Thus, dissolution of a partnership is relatively easy—but notice, I did not say it was painless. A business advisor may steer you away from such a venture. The problem is that a partnership has unlimited liability. So does a sole proprietorship, but many designers will tell you that sole proprietors work to preserve their own best interests. With a partnership, there's another individual ostensibly acting as part of the team. Sadly for many failed partnerships, this teamwork turns out to be pure illusion.

A partnership could be equated to a working friendship (and we all know the joys and pitfalls of close friendships). Perhaps a more appropriate metaphor is to compare a partnership to a marriage; just like a spouse, you'd better know your

SELECTING A LAWYER

Use the following guidelines when looking for your personal legal eagle:

➡ Obviously, look for a lawyer with some experience with graphics arts issues, such as copyright, work-for-hire, and intellectual property rights.

➡ Don't wait for push to come to shove. Have your legal representative on call before you go into business. You'll also need this individual to draft papers of incorporation or partnership if you decide that you want to structure your business in one of these ways.

➡ Don't engage a "babysitter" to calm your jangled nerves. You need to hire a lawyer who knows his way around the courtroom. You want a lawyer who can draw up a bulletproof agreement.

➡ Can we talk? Good communication skills are important. Your attorney should fully explain strategies and unfamiliar terminology and never sound patronizing.

➡ A referral makes for a nice lead, but not a blind decision. Shop around and interview three lawyers, at least. Spend money on an initial consultation—it will be worth it in the long run.

➡ Avoid a lawyer who shuffles your case to a junior partner after your interview. Ask at the interview stage who in the firm would be handling your case.

➡ If the lawyer is not upfront about his billing of services, don't hire him. An honest lawyer will return unused portions of the retainer you paid at the start of the case when the case is closed or terminated.

➡ Don't hire a litigation-happy barrister. You don't need or want a Perry Mason wannabe. If an attorney says he rarely settles out of court, he may prolong your case and drain your wallet.

➡ Study the lawyer's contract. Negotiate terms, if need be, and don't be in a hurry to sign.

➡ If he makes the point that he's "too busy," "swamped," or "overworked," forget the guy. Move on to your next interview.

business partner. Married life can be pain and/or pleasure. Divorce is invariably traumatic and devastating. So goes a partnership. Writing in *HOW* magazine, Joyce Stewart recommends, "Never just 'become partners' with another designer without developing a formal business agreement for the partnership. That's like marrying a blind date before you've met!"

Be smart. Write a practical, detailed document that will govern the arrangement of a partnership and address the very real issues of organization (who, what, when, where, how); goals and purpose; assets and contributions; how you will share profits (and losses); how you will divide responsibilities; accounting procedures; specifications of legal and financial powers; grievance procedures, dispute resolution, mediation and arbitration; dissolution procedures because of sale of interest, business termination, withdrawal, death, or expulsion of a partner; and growth procedures.

While it seems an exercise in morbidity to discuss some of this in those heady first days of the firm, that's exactly the right time. Change is inevitable, so be prepared.

I recommend reading *The Partnership Book*, by Denis Clifford and Ralph Warner (Soquel, CA: Nolo Press, 1997). And a last note: If you are thinking about taking on a partner, make sure you pick a person with similar business ethics and priorities. Be certain you share the same long-term objectives and the plans to achieve those goals.

FINDING VENDORS AND SUPPLIERS

No designer is an island, so to speak. No matter how digital your operation, you're not going to be able to do a job completely in-house; you will need to use outside help at some point. Evaluate your needs and where to find that support team (copywriters, editors, printers, service bureaus, photographers, illustrators, calligraphers, art supply stores, etc.). What contacts do you have already? How do you find vendors if you don't already know them?

Most support services are discovered through some rather basic sources: leafing through the yellow pages, recommendations from or networking with friends, family, or other professionals, or by the way of support services' promotions or advertising. Employ these traditional avenues to locate the crew you require. When you've located some supply sources, organize yourself by making a list and categorizing it into specific areas:

- *Studio Help:* Includes freelancers, part-timers, and clerical workers. These are individuals who can pick up the load when you have more than you can handle.
- *Professional Help:* Includes photographers, illustrators, calligraphers, and copywriters—other creative professionals who supplement your capabilities by providing special talents.
- *Printers, Production, and Special Services:* Includes all prepress, print, and finish capabilities—service bureaus, color separators, plus a range of printers, from quick-print shops to commercial printers. You never know when you will need a company that specializes in embossing, the little operation that does custom embroidery, or a screen printer for a special-

ty job. Keep a record of what each vendor does best (and/or cheapest and/or quickest), and note the equipment available.

Set up a resource file for the above categories that includes information on each of the supply sources you are currently using or would like to consider for the future. You'll want to have alternatives and plenty of sources to choose from when trying to obtain the best value for a particular service (value being the best quality and service for the price).

Use your files to keep track of quotes you received from each of your current and potential suppliers. Generally, the word on the street will lead you to the supplier with the best deal, but be careful. Sometimes vendors will lowball with a first job to get your business and, once they've proven themselves, will jack up their prices to the level of their competition. When you receive a promotion from a new supplier, file it under the category of "potential supplier." This will be a great way to build up a handy network of vendors.

WILL YOUR PLAN WORK?

Are your plans practical? Is your business truly viable? No matter what you want to do, you aren't going to work twelve hours a day, seven days a week—at least not without going crazy or getting sick. If it takes that kind of effort, your plans aren't realistic. If you can't write good ad copy now, while you're working as an employee, you won't magically be able to when you're on your own, and so on. Your time is valuable, so examine your goals in the light of your knowledge, talents, strengths, and weaknesses. Be blushingly honest with yourself. Your future business will depend on an accurate assessment of what you want and your capabilities to accomplish that charge.

How will you survive tough times? Should business go sour, can you borrow money, live with family, sell your car, have a studio garage sale, cut back on personal and/or business expenses? Could you freelance in someone else's agency, department, or studio for a while? Share studio space or rent a portion of your space to someone else? Market another capability (like shooting stats for other designers/studios, etc.)? Rent out computer time to other designers or writers? Input data or do typesetting for other writers and designers? Start a résumé service or custom greetings/stationery shop? Write and design custom love/hate/complaint letters ("Two Macs—no waiting! No emotion too small!")? However, in all seriousness, you might have to think of other options to support yourself if your business goes through a dry spell.

YA GOTTA HAVE A (BUSINESS) PLAN

Whether it be short and sweet or the size of *War and Peace*, an effective business plan must clearly detail your particular venture. Your business plan will help you to determine your future success by defining your goals, analyzing the competition, and determining your risks. Your business plan says who you are, how you got here, and where you're going. It is a personal, professional, and financial yardstick that gives you a place to start, keeps you on track, and helps you grow.

Because designers often start as one- or two-person operations, they often start without a business plan. Writing a plan seems to be another formidable part

WOW, WHAT I DID WRONG!

Your business will fail when (or if) you can't generate income. It will fail if you are not competitive in your pricing or do not provide quality service. Your business will fail if you are not aggressive enough when marketing your services or product. There are those who are just not cut out to be businesspeople. Some folks go into business and live to mutter about it: "Wow, what I did wrong!" I checked with other designers and illustrators and came up with a top fifty list of complaints, excuses, and famous last words:

1. I chose a terrible location.

2. I don't need an accountant or a bookkeeper!

3. I shouldn't have rushed into this.

4. I got off to a lousy start.

5. I have no financial cushion to fall back on.

6. Poor cash flow.

7. I picked a bad partner.

8. I didn't write a partnership agreement.

9. My credit rating is lousy.

10. Getting a loan is going to be a piece of cake.

11. I didn't get enough funding.

12. I was underqualified at some things, overqualified at others.

13. I don't need any clients before I start.

14. I thought credit screening was a waste of time.

15. The business can run itself; I'm going to Bermuda.

16. Unrealistic? Me?

17. I got too big too fast.

18. I kept small too long.

19. I didn't know I was required to do that.

20. I advertised in the wrong place.

21. My ads stunk.

22. I suffered from promotional overkill.

23. I suffered from promotional underkill.

24. There was too much competition.

25. I was underpriced.

26. I was overpriced.

27. Luck is everything.

28. Timing is overrated.

29. Legalities? What are those?

30. Ethics? What are those?

31. I took checks that bounced higher than the Empire State Building.

32. I don't think I'm good enough.

33. I was overconfident.

34. I don't have to hire anybody—I can do it all.

35. I don't want to delegate—I can do everything.

36. I took unneeded insurance.

37. I didn't have enough insurance.

38. Eventually I'll succeed, because I deserve it.

39. Going into business won't be that expensive.

40. I really need all this fancy equipment and furniture.

41. Who needs a business plan?

42. I couldn't handle the politics.

43. Buyers around here sure are cheap!

44. They don't appreciate quality.

45. I couldn't compete with the price cutters.

46. I'll make it up on the next job.

47. Ya gotta spend money to make money.

48. I'll just keep going; things are bound to get better.

49. They said they had plenty of money and lots more work to come.

50. They stole my ideas and gave them to some hack.

51. _____ (you fill in the blank).

of that bugbear called "business." Hey—all you need is a drawing board, some talented hands, and a good printer at your disposal, right? Is that your final answer?

When the cash flow stops trickling in, when you're getting no response from your latest mailing, when it's your time in court after not being able to pay your printer, then you'll wish that you had planned your business more carefully. A business plan won't solve all your problems for you, but it will give you a clear idea of what your problems might be and how you can prevent them from happening.

Understand the objectives. And as Roger Brucker advises, "Know your mission—what are you in business to offer? To whom?" Your business plan is a personal statement of your goals. It can vary from a short summary to a full-blown document filled with marketing and financial projections. The length is up to you, but every business plan has six essential elements: where, why, how, when, who, and what.

Where the business is to be located can be determined by its purpose, the competition, and its overall opportunities for success.

Why the business will succeed is determined by identifying your potential clients and why you have an advantage over your competition.

How describes the company's resources and its ability to carry out the plan.

When is indicated by milestones measured in profits, billings, number of clients, number of employees, and so forth.

Who defines each person's specific responsibilities (and qualifications) for accomplishing the goals of the business.

What it costs is indicated by the cash flow projections.

You'll find more specific information in this book on how to pull together the details that will go into this plan. You will find out how to determine the most advantageous location for your business. You will learn how to identify prospective clients and how to convince them to use your services. You will find out how to make cost and income projections to help in the completion of this plan. But remember, change is constant. Revise your plan as needed to keep it timely and doable. Modify your operations accordingly.

PROFESSIONAL ⬇ VIEWPOINTS

Get a job in a small design firm to see, firsthand, just how tough it is to run your own business.　　　—Rick Tharp, Designer

We must all ask ourselves: What do we want to get out of our business? What type of market do we want to create? Some of us have a need to make a big splash for some dumb reason, so I think we must remind ourselves that we got into this business to have a little fun. It can be an extremely fun-filled business.

　　　—Mike Quon, Designer and Illustrator

You can't have a business without the desire, without the soul. But you can't have this spirit unless it's supported financially. You have to have the heart and the head. The most important thing about running a successful creative business is that balance.

　　　—Kim Youngblood, Designer

The most important question to ask yourself before starting your own business is this: "Do I want to be in charge of everything?" Most likely, you will be the salesperson, the business manager, the per-

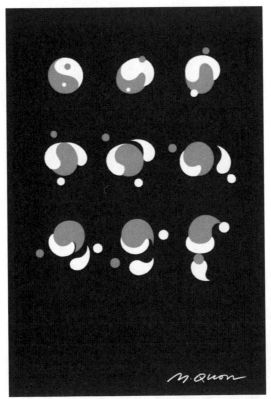

sonnel manager, the art director, the production manager. Unless you have a partner, there won't be anyone to bounce ideas off . . . do you really want all that responsibility? —Ellen Shapiro, Designer

Of course, getting sound advice from my friends and accountants, as well as other established designers, saved me from having to learn many things the hard way.
—Bennett Peji, Designer

Merely possessing design talent doesn't necessarily mean you will have a successful business. So much depends on how you structure your firm, how well you plan and budget, and how effectively you reach out. —Arthur Ritter, Designer

There's a feeling of isolation and loneliness—you have nobody to interface with or consult with . . . There's also a tendency to become compulsive—to feel guilty about taking time off. One has less time for a social life. —Mary Ann Nichols, Designer

[Partners] complement your work style and fill in the gaps. Are you a specialist? Then look for a generalist. If you're the creative type, an ideal partner will have business and sales skills. Find someone with the qualities you don't possess.
—Valerie Ritter Paley, Designer

chapter 5

SETTING UP
SHOP

I created an environment I enjoy working in.

— Jilly Simons, Designer

I wanted to get away from the studio once in awhile, so I set up in an office.

— Rick Tharp, Designer

If you've always worked for someone else or are just getting out of school, you've probably never had to think about what equipment and supplies a studio needs. One of the joys of having your own studio is that now you can have exactly what you want—if you can afford it.

Before you run out and rent fancy office space and buy expensive furniture and equipment, you should determine what you'll need and why. Your first decision will be choosing where you want to work—at home or in a studio away from home—and what you must have to get your work done, including a computer (a big, but absolutely key investment). Then, you can start to plan for your own opening day in the space that's right for you.

DECIDE WHERE YOU'LL WORK

You need a place to work. In theory, that can be anywhere you can get the work done. But in practice, your studio space must provide a professional atmosphere (especially for meeting clients). It must be an affordable place where you can concentrate and have enough room to do the job well.

Many designers feel they must have a fancy address in order to succeed, but that's simply not true. Although a ritzy-sounding address may attract certain clients, a prestigious address is not synonymous with premier design. However, working in a clean, safe neighborhood will obviously help your credibility. You certainly don't want to set up shop in the heart of the high-crime district or in the middle of a heavily-polluted industrial zone.

Your studio's location must also be practical. Consider proximity and access to clients, vendors, and suppliers (and be sure your studio is within range of those suppliers who deliver). You want to be close enough to your clients so you can easily visit them, and vice versa. You should be able to pick up supplies or drop off a job without having to drive long distances.

Home Sweet Office: Working At Home

Some designers caution against the home studio, citing the major distractions of house, family, and neighborhood. Throw in the potential client attitude that anyone working out of the house is not a true professional, and you have a big red flag. But a good proportion of designers I interviewed for this book at least began their businesses working out of their apartments or houses. And the designers I interviewed who still have home studios wouldn't have it any other way.

Let's first look at the pros and cons of working at home. On the positive side: You don't have to pay for office space, and you won't have extra utility and phone-line costs. A home office is tax deductible (for example, a one-room studio in a five-room house garners you a 20 percent deduction off mortgage and utility costs). You can take care of business and chores. You can save on child care. You don't have to get dressed up each day, and you can easily schedule work to suit your convenience, plus you save time and gas money by not commuting from home to work.

The cons? You can't leave the office behind. Family and friends can interrupt a lot, and housework and family responsibilities can distract you. You'll appear less professional. You can spend too much time goofing off. Your work space may be inconvenient. Your work interferes with your personal life, and your personal life interferes with your work.

There are, of course, ways around the negatives if working at home is important to you. Don't try to set up a studio in the center of a bustling household. You must have privacy in which to work and a way to protect jobs in progress. You need a door you can close on the design world, as well as on the living room. To appear your most professional, you can always meet clients at their offices (they'll probably love you for that) or have a separate door to the studio portion of your home. Or perhaps you can simply explain, "I hope you don't mind, but the studio's at the house. Be prepared for a warm, fuzzy, and thrilling experience . . . no extra charge!" In some cities, corporate office centers offer meeting parlors rented by the hour.

Current technology and services have made the home office far more accessible than ever before. Indeed, the Net and computers, information and communication systems, fax machines and express mail couriers have revolutionized the size and scope of the marketplace. Local studios, and cottage industries in general, have been transformed into viable national (if not international) concerns.

A small, but key issue will be the business phone/home phone dilemma—the number of telephone lines you will need to maintain business communications (and that all-important professional atmosphere). Obviously, your three-year-old shouldn't answer your business phone—or any phone, if you have only one line—during business hours. But can you afford two (or more) lines?

One bona fide conflict of interest will be if your home or office Internet connection is on the same line as your business phone system. You can't make or take business calls if someone is surfing the Net. Separate phone lines make sense here, or you can go the cable modem route.

You may certainly want to look into what is called a "DSL line." DSL provides a connection using a *digital signal line*. The digital line needs certain ingredients to work, and older homes may not have the correct phone set-up. This will require the DSL installer to bring in a digital line, which, of course, can add to the total cost.

The digital line also has a physical distance limit. You must be within a certain distance to the phone company's central office. However, the DSL line does provide a dedicated, high-speed connection, whereas the cable modem is a shared connection. For a business, a DSL line is a smart idea. If necessary, you could always add an Internet routing system to connect multiple computers to the DSL line.

And you may consider two phone lines a decided benefit if you fax frequently, dedicating one line exclusively to your fax. However, you needn't have two lines to accommodate a fax. Many fax machines are able to decipher between a fax and a voice message and route a signal to the proper destination (voice messages to the telephone, fax signals to the fax). If you decide your volume of calls and faxing only warrants one line, consider the various call-waiting options to inform you of incoming calls while you're engaged in a conversation (for instance, many phone companies offer a service that accepts and stores faxes when your line is busy). You could also look into a cellular phone as your "second phone line."

You never want to take a chance on missing an important call because the other party is turned away by a busy signal. By that same token, don't forget the good ol' answering machine for fielding calls when you're not around or unable to answer the phone. Some folks swear by Caller ID to screen calls (and for call waiting, as well).

Finally, consider other core issues when evaluating the home studio: Does your home provide adequate space (and wiring) for your equipment? Can you maintain regular office hours at the house? How well will you be able to deter interruptions?

Office Sweet Office: Working Away from Home

Now, let's evaluate the pros and cons of working away from home. Obviously, you have a fixed center of business and communications that provide a professional atmosphere (for you, any staff, and your clients). Your environment is conducive to work (and reasonably free from the disturbances of family obligations). You project a more professional image. Your work and personal lives are separate. You have better accessibility to vendors and delivery service with a location in a commercially-zoned area.

But working away from home is more expensive—you're paying rent twice and shelling out extra bucks for utilities and furniture. You may need child care; you may miss your kids and the interaction with your spouse. You may not be able to dress casually or as comfortably as you prefer. Your work space may not be in your desired location of choice. Time will be spent commuting between your home and studio. You may not have as much flexibility to work when the mood strikes you or at odd hours.

You may want to consider a studio that, as real estate agents optimistically say, "needs some work." These work spaces, due to neglect or location, are in subpar condition. If your future office is the proverbial "handyman's special," evaluate how much time, energy, and resources will be spent to get the place up to safety code and to suit your needs. If your goal is to get your business quickly up to speed, I would discourage you from going this route. There's only so much of you to go around, and I believe your energies should be directed towards becoming a freelance designer, not Joe Contractor.

You may want to look into leasing or owning a condo, renting part of an office suite, or sharing space with another designer or a photographer (or an even larger group). There are benefits in mutual space: a common receptionist and conference room, sharing large equipment, splitting expenses and overhead, and there's valuable camaraderie, in-house feedback, and a ready-made support system.

A business incubator just may work out for your particular situation. Here, single-room offices are rented out to a variety of one- to two-person companies who don't know each other. As in the above, everybody shares a receptionist, conference room, photocopier, etc., but you don't have to find (or know) your office mates first.

Whether you found the ideal office, or you simply know your home is just perfect, look at your potential studio and ask some critical questions: Are the space and facilities really right for your purposes? How's the storage? What about plumbing and sanitary facilities? How will you handle clean-up and waste removal? Do you have plenty of daylight, interior lighting, and wiring? Is there parking? What's the traffic like at your location? Is the studio easily accessible by standard modes of transportation? Is there adequate security?

The Lease You Can Do

You've found this great loft space north of Rialto, just off the Dakota district—very close to Joanne's Art Supply. Good light, lots of room. A perfect space for the office. The landlord smiles and says, "Just sign on the dotted line, Ms. Designer; don't worry about all that stuff down there. Pay no attention to that little paragraph set in tiny type. Oh, that clause? It's nothing, nothing at all."

Hold on. Study your entire lease very carefully. Remember that the lease was prepared for the landlord, so it's written with his needs and not yours in mind. A lease is, however, subject to negotiation.

Even though this office is to die for, show the lease to your lawyer before you sign. Examine the lease together. Be sure you truly understand the terms. Can these terms somehow change during the course of your lease? Can the landlord legally cancel your lease—how and why? Can you legally break the lease—how, when, and why? Here's a checklist of points you should be aware of in addition to the monthly rent:

- ➡ What is the length of the lease (shorter is better)?
- ➡ When and how may the deposit be forfeited?
- ➡ Are there restrictions on how you may use the space?
- ➡ What are the zoning requirements?
- ➡ Is there an option to continue or renew the lease?
- ➡ What is the cost for continuing or renewing the lease?
- ➡ Can you sublet or assign the lease?
- ➡ Who is responsible for cleaning and repairs?
- ➡ Who is responsible for what utilities?
- ➡ Who is responsible for maintenance?
- ➡ Does the landlord have the right to move tenants?
- ➡ How are disputes handled?

Obviously, it makes good sense to take care of the lease up front. This will enable you to focus on growing your business, rather than legal issues, unexpected expenses, or moving your office—*again*.

COMPUTERS, BUY AND LARGE

Your computer is invaluable and indispensable. Fast, powerful, and versatile creative tools, computers also streamline the business end of your illustration and design. It's safe to say that you'll buy a computer for tracking expenses and time, communications and research (e-mail and the Internet), billing, record keeping, and project storage.

A needs assessment can be very helpful in determining just what equipment to purchase. Consider what you want the system to do, your available resources (both skill and money), and the time frame available for making the decision and implementing your system. Time is important. A common error is to wait for the "latest and greatest" and never get started. Don't be a digital wannabe, and don't make excuses—jump in.

Years ago, I bought my first Mac for a graphics solution, but it quickly became a business lifesaver as well. Easy to learn, yet a most challenging and interesting work device, the Mac provides a happy marriage of process and product that's extremely satisfying. Although my Mac can never replace the rush I get from the flow of watercolors or the scratch of a pen on good paper, it's a high-powered instrument that adds a lot to my toolbox.

Let's establish some background about what systems can contribute to your creativity and business. We'll also discuss what to look for and what to ask when window shopping and then buying (or leasing) a computer. First, though, a word of caution: As mentioned above, computer technology roars by the consumer like a rocket. Roger Brucker comments that the velocity of computer technology is on an eighteen-month cycle. "As speed and storage go up," he says, "price goes down." Prices as well as hardware and software will most certainly have changed between the time of this writing and the time you read this. Use this info only as a shopping aid, not as a definitive buying guide.

Why Buy?

It's almost a given these days that everyone has a computer. We buy computers to gain greater control of the production processes and to enhance our creativity. Digital corrections and client changes are faster and cheaper. The designer can see how "real" type, copy, and visuals look on the page instantly and explore more variations in less time. And speaking of which, working digitally enables you to get more done in *less* time; you cut down studio hours and production costs, while reducing paperwork and streamlining procedures. All of this helps you keep up with or get ahead of your competition.

Editorially, I won't beat the drum for either the Mac or PC-compatibles. But if we talk shop, what's better professionally? Is it simply a matter of right brain versus left? Will the Mac actually be faster and easier to use than a PC? Are MS-DOS/Windows systems really cheaper and more powerful than Macs? It depends on how you're most comfortable working and what you want to do.

Just for the moment, let's enjoy the luxury of speaking in digital generalizations. Those "arty types" interviewed for this book employ a Mac as a creative, production, and business tool. The Mac appears to be the computer of choice for designers and illustrators, so there's an extensive support network for those just beginning or testing the waters. The Mac's high-resolution visuals, icon-based interface, the consistency of the command sets for all software, and the availability of design- and illustration-related software have made it the darling of the design and illustration world.

On the other hand, the lawyers, accountants, and tax specialists I talked to employed PC-compatibles. The PC crunches numbers, juggles data, and does word processing and text editing skillfully. It's a seasoned veteran with plenty of software available. Lump in speed, power, proven technology, and price, and PCs may have the edge over the Mac as a general business machine.

Now, if we switch the words "PC" and "Mac" in the above paragraphs, guess what? Basically, you'll have the same truisms. The debate about what system is the best is pointless and never-ending; all those experts out there have their own opinions (and seldom mutually agree on anything). Truth is, over time, the Mac and the PC have moved closer to each other. Powerful word processing and business-related software are available for both formats. New operating systems and redesigned software emphasize easy-to-use operating systems, icon-based interfaces, and sparkling graphics. The distinctions are blurring. It all comes down to a question—and the accurate evaluation—of your situation, preferences, time frame for growth, and available funds.

There is a groundswell of enthusiasm (and much hype) about new models for every computer manufacturer. Innovative and beautiful pieces of equipment boasting great power and features can satisfy most wish lists. Quality and performance can be found at all price breaks, and computer prices always drop over time. Every generation of computers is more powerful, efficient, and less expensive than the original machines.

Investigate a variety of systems. Inexpensive computers more limited in power and expandability still feature fine color and graphics capabilities. These computers should be considered the entry into economical digital art. So, along these lines, evaluate buying last year's model (or earlier). Remember, classic machines—used, refurbished, or discontinued—were at one time (and not too long ago, in computer years) the cutting edge, the most powerful, fastest, feature-laden boxes on the block

Today's Macs and PCs offer truly breathtaking speed, awesome power, and amazing grace. As you grow into your business and skills, you can always move up into the rarified digital atmosphere.

Compatibility

What type of files will you need to exchange with your clients and vendors? What types of media? Even more importantly, what "stuff" do your service bureaus and printers use? "Service bureaus and printers significantly prefer Macs over PCs," says designer Larissa Kisielewska. "The Mac has been around in the design world that much longer—much more development in font management and color matching has taken place for the Mac. Service bureaus can rip Mac files much easier, faster, and with far fewer glitches."

I must agree, but zealots for either system can escalate the debate to Defcon 3. So, of course, there's always the universal fine print here: Your results may vary (and you may just have to be a switch hitter). Do *your* homework, and someday next week, we'll compare notes over a triple mocha latte over-easy, covered, and smothered.

Illustrator Robert Zimmerman tells this interesting story: "I'll never forget the first time I walked into the offices of *PC World* magazine. I expected, literally, to see a world of PCs, I suppose. What I found was a world of Macs—not one PC to be seen in the entire art department. It dawned on me then that the industry standard for graphics of any kind was Macintosh. To this day, I've never worked with an art director that wasn't running Mac OS, and I doubt I ever will."

Software and Tear

But no matter how fancy the computer system, the most powerful machine remains humbled without the right software. As an artist and businessperson, you will need a variety of applications to effectively run your complete studio: design and illustration software, word processing and e-mail software for correspondence, a database for file-keeping, accounting and/or bookkeeping programs, and organizational software for your office management.

When it comes to graphics software, it's a real buyer's market. Creatives can pick and choose from many possible options. There are programs for basic design, page layout, typography, drawing, and technical rendering. You can find paint programs to do everything from random doodles to highly-polished, final art. Web design and site management programs, 3-D animation packages, and presentation software galore are widely available.

You'll find a variety of entry-level, mid-range, and high-end applications (determined by a combination of price, degree of difficulty, and features). No matter where you are on the learning curve, you should be able find software to meet your needs.

What does the small design studio need in terms of business software? As mentioned earlier, electronic spreadsheets, databases, communications software, and accounting packages can help the artist manage an efficient and organized business. Look into integrated (all-in-one) packages or bundled software that combines the basic business applications—text, spreadsheet, database, and tele-communications. At this writing, some software to evaluate would be AppleWorks and Microsoft Office.

Specialized programs or general-purpose applications designed to handle most of your business chores can be found right on the shelf. With a bit of research, you can get great performance and good value. If you can't get to the store, you need go no further than the current computer magazines, or shop on the Net. Window shop a few issues and Web sites, read the reviews, and/or call the mail-order houses for recommendations.

Make an educated decision and purchase. Remember, even a bit of information can go a long way. Whether you're buying graphics, business, or word processing software, get plenty of input first. Surf the Net, call your friends, call or e-mail those professional contacts. Consult user groups, chat and message boards, and books and magazines to find out what's hot and what's not.

Compare features and prices before you buy, and always test-drive the program first to make sure it does what you want it to do (and is compatible with the software used by your clients and vendors). Fool around with the program on a friend's computer. Take it for a spin at your local dealer. Borrow from a friend, or download a trial version from such sites as Tucows.com. One last word about buying from vendors: Educator and computer consultant Ryan Osborne reminds us that federal law prohibits any return of opened software or other recorded media to the seller, except for replacement with the same title.

Just Tell Me What You Want

All time expended assessing your needs before you buy is time well spent. Here's an inventory of points to consider and questions to ask before you purchase a computer and related peripherals:

Who will use it? Just you, or you and your partner or staff? Why are you planning to buy—what specifically do you expect a computer to do for you? If you want to improve productivity or cut costs, how will a computer help you do that?

What exactly will you use it for—bookkeeping, typography, creating illustrations, page design and layout, word processing, etc.? What quality of output do you need—high quality (1200 dots per inch [dpi]), mid-range (600 dpi), or low quality (300 dpi or lower) printing? Do you need to output color? Is your work for the computer screen or for paper?

Where will you do input and output? One workstation or more? Will you need to deliver material to a service bureau frequently? What kind of scanning will you do (flat art, slides, photographs, transparencies; color or black-and-white line art), and how much will you be doing? Do you need to network your computer to other machines?

When do you want to be partially or fully computerized? How much will it cost? What can you afford? Where will you get the money?

How will your system be supported: Who will train you, help you solve problems (technical support), and fix your equipment when it's not working? If you can afford the services of one, a consultant is an invaluable ally (see below for more on consultants). Don't underestimate the time and money involved in keeping your computer system up and running effectively.

Talk to Me

Whatever (and wherever) you buy, consider working with a consultant. If you can afford one, it's to your definite advantage to have a consultant on tap. Find a people-oriented expert who knows the hardware and software and who will be there when you need support, training, or advice. To locate a consultant, talk to friends, check the phone book, and then interview. You might also consult vendors or user groups, even though it's a slight conflict of interest (vendors will naturally promote use of the hardware and software they sell; user groups, in the effort to promote computer literacy and autonomy, will steer you toward what they know and use).

You may be able to find a Value-Added Resaler (VAR), a person or dealership authorized to sell some particular equipment, who will act as your consultant. These may be small stores, larger operations, or chains. In either event, look for an operation that emphasizes the relationship they build with the client after the purchase as part of the purchase. This is the best of all worlds—sales, service, and support all in one. It's worth the search and possibly higher prices to find such a vendor.

Ryan Osborne says, "Get someone local! Especially with Macs. Most chains or superstores lack Mac expertise and in-house support and service."

The Path of Lease Resistance

Should you lease your equipment instead of buying outright? That depends on your financial and tax situation. There are advantages and disadvantages to leasing. Leasing may give you lower monthly payments over a longer period of time than an outright purchase. You can buy your machine at the end of the lease (terms will vary), renew the lease, or trade up to newer and better equipment. Understand, however, that because you may have to pay top dollar for a system, this can be a more expensive way to go.

But many dealers include a service contract and access to some technical support as part of your lease (not all do, so be sure to read your lease carefully). Otherwise, you'll be responsible for repairs. The cost of your lease is tax-deductible annually, which may be a better deal for you than taking the depreciation allowance from an outright purchase. If your accountant suggests leasing as an option, check it out.

Making the Buy

Remember, it's a common complaint that the buyer can't keep up with technology. Hardware and software improve so dramatically and so fast that many users moan that a system becomes obsolete as soon as you crack it out of the box. Because of this situation, any specific information given at this writing may well be ancient history by the time you read it. Therefore, we must approach the market in general terms.

Evaluate what you want to do, but don't overbuy. Mix and match speed, power, memory, and storage with some expandability—keep an eye on your future. Get plenty of memory and storage—at the least, 256 megabytes (mb) of random access memory (RAM) with a 20-gigabyte hard drive.

If there's one truism in the world of computer technology, it is this: *You can never have too much RAM.* Invest in this absolute essential. Another rule of thumb here is that you can never have too much storage space. Trust me on this—make it a priority. Get as much RAM and the biggest hard drive you can afford. Oh, yes, my mother would also remind me to tell you to back up your data files constantly and consistently. (Please be a good little designer and illustrator and listen to my mother. Please.)

Purchase a monitor with a screen as large as you need. For graphics, a seventeen-inch monitor is where you start looking. There are good buys out there on nineteen- to twenty-one–inch screens, but they will be more expensive, of course.

Consider speed and power, too. Processor speed increases every three to six months, and prices fluctuate with the validity of the market. At this writing, and in today's world, a low-end Mac system costs about $2,500 to $3,000 and includes a monitor, scanner, basic printer, a Zip drive (to transfer information and for modest external storage), and some software (entry-level word processor, paint and/or draw programs, and database). A medium-range system runs in the neighborhood of $4,000 to $7,500. Options here would be a more powerful CPU (central processing unit), a moderately-priced laser printer and/or faster, better color (or tabloid-sized) printer, a larger monitor, a CD/DVD-writer, a better scanner, perhaps a digital camera. Your wish list could also include a digitizing tablet, more RAM, a slide scanner, Jaz drive, etc.

A high-end, state-of-the-art Mac with all the bells and whistles, gadgets du jour, software, plus rocket-powered peripherals your heart desires starts at about $6,000 and goes straight up.

A good shopper can make the actual numbers vary dramatically, and the scenario for a PC purchase will play the same—you pay more for extra and better equipment. You do better if you buy smart and shop till you drop.

Where to start your shopping? Do your homework and go on a reconnaissance mission. Hit the library; browse the Net. Talk with friends, buy a few periodicals, cruise the stores, and—perhaps most importantly—check with other designers who use computers and software that interest you. Learn what available hardware and software meet your needs and budget.

Then, seriously shop around. Many, if not most, vendors offer on-line shopping. It's easy, fast, informative, and fun. You can buy both software and hardware at that store in the mall, by mail order, or over the phone. You can purchase through a VAR or from a consultant in your local area. Each of these outlets has its fans and critics. Unless you network, comparison shop, research and read (including the fine print), ask questions, weigh the pros and cons carefully, and know exactly what you want, you probably won't get a good deal anywhere. But this is true of buying a car, furniture, or stove. The old caveats apply even more to our new high-tech gear: Buyer beware, buyer prepare.

While price is important, it's not the only consideration. A great bargain may not be the best computer for you. Inquire about how long the vendor/dealer/VAR/consultant has been in business. How accessible are customer service, repair, and training centers? Can the vendor/dealer/VAR/consultant supply references from previous customers?

What's the cost of the basic system components (versus your budget and in general)? What equipment is really included in that price? What kind and amount of software is available for and compatible with your hardware—at what prices? What add-ons are available?

What are the system's requirements in terms of power, space, and ventilation?

Check out the kind of training and support available. Do you get any free training? How much? How long does it take most users to learn this system?

Get a sense of the top limits on what your hardware and software can handle (number of users, programs, and projects). How are upgrades (customizing to create a bigger, better machine) and trade-ups (swapping to acquire a bigger, better machine) handled?

Can you network your system and software easily? Are there compatibility issues with both Macs and PCs on the same network?

What are the policies on returns? What is the system's or software's record for reliability? Can it be serviced locally, or will it have to go back to the manufacturer? Are service contracts available, and how much will they cost?

Apples and Oranges—Comparison Shopping

Getting the lowest possible price shouldn't be your sole prerequisite for buying a certain computer at a particular store, but you should shop around. For smart and efficient shopping, organize your information by adapting the buyer's guide found in chapter 7; this will help you pinpoint the best deal and where. Computer consultant Steve Ledingham uses these guides to make recommendations to his clients. It's easy: Vendor information goes on top. Next, info on each component is gathered over the phone, through the Internet, in person, or from want ads and store advertisements. Remember to research both new and used equipment (if available).

CHOOSE YOUR SUPPLIES AND EQUIPMENT

"Like a kid in a candy store" may accurately describe the designer at the art/office supply house, but it's important to realistically assess—and choose—only what you actually need, can afford, and what can fit into your space. Of course, you'll need more furniture, etc., if you're starting up with a partner or associates than if you're all by yourself.

A list of supplies and equipment could go on and on. Here are some obvious wants and needs (in no particular hierarchy):

Can't Start Without

- Drawing table
- Work table
- Fax machine
- Light table or light box
- Storage: shelves, cubbyholes, boxes, etc.
- File holders or filing cabinets
- Chair(s)
- Lights, lamps
- Waste basket(s)
- Art and production supplies
- Paper cutter
- Mounting facilities
- Office supplies
- Address file (simple Rolodex) or Personal Digital Assistant (like a Palm or Visor)
- Basic cleaning supplies and equipment
- First aid kit
- Computer, related hardware and software
- Phone(s) and appropriate phone lines for you
- Answering machine
- Stationery
- Some promotional material
- Business cards and forms

Handy to Have

- Coat rack or closet
- Additional work surfaces
- Desk (a real one, above and beyond your old drawing board)
- Flat files or racks
- Photocopier with reduction/enlargement capabilities
- Guest chairs and table for meeting with clients
- Bulletin board(s)
- Presentation software and hardware
- TV and VCR
- Digital viewing system (CD, DVD)
- Basic kitchen supplies, coffeemaker

- Multiline phone
- Music system

NEW, USED, OR LEASED

In my discussions with the designers and illustrators in this book, we identified a malady common to artists everywhere: the craving to have only the newest and best of everything. (Is this ailment exclusive to the art world? Certainly not, but let the plumbers complain about it in their own book.)

If you have the cash available (see chapter 6 on calculating and monitoring your cash flow), an outright purchase is cheaper. You own the furniture or equipment without the hassle of payments—and there are no interest charges. But will you be able to sell an obsolete piece of equipment (if you can't trade or upgrade it) or used furniture to recover part of your investment?

Is used equipment or furniture a good alternative? That's a big "maybe." "Buyer beware" says it best. Cheap, previously-owned equipment may look like a bargain, but do your homework and shop around before you say "yes." Definitely negotiate for a trial period, a repair warranty, and terms for return. It's also wise to have the item thoroughly, professionally inspected before you buy.

Before you decide, get your accountant's advice. As we mentioned before, it sometimes makes more financial and tax sense to finance or even to lease big-ticket items. A leasing company may decline to lease you equipment if you haven't been in business a certain number of years (an indication of stability and ability to pay). They may demand a personal guarantee.

Leasing has tax advantages—you can write off your entire payment—and does allow you to upgrade your equipment with a minimum of fuss. Often, you'll have the option to buy at the end of the lease. Investigate interest rates carefully, especially when choosing between leasing and financing a purchase.

PLAY BALL! OPENING DAY

You'll need to gear up for that first day of business. The preconception that a designer or illustrator just casually strolls into a new workspace and becomes a business is woefully wrong. But any dread of the work required—or planning involved—is also unnecessary. To get a handle on what to do before your doors open, I've grouped items and set up a table (see chapter 7) sequentially to help you prepare for your big day. You'll find more information on these aspects of starting your studio in other chapters, so I'll only hit the highlights here. For example:

Five weeks to a month prior to opening, you should visit your accountant; work up your first promotion, business forms, cards, and letterheads; acquire all permits and licenses; lay down the rent deposit, and get the keys. The timing may not be right for fingers to do the walking, but I'd secure a listing in your local yellow pages at this time, too.

One month to three weeks before opening day, you would see your lawyer; create your business sign or have it made; print the promo, business forms, and the identity. Business gizmos like refrigerator magnets or stickers should be done now.

BUY, CLAUDIUS (HARDWARE AND SOFTWARE TO CREATE YOUR WEB SITE)

If you're purchasing computer equipment with an eye towards Web marketing, think about the following:

▶ Window shop at places like Dealmac (*www.dealmac.com*), DealNN (*www.dealnn. com*), and Smalloffice.com (*www.smalloffice.com*) to find the best deals, plus terrific product information and insightful reviews.

▶ Evaluate if you can simply upgrade your present system. More RAM, a faster processor, another hard drive—maybe this is all you really need? Consider what your computer will do, then investigate a variety of systems. Inexpensive computers usually mean limited power and expandability, but still boast fine features and graphics capabilities—can these machines do the trick? Today's Mac and PC product lines offer great combinations of speed, power, capacity, and growth potential. Grow your business and computer systems simultaneously.

▶ I've said it before, but the most crucial element in the mix is memory. Get as much RAM as you can (again, at least 128 to 256 megabytes). Sure, processor speed is important. But this is a race that never ends, and there's a speedier chip coming up right behind you.

▶ We've all heard that size doesn't really matter, but get a BIG internal hard drive—as big as possible. And buy a removable hard drive (like an Iomega Zip drive) for both portability and headroom.

▶ Find a comfortable and functional keyboard.

▶ Monitors? You'll want a monitor with a resolution of no less than 640 x 480 pixels and a refresh rate (the number of times per second it takes to redraw an image on a screen) of about 60Hz (hertz). Size is measured diagonally: 14-inch to 21-inch sizes are widely available.

▶ There are various ways to connect to the Internet. You'll be looking at analog and cable modems, ISDN (Integrated Services Digital Network) lines, and DSL (Digital Subscriber Line) service. Each step up the ladder offers faster connections, entails further installation, involves more hardware and software, and, of course, means more expense.

- ☑ Chances are, your computer will have a CD-ROM drive installed. Better yet, buy (or purchase a computer with one built-in) a writeable (CD-R) or rewriteable (CD-RW) CD drive. At this writing, DVD-ROM (read only) drives are becoming standard on most computers, and DVD-RAM (writeable) drives are turning up in high-end machines.

- ☑ Get a surge suppressor, and plug into three-prong grounded outlets (that are, hopefully, truly grounded by three wire cable; you may have to hire an electrician to upgrade your wiring). Look into an uninterruptible power supply (UPS). This device provides a few extra minutes of power during blackouts or storms, thus giving you the time to save or back up data and shut down properly.

- ☑ You will need Web page design and production software (for instance, Adobe GoLive or Macromedia Dreamweaver, Macromedia Fireworks, and Flash); a word processor, like Microsoft Word; and graphics programs, such as Adobe Photoshop and Illustrator or Macromedia Freehand. I'd also look into accounting software, such as Microsoft Excel.

- ☑ Investigate training and obtain technical support, and as you upgrade your equipment, do the same with your insurance coverage.

Two weeks to opening, mail the promo; place your advertising; buy a phone (and fax) and get your phone line(s) hooked up; hand over your deposit, and have the utilities turned on; build shelving, etc.

One week to "D-Day" finds you picking up your business forms and identity materials; installing the store sign; signing up for cleaning services, etc.

Adapt my form (found in chapter 7) to suit your own needs. You will find that following this basic road map will get you down the path to opening day easily and efficiently. Of course, you also need to plan these expenses carefully, so you don't end up over your head in debt before you even open. You don't want your gala opening to be followed immediately by your going-out-of-business party. (For more on calculating and budgeting for your start-up costs, see chapter 4.)

PROFESSIONAL ⬇ VIEWPOINTS

It's amazing how much storage and work space is needed for this type of business!
—Mike Quon, Illustrator and Designer

I converted a detached, one-car garage into an office. Cold in the winter, but great most of the year. I wanted to keep costs to a minimum, as well as have the convenience of working out of my home. My mother thinks I started freelancing so I could spend more time with my cat (only partly true).
—Vicki Vandeventer, Designer

Having an office [in the house] is worth all the hassles of living with the mess, and I would do it all again. Having my own time schedule, being my own boss, and being able to work comfortably supersede the need to have perfect work conditions.
—Peg Esposito, Designer

I can stretch any job to fill all my time—especially if the alternative is housework. Where's the choice in, "Should I dust or design?"
—Peg Esposito, Designer

I can't work unless it's in an environment that's "perfect." Everything, from the sofa slipcovers to the cabinet handles and the paper napkins in the kitchenette, has to meet my exacting standards. I guess most graphic designers can relate to this, but sometimes I wonder where my priorities are. Like, why was I out shopping for picture frames when I should have been out getting more clients?
—Ellen Shapiro, Designer

I moved our office last May and, for the second time, have created an environment that we can enjoy working in. We're not a chichi office and have sacrificed certain typical things, like a conference room, for a practical, organized space with good storage and systems.
—Jilly Simons, Designer

I highly recommend starting at home—if you have the space and can isolate a studio. I have a child, and working at home has allowed me to be there and work in a wonderful, comfortable space. My clients think it's great.
—Alyn Shannon, Designer

I can make a strong argument for buying used computers (I do all the time) and about passing down older models for administrative tasks when getting new equipment (your bookkeeper doesn't need a G4).
—Larissa Kisielewska, Designer

Phone calls incessantly interrupt, car pools and meetings need to be arranged, shopping and household tasks demand attention, and, of course, children have their own set of needs, which no one can afford to ignore. I used to find myself thinking, "I don't even have time to die, too many people depend on me."
—Ilene Winn-Lederer, Illustrator

THE 3 RIVERS JUGGLING FESTIVAL 1996

© Ilene Lederer 1996

chapter 6

DEVELOPING YOUR FINANCIAL PLANS

A lot of younger designers seem confused or concerned; often, they are not interested in planning or preparing budgets, but I found the business end of things to be rather creative. It's the process that I was always somewhat attracted to.

— Jilly Simons, Designer

You need to have a financial plan. It's dangerous to start out underfinanced, yet you don't want to spend too much money at first.

In this chapter, we'll assess how much money you will need, how much you can realistically plan to earn, and where and how to get the needed capital. You'll also find out how to create a working budget to maintain a cash flow that will keep your business in the black.

FIGURE OUT HOW MUCH MONEY YOU'LL NEED

Get a handle on just what it will cost you to be in business by figuring out first what your start-up expenses will be. This would include all one-time expenses involved in beginning a business. Factor in fixtures, equipment, and installation; office supplies, decorating, and remodeling; rent, phone, and utilities deposits; legal and professional fees; licenses and permits; advertising and promotion; and operating cash.

The bottom half of the start-up worksheet (in the following chapter) can be adapted to fit your needs and give you an accurate picture of what it will cost to get your firm off the ground.

After calculating start-up costs, you'll need to figure out what your expenses will be on a monthly basis and enter them on the top half of the start-up worksheet. You can break this down into monthly, fixed expenses: rent, utilities, loan payments, parking, your salary (if any), etc. Add to these your variable or operating expenses, or what you think it will cost on a per-month basis for items such as supplies, postage, entertainment, and transportation. If you will have purchases that will need to be made only once or twice a year—for example, you estimate a roll of acetate will last you about twelve months—take the cost of the roll and divide it by twelve to come up with the monthly cost for this item. Do this with the rest of your equipment and supply costs, and you should have a pretty good idea of what your monthly expenses will be.

Don't include items such as copywriting, photography, printing, illustration (if you're a designer), or design (if you're an illustrator) in your monthly tally. These job expenses should be billed to the client for each job they are purchased for. An exception would be service expenses incurred for your own promotional pieces. Here, the copywriting, photography, printing, or illustration charges are indeed operating expenses and should be factored into the equation.

ESTIMATE HOW MUCH YOU THINK YOU'LL EARN

You have a number of potential clients with a certain amount of business to give you. Think about their needs and how you can fulfill them in order to get a realistic picture of how much and what kind of work you could be doing for them.

Based on the soul searching you did earlier in this book, you should now have some idea of what skills you should be marketing and where they can best be applied. You'll need to have a practical estimate of how much business you can expect and where it will come from.

Start by thinking how you can build on existing business. Let's assume that one of your prospective clients is starting up a business and that you're going to be developing a logo for him. Certainly, there's the potential for developing other business and promotional materials as well. Are there other potential clients out there for whom you could be doing similar work? Do you stand a good chance of building on this business through referrals? Is there a good possibility you could be doing a substantial amount of logo or identity work? If this is the case, make a list. Project how many logo jobs you think will come to you in a given year. At a cost of $1,500 each (if this is what you think your average charge will be), what does this come to annually? Figure from there how much of this business will spin off into collateral work for each of your logo clients, and attach a monetary value to all of it.

Do the same for any other type of work you think you will be doing. Figure out how much business in this area you can realistically be able to get, as well as what you are capable of doing in a year. Think in terms of projects on an annual basis, and after you have made a list and totaled it, divide this figure by twelve to get an idea of what your monthly gross profit will be.

CAN YOU MAKE ENDS MEET?

You will need to compare costs and income to see if your business plan is viable. A lowball or highball scheme built around inaccuracies won't get you very far in actual practice, so make sure your projections reflect real-world facts and figures.

Bone up! Research the numbers by talking to both buyers and sellers of graphic design and illustration. Compare notes with your professional friends; brainstorm with family. Hit the library and bookstore to study pertinent texts.

Now, create a hypothetical budget. A budget is *important*. It's absolutely vital that you have a handle on expenses and income—and it's best to have it on paper. Otherwise, you'll have no idea how you're doing financially or where (and why) your money is going.

Check out the budget template in the chapter 7. Doing just the "estimate" column would give you what's called a cash flow statement or budget projection. You could do a monthly, quarterly, or yearly projection using our format. On the yearly projection, you could also tack on a preopening column, if you desire. Use the "actual" column to gauge how good your estimates are and fine-tune future projections.

Here's a formula you can use to calculate your break-even point: Let's assume that your expenses add up to $2,000 per month. You know that every week you have to bill $500 worth of design fees to break even (or $2,000 every month). The break-even point is what you have to bring in for your business to survive. It's pretty simple math. If you want to end up with a $12,000 profit at the end of the year, figure on billing $3,000 every month or $750 every week.

You can take this formula a step further and figure out your billable rate as well. If you can manage twenty-five billable hours out of every week (it's reasonable to assume that that you can squeeze five billable hours of work out of every day), you will need to bill your time at $30 per hour in order to cover expenses and achieve your goal of a $12,000 at the end of the year.

Of course, all of this figuring is done on an average basis. It's impractical to assume that you will bill $750 on a regular basis. More than likely, you won't bill a cent during some weeks and then bill a number of projects within a given week to make up for the previous week's slack. This is why it makes more sense to figure out what your income will be on an annual basis and then divide this figure by twelve to balance this against your monthly expenses.

GETTING THE MONEY YOU NEED

When most people consider possible cash sources, they think first of borrowing from the bank. Yes, a bank loan is a possibility, but the chances are, at best, slim. To explain why, we'll detail the process of getting a bank loan, exploring what's involved in proving the viability of your business and establishing your credit and credibility—in short, convincing the bank to loan you money. This will include profit and loss statements, net worth of the individual starting up a business, etc. We'll look at some other possibilities for obtaining capital, too.

First off, you'll probably have better luck pursuing a loan from a small bank. And let's be frank, up front, right now. When you ask for a loan from any bank of any size, the first question this institution may ask you is, "Why did you quit your full-time job?" Sit down—here are some other facts of life when it comes to banks and loan acquisition.

Banks look upon a freelancer as a rather unstable commodity and are well aware that new businesses frequently fail. Lenders are hesitant, especially in today's economy, to loan any money to a service business, because, frankly, there's nothing they can touch should the business go belly-up. You won't be able to use your fledgling design studio as collateral for that same reason.

If it's a nonsecured loan, a bank will be unwilling to "give" you money unless you can bring other assets to the table—a car, your house (a second home mortgage), a working spouse (as cosigner), the birthright to your next-born child (only kidding . . . I think).

If you can get a bank loan, you will have to personally guarantee it (even your vaunted corporation status may not exclude you). You may also face sky-high interest rates and unfavorable terms.

What all this means is that your chances of obtaining a loan as a freelancer or new small-business owner drop automatically. But don't totally eliminate the possibility of obtaining a bank loan at some point in the future, after your business is established.

Accountants Todd Williams and Kevin Horner advise you to keep your money in your company. "This looks good when applying for a bank loan," Horner says. "After three to four years of retaining profits (and keeping salary low, if possible), you can more easily obtain a loan to expand business and salary."

Somewhere down the road, your great reputation will be well-earned through quality work. You will have cultivated a cozy rapport with your banker and built a solid credit history with a positive net worth. You'll hold substantial security, and, of course, the studio will be turning business away. You may then have a good chance at getting that loan. But even then, it's no sure thing (and you'll probably still have to personally guarantee the debt).

What can you expect when you apply for a loan? There are certain criteria a lender will use to determine if you're a good risk. Let's say you have one golden minute to state your case. What would a lender want to know in sixty seconds? She'll ask five basic (but oh, so big) questions: What is the service or product you're trying to sell? What's your experience and track record? Who are you, and what's your credit history? What is your ability to repay the loan? What is my security or collateral for the loan?

The first two questions are the icebreakers, but questions three, four, and five are the nutcrackers—the ones the loan officer really cares about. These are the fabled "three C's," representing character, capacity, and collateral.

If you have a checkered past with a dubious credit history, that's bad character. If you don't look like you have a good way to repay the debt, that's poor capacity. If you can't bring enough security to cover it, that's inadequate collateral. You're not going to get the loan if you rate poorly in all categories—it's that simple.

CREDIT RATINGS

You might want to keep tabs on your credit rating by sending for a credit report from agencies such as TRW, Trans Union, and Credit Bureau. You can find these services in the yellow pages. There is a company called Credit Alert that will send you copies from each of these agencies in one single statement.

Even if you have a perfect credit record, sometimes incorrect information can end up in your credit file, so get a credit report before applying for a loan to ensure that you won't be turned down. Refusals become part of your credit history, and several refusals will look bad in your credit report. If you are ever turned down for a loan, make sure you get the name of the credit bureau your lender used. The lender is required by law to make this information available to you, and the credit company, likewise, is legally obligated to tell you over the phone, free of charge, what is in your credit report.

BEYOND THE BANK: OTHER LOAN OPTIONS

We can conservatively estimate that it's going to take six to twelve months (or more) of working capital for a start-up business to survive. This is without spending a dollar generated by that business (and don't forget—you'll need living expenses, too). What are some sources of funds? A bank may be the place to start, because you want to develop a relationship with a banker as you start growing your studio, but remember: If you're fresh off the bus with no experience, savings, or equity, your chances are marginal. Here are some alternatives:

- ▶ *Personal Reserves:* Tap into your own savings for start-up money. The way to build a nest egg is to sock away as much money as you can while you're still employed.
- ▶ *Loans from Family and Friends:* The interest rates and terms are usually great, and you're intimately acquainted with your "banker." Should there be problems, you know the lender is looking out for your best interests. However, this is still a business loan, to be repaid in a timely manner. Writing up a formal document might be a good idea.
- ▶ *Credit Unions:* These are people-oriented, nonprofit co-ops that generally stay away from commercial investments and business loans. But if you're a member and meet the criteria, a credit union would give you an unsecured (often called a personal or "signature") loan. Most credit unions will look at your employment record, check your credit rating and mem-

bership status (you should be a member for at least one year), and will calculate your debt-to-income ratio.

◆ *Borrow against Your Life Insurance Policy:* If you have enough equity, this is a relatively easy way to get some cash. Like any loan, there is interest involved, but the rate is usually very reasonable. And understand that, if the loan is not repaid before your untimely demise, the debt would then be deducted from your benefits.

◆ *Borrow against Your Savings:* Use your savings as the collateral for a loan (thus creating a secured loan). What you are doing is borrowing your own money (and be advised that you'll be paying interest on the use of money you already have). In this situation, your account balance and your loan balance must be the same. As you repay the loan, the principal goes down, allowing you to then dip back into your savings. The lender won't let you fall below the loan balance (they'll put a hold on your savings before that happens). If for some reason you can't make the payments, your savings will be used to pay off the loan.

◆ *Get a Partner and Pool Resources:* Some designers swear by their partners; some swear at them.

◆ *Get a Small Business Administration Loan:* If you qualify, this might be just the ticket. Write for official SBA guidelines, or locate a bank that does this type of loan.

◆ *Commercial Finance or Credit Companies:* Your junk mail is already seeded with mailers from such places. Yes, you'll find attractive, flexible plans, but you'll find short-term secured loans with higher interest rates. And expect the lenders to be more interested in that collateral (as in "easily liquidated") than the health of your business. If you want or need the money badly enough, go ahead, but go in with your eyes open.

◆ *Credit Cards:* Convenient, but inadvisable because of extremely high interest rates (16 to 25 percent). Sure, your mailbox is probably jam-packed with those low, zero-percent (or slightly higher) card offers, but these deals usually last about three to six months, then a higher interest rate kicks in. And do read the fine print to review some often-interesting terms of agreement. Think of your credit cards for short-term financing only. You can build a credit history with credit cards, but be aware that if you ever obtain a bad rating, this can mean big trouble for establishing credit with vendors or when looking for a loan.

Don't Give Up

The road to landing a loan is rough, even for established designers who've been around the block a few times. With a start-up, it just might be an impossible dream. If you're still employed and want to start your own business, you might apply for a loan while you still have a job, and start your business as a moonlighter. A bank may look at your day job as the capacity to repay a loan. Freelance on the side, and grow your business as you simultaneously grow your bank account. Eventually, use this reliability, experience, track record, and equity to show a bank you're a good risk.

Although a loan may be out of reach initially, look ahead. Form a relationship with your bank as you shape your business and career. While a bank loan might be hard to get at first, it may be a different story once you've established credit, built a good reputation, and have a solid business.

Accountant Grant Perks asks us to consider these old axioms: Borrow before you need it; banks like to loan money to people that need it least (to avoid undue risk). And remember these last words from accountant Gary Teach: "Once you line your ducks in a row, and *if* you succeed in collaring the loan, make sure you obtain the right amount of money the first time. We've established that getting a loan is no picnic, but going *back* to the well will be hard labor indeed."

ESTABLISHING CREDIT WITH VENDORS AND SUPPLIERS

You will want to establish credit with suppliers, such as printers, typesetters, supply houses, etc. The best way to do this is simple, short, and sweet: Pay up and on time. Develop rapport and a great track record. Keep those bills paid, and pay them quickly.

If you're trying to get credit, many vendors will ask you to fill out a credit form. This form asks where you do your banking and for references (two or three vendors you've used in the past). Once they've checked your references—and you check out—they will extend credit (another great reason to pay your bills on time).

SEEK AN ACCOUNTANT'S ADVICE

If you're just starting out, or are in your early years of doing business, you should hire (or, at the very least, consult) an accountant.

A good accountant can be the lynchpin of your business. He or she can review your situation and tell you if you need a lawyer, and then make recommendations and referrals. An accountant can apprise you of government regulations and requirements, set up your bookkeeping system, and be your financial advisor and tax consultant/preparer.

Find a person you can rely on year-round—don't be tempted to hire a moonlighter around tax time. You'll need to find someone who is well-qualified and whom you can trust, because ultimately, you will be responsible for this individual's mistakes. You may think you will save some money by going to "Taxes 'R Us" for your tax return, but it may cost you much more in IRS penalties when you find out what Ronald Maccountant didn't understand about tax law. As a designer with a new business, I'd go to a public accountant, an enrolled agent, or a CPA specializing in accounting and tax preparation for graphics professionals and/or small businesses.

As designer Tom Nicholson says: "Your accountant is probably the centerpiece of it all. An accountant can refer you to most of the other professionals. A designer can do his own bookkeeping, but you don't want to deal with tax situations on your own. For that reason alone, an accountant is a mainstay of your operation."

Your Graphic Artists Guild chapter may be able to give you a referral for an artist-savvy accountant; just ask.

Why Not Do It Yourself?

So, you bought a green eyeshade, and you're going to do your own tax return. Here are four well-chosen words: I'd advise against it. I can even make it simpler: *Don't!* Personal tax preparation is elaborate enough. Due to your start-up situation, you could make some mistakes; there may be some advantages, and some requirements, of which you might not be aware. Besides, you're a designer, not an accountant. Maybe you can do the job, but you really don't have the knowledge, experience, or expertise to do the job right (this is akin to having your CPA handle your design jobs). And finally, how much creative work will you accomplish away from the board, and what's your time worth?

How to Choose an Accountant

You'll want to find an accountant or firm with small business experience. Obviously, if you can, find someone who's familiar with designers and illustrators. It's best to get referrals from others in your situation who have a comparable income to your own.

There are four basic levels of experience that you can use in gauging the expertise of anyone you're interested in hiring:

- ▣ *Accountant:* Usually has a four-year degree in accounting, but doesn't necessarily *have* to have any training, much less a degree, license, or track record. Anyone can call himself an accountant—just like anyone can call herself a designer.
- ▣ *Enrolled Agent:* Certified by the IRS itself (but does not work for the government). Upon meeting official requirements and passing a number of exams, enrolled agents are the only other individuals (along with lawyers and CPAs) authorized to represent clients before the Internal Revenue Service.
- ▣ *Public Accountant:* If you can find one these days, a public accountant usually has a two- or four-year degree in accounting and is licensed by the state. He or she has probably passed a practical exam in the areas of accounting and tax, but each state will have different rules and regulations regarding who can call themselves a public accountant.
- ▣ *Certified Public Accountant:* The highest degree of professional accreditation. A CPA has a four- or five-year degree in accounting and at least one year of public accounting experience. Most important, all CPAs must pass an extremely rigorous exam.

Consider at least three to four possible candidates. Talk to both accounting firms and sole practitioners. When you interview accountants, evaluate each by considering:

- ▣ *Rapport:* Could you work with this individual? Do you like her? Do you like her style? Do you trust her?
- ▣ *Communication:* Can you understand him? Does he use plain language? Is his advice clear? Does he understand you? Will he fully comprehend both your personal and business needs?
- ▣ *Knowledge and Expertise:* Check this individual's credentials and accreditation. Find out how she maintains her knowledge base and continues

her education. Prepare questions and present data relevant to your business scenario. Do her recommendations make sense for your situation?

■> *Fee:* Finally, find out what this individual's fee will be for general advice, preparing quarterly reviews of your tax situation, and preparing a tax return. You will also want to find out if this individual will work with your bank, lawyer, and financial planner.

KNOW THE SCORE

Sponsored by the SBA, SCORE stands for the Service Corps of Retired Executives. It's a volunteer organization of men and women who counsel small businesses at start-up and offer business education programs. It can be a great clearinghouse of information from local professionals. As these folks have been there, they know and can help a small business through the rough spots, too. And guess what—their services are free! Check out the yellow pages for your local phone number.

■>

PROFESSIONAL ⬇ VIEWPOINTS

The number-one reason to be in business is to make money. The number-one reason to do illustration is to stay out of the mental hospital and, hopefully, have some fun doing it. If you're not independently wealthy or have values left over from the sixties (which is not entirely bad), then you're going to have to make a living. For me, freelancing is a marvelous way to do just that—you can make a lot of money!

—Bill Mayer, Illustrator

We met with an accountant and created a plan. A financial plan forces you to be realistic. It makes you put down on paper what you think your overhead is really going to be, how much it's going to take to meet that overhead and make enough money to live on. A plan helps you focus and organize. It would have been kind of frightening to have never gone through that process or do it the day we opened our doors.

—Don Sibley, Designer

In my experience, banks often ask for collateral in the same dollar amount that you're asking to borrow—a cold, hard fact, but it illustrates the unlikeliness of bank loans.

—Larissa Kisielewska, Designer

At our bank presentations, we found that they weren't really concerned about the creative end. Basically, what they were interested in was our ability to make good on the loan—they wanted to know what our personal and financial situations were.

—Don Sibley, Designer

Big is not better. Often, quality suffers with growth. But really, it's all relative— what is big? Is big one [person]? A staff of five, or ten? Some folks consider my firm, Pinkhaus, to be a "big" design firm, but I don't.

—Joel Fuller, Designer

Don't overspend. Don't overbuild. Be cautious as you expand—take small steps. Avoid runaway growth. Keep your overhead low. Think flexibility—plan ahead for expansion.

—Mike Quon, Designer and Illustrator

I made it a point to come up with a cash flow projection every year and base my growth strategies on this projection. I review this annual projection every three months and revise my plan and future projections, if necessary.

—Lori Siebert, Designer

Don't be in it for the money—know that you're working for your personal survival fund and that there's always another job coming down! Think of yourself as a business, and you're trying to enhance, market, sell, and promote that business.

—Fred Carlson, illustrator

Knowing what's happening (from a dollar standpoint) at any time, keeping close tabs on your costs is essential. It's really the most important part of operating a business, whether it's a one-man shop or a ten-person operation.

—Read Viemeister, Designer (deceased)

chapter 7

FORMS
CHARTS
TEMPLATES

A One-Year Projection (or Work Plan for Your Time)

	PROMO	BILLABLE	ADMINISTRATIVE
January	90	20	50 (setting up)
February	80	50	30
March	60	70	30
April	60	70	30
May	60	70	30
June	60	70	30
July	50	80	30
August (less 40 hrs.)	20	70	30
September	40	90	30
October	20	110	30
November	20	110	30
December (less 20 hrs.)	10	110	30

Here's an example of how a one-year projection (also called a work plan) for your time might look.

VENDOR NAME: _____				FOR Company Name: _____		
Phone: _____				Phone: _____		
Contact Person: _____				Contact Person: _____		
Date of Contact: _____				Date of Contact: _____		
Address: _____				Address: _____		
City/State/ZIP: _____				City/State/ZIP: _____		
Source: _____						

CPU				PRINTER				STORAGE		
Model	New	Used		Model	New	Used		Model	New	Used

KEYBOARD			APPROXIMATE TOTAL COST		
Model	New	Used	Item	Model	Amount
			CPU		
			Monitor		
			Keyboard		
			Card(s)		
			Drive(s)		
			Storage		
			Printer		
			Cables		
			Additional		
			Subtotal I		

MONITOR					
			Setup		
Model	New	Used	Consultation Fee		
			Subtotal II		
			Training		
			Technical Support		
			Subtotal III		
			Software		
			TOTAL		

This computer-buying worksheet, based on guides created by Steve Ledingham, will help you comparison shop for the best deal on your computer setup. Fill out one sheet for each vendor you contact. Try to keep the components in the same order in each section, so you don't end up accidentally comparing a high-priced computer with a lot of memory with one that has a lower price because it has less memory.

TASK	WEEKS BEFORE OPENING AND ANY CASH REQUIRED				OPEN	WEEKS AFTER OPENING AND ANY CASH REQUIRED			
	5-4	4-3	2	1	0	1	2	3	4
See lawyer									
See accountant									
Do initial ad									
Place ad									
Do/print promo									
Send promo									
Phone hook-up									
Get city permit									
Buy fax									
Utilities on and deposit									
Yellow pages listing									
Pay deposit and get keys									
Sign made									
Sign installed									
Do card and letterhead									
Do business forms									
Print all									
Pick up printing									
Refreshments for open house									
Sign up cleaning service									
Build shelves									
Cash Needed									

Use a task chart like this to plan your grand opening. Place an X in the corresponding column for each item, or enter the costs for each in the appropriate space.

START-UP COSTS		
Monthly	**Estimate**	**Actual**
Rent or Mortgage		
Legal		
Adv. and Promotion		
Supplies and Materials		
Acct./Bookkeeping		
Other professional fees		
Insurance		
Owner's Draw		
Shipping and delivery		
Telephone/Fax		
Utilities		
Loan and Interest		
Maintenance/cleaning		
Auto/travel		
Other		
Subtotal		
One-time Only	**Estimate**	**Actual**
Operating cash		
License and permits		
Deposit for Utilities		
Decorating/Remodeling		
Fixtures and Equipment		
Installation of Equip.		
Rent Deposit		
Legal Consultant		
Accountant Consultant		
Initial Adv./Promo		
Miscellaneous		
Subtotal		
Total cash needed		

This start-up worksheet will help you figure out such initial expenses as deposits for utilities or printing letterhead, and ongoing expenses, such as supplies and materials or telephone bills.

Year:	Month:				
Budget		**Estimate**	**Actual**	**Estimate**	**Actual**
INCOME:	Cash on hand, first of month				
	Receipts				
	Loans				
	Savings				
	A. Total Cash Available				
EXPENSES:	Rent/Mortgage				
	Health/Life/Business Insurance				
	Supplies and Materials				
	Shipping				
	Utilities				
	Telephone/Fax				
	Repairs/Maintenance				
	Legal				
	Travel/Transportation				
	Meals and Entertainment				
	Advertising and Promotion				
	Equipment				
	Cleaning				
	Dues and Publications				
	Accounting/Bookkeeping				
	Other				
	Subtotal				
	Loan Payment With Interest				
	Owner's Draw				
	Capital Purchased (depreciated items)				
	B. Total Cash Paid Out				
	Subtract Total B from Total A (+or-)				

This budget worksheet will help you see how much money you must make to cover your expenses—or how little you can afford to spend. First, estimate how much actual cash you will have on hand each month (when in doubt, go low). Then, list what you'll need to cover expenses. If you can't make ends meet on paper, you won't in real life either. Keep refiguring your expenses until you get a workable result. Once you're up and running, track your actual *expenses and see how your budget is working out. How we doin'?*

< Illustrator's Letterhead >

PROPOSAL FORM

Client Name _____ Date _____

Project Title _____

Nature of Project _____
_____
_____
_____

Project Plan _____
_____
_____
_____

Itemization of Expenses
Nature of Expense _____ Fee _____
_____ _____
_____ _____
_____ _____
_____ _____

Reimbursables to be billed with a _____% Markup _____

Schedule of Payment _____
_____
_____
_____

Fee Upon Completion of Project _____

Client agrees to the above stated schedule, plan, and charges. Any desired changes expressed by the client to be made following the commencement of the project will require additional compensation to the illustrator or designer, in addition to the payment of whatever costs are incurred to the illustrator or designer as a result of the client's change. (See the "Notes" section of this form for additional stipulations regarding client changes.) Any additional work done by the designer that is not outlined in this form will be billed in addition to the expenses stated above.

Notes _____
_____
_____
_____

Client Signature _____ Date _____
Company Name _____

A proposal, like the example form here, should clearly define the design services to be provided, describing them in enough detail for the client to know easily what will be done and when.

Proposals can vary in length and content, depending on the client and the nature of the project. In any scenario, certain key features are common: Expenses will be itemized and the billing schedule established. The document should spell out how client changes will be handled (and include a request for the client's signature to acknowledge agreement with these costs for work to commence). It should be clear that work not described in the proposal (such as extra presentations) would be billed in addition to the expenses listed in the proposal.

< Illustrator's Letterhead >

Estimate

Client _____ Date _____

Address _____

Client Purchase Order Number _____ Job Number _____

This Estimate is based on the specifications and terms that follow. If the Client confirms that the Illustrator should proceed with the assignment based on this Estimate, it is understood that the assignment shall be subject to the terms shown on this Estimate and that Client shall sign a Confirmation of Assignment form incorporating the same specifications and terms. If the assignment proceeds without a Confirmation of Assignment being signed by both parties, the assignment shall be governed by the terms and conditions contained in this Estimate.

1. **Description.** The Illustrator shall create the Work in accordance with the following specifications:

   Subject matter _____ .

   Number of illustrations in color _____ Number of illustrations in black and white _____

   Size of illustrations _____ Medium for illustrations _____

   Other specifications _____

2. **Due Date.** Sketches shall be delivered within _____ days after either the Client's authorization to commence work or, if the Client is to provide reference, layouts, or specifications, after the Client has provided same to the Illustrator, whichever occurs later. Finished art shall be delivered _____ days after the approval of sketches by the Client.

3. **Grant of Rights.** Upon receipt of full payment, the Illustrator shall grant to the Client the following rights in the finished art:

   For use as _____

   For the product or publication named _____

   In the following territory _____

   For the following time period _____

   Other limitations _____

   With respect to the usage shown above, the Client shall have ❏ exclusive ❏ nonexclusive rights.

   If the finished art is for use as a contribution to a magazine, the grant of rights shall be first North American serial rights only, unless specified to the contrary above.

   This grant of rights does not include electronic rights, unless specified to the contrary here _____ in which event the usage restrictions shown above shall be applicable. For purposes of this agreement, electronic rights are defined as rights in the digitized form of works that can be encoded, stored, and retrieved from such media as computer disks, CD-ROM, computer databases, and network servers.

4. **Reservation of Rights.** All rights not expressly granted shall be reserved to the Illustrator, including but not limited to all rights in sketches, comps, or other preliminary materials.

5. **Fee.** Client shall pay the purchase price of $_____ for the usage rights granted. Client shall also pay sales tax, if required.

6. **Additional Usage.** If Client wishes to make any additional uses of the Work, Client shall seek permission from the Illustrator and pay an additional fee to be agreed upon.

7. **Expenses.** Client shall reimburse the Illustrator for the following expenses: ❏ Messenger ❏ Models ❏ Props ❏ Travel ❏ Telephone ❏ Other _____. At the time of signing the Confirmation of Assignment or the commencement of work, whichever is first, Client shall pay Illustrator $_____ as a nonrefundable advance against expenses. If the advance exceeds expenses incurred, the credit balance shall be used to reduce the fee payable, or, if the fee has been fully paid, shall be reimbursed to Client.

8. **Payment.** Client shall pay the Illustrator within thirty (30) days of the date of Illustrator's billing, which shall be dated as of the date of delivery of the finished art. In the event that work is postponed at the request of the Client, the Illustrator shall have the right to bill pro rata for work completed through the date of that request, while reserving all other rights. Overdue payments shall be subject to interest charges of _____ percent monthly.

9. **Advances.** At the time of signing the Confirmation of Assignment or the commencement of work, whichever is first, Client shall pay Illustrator ____ percent of the fee as an advance against the total fee. Upon approval of sketches, Client shall pay Illustrator ____ percent of the fee as an advance against the total fee.

10. **Revisions.** The Illustrator shall be given the first opportunity to make any revisions requested by the Client. If the revisions are not due to any fault on the part of the Illustrator, an additional fee shall be charged. If the Illustrator objects to any revisions to be made by the Client, the Illustrator shall have the right to have his or her name removed from the published Work.

11. **Copyright Notice.** Copyright notice in the name of the Illustrator ❏ shall ❏ shall not accompany the Work when it is reproduced.

12. **Authorship Credit.** Authorship credit in the name of the Illustrator ❏ shall ❏ shall not accompany the Work when it is reproduced. If the finished art is used as a contribution to a magazine or for a book, authorship credit shall be given unless specified to the contrary in the preceding sentence.

13. **Cancellation.** In the event of cancellation by the Client, the following cancellation payment shall be paid by the Client: **(A)** cancellation prior to the finished art being turned in: ____ percent of fee, **(B)** cancellation due to finished art being unsatisfactory: _____ percent of fee, and **(C)** cancellation for any other reason after the finished art is turned in: _____ percent of fee. In the event of cancellation, the Client shall also pay any expenses incurred by the Illustrator and the Illustrator shall own all rights in the Work. The billing upon cancellation shall be payable within thirty (30) days of the Client's notification to stop work or the delivery of the finished art, whichever occurs sooner.

14. **Ownership and Return of Artwork.** The ownership of original artwork, including sketches and any other materials created in the process of making the finished art, shall remain with the Illustrator. All such artwork shall be returned to the Illustrator by bonded messenger, air freight, or registered mail within thirty (30) days of the Client's completing its use of the artwork. Based on the specifications for the Work, a reasonable value for the original, finished art is $_____.

15. **Permissions and Releases.** The Client shall indemnify and hold harmless the Illustrator against any and all claims, costs, and expenses, including attorney's fees, due to materials included in the work at the request of the Client for which no copyright permission or privacy release was requested or uses that exceed the uses allowed pursuant to a permission or release.

16. **Arbitration.** All disputes shall be submitted to binding arbitration before _____ in the following location _____ and settled in accordance with the rules of the American Arbitration Association. Judgment upon the arbitration award may be entered in any court having jurisdiction thereof. Disputes in which the amount at issue is less than $_____ shall not be subject to this arbitration provision.

17. **Miscellany.** If the Client authorizes the Illustrator to commence work, the terms of this Estimate Form shall be binding upon the parties, their heirs, successors, assigns, and personal representatives; the Estimate Form constitutes the entire understanding between the parties; its terms can be modified only by an instrument in writing signed by both parties, except that the Client may authorize expenses and revisions orally; a waiver of a breach of any of its provisions shall not be construed as a continuing waiver of other breaches of the same or other provisions hereof; and the relationship between the Client and Illustrator shall be governed by the laws of the State of _____.

Illustrator _____

19 West 44th Street, Suite 1500 • New York, New York 10036 • 212.221.7559

OPTIMUM
design & consulting ▯

ESTIMATE NUMBER: 16-2-A.1367

DATE: 20 February 2001

DESIGNER: Rebecca Blake for
Optimum Design & Consulting
I.D. No. 11-3110325

CLIENT: American Express

OF: World Financial Tower, 200 Vesey Street, 37th Floor
New York, New York 10285-4817

CONTACT: Teresa Legree

JOB: SBS Lending Products sales kit

ACCOUNT NUMBER: 88AE.540P

ASSIGNMENT DESCRIPTION: Design and produce a 9x12" four-color one-pocket folder with text printing on the inside cover and nine insert sheets consisting of client-supplied text and graphics. Design should be clear and concise but attractive, and should appeal to an ethnically diverse audience of small-business owners.

ITEMIZED EXPENSES

DATA ENTRY OR COPYWRITING	$50.00	PROOFS	$649.25
ILLUSTRATION	$0.00	MATERIALS AND SUPPLIES	$0.00
PHOTOGRAPHY	$0.00	PRINTING AND FINISHING	$5,546.45
SCANS	$0.00	SHIPPING AND MESSENGERS	$165.00
IMAGE MANIPULATION	$0.00	MAILING PREP AND POSTAGE	$0.00
DESIGN	$1,080.00	TRAVEL	$0.00
MANUAL OR ELECTRONIC PRODUCTION	$450.00	CONSULTING AND TRACKING	$405.00
STATS, FILM AND SLIDES	$956.80	SALE OF RIGHTS	$0.00

DESIGN AND PRODUCTION FEE INCLUDES

Creation of materials based on client-supplied text provided in IBM format and nine client-supplied graphics; presentation of up to three comprehensive layouts showing format; production of camera-ready film and color proofs; and coordination with chosen printer.

PRINTING FEE INCLUDES:

500 9x12" four-color one-pocket folders with nine individual 8.5x11" four-color sheets printing with bleeds in full color on bright white coated stock. One blueline proof is included in the price.

DESIGN AND PRODUCTION FEE: $3,756.05

PRINTING FEE: $5,546.45

PLEASE MAKE CHEQUE PAYABLE TO: OPTIMUM DESIGN & CONSULTING
Please sign both copies of this estimate and return one to Optimum Design & Consulting. Half of this fee is to be paid upon signing this document, the remainder upon delivery.

THANK YOU.

FOR OFFICE USE ONLY: MC ☐ V ☐ AE ☐   ACCT.#: _____ EXP.: _____ SWIPE ☐
T.E.☐ CASH ☐ CHEQUE ☐ DEPOSIT: _____ DATE: _____ CHEQUE #: _____

Designer Larissa Kisielewska uses this simple estimate to spell out what will be done, what it will cost, and when payments are expected, as does the estimate template from Business and Legal Forms for Illustrators. *Whether part of a proposal or presented separately, an estimate—like any good business form—will cover all the necessary details to help keep the business side of the studio running smoothly. © Larissa Kisielewska 2001, Optimum Design & Consulting*

Confirmation of Assignment

AGREEMENT entered into as of the _____ day of _____, _____, between _____ (hereinafter referred to as the "Client"), located at _____, and _____ (hereinafter referred to as the "Illustrator"), located at _____, with respect to the creation of certain illustrations (hereinafter referred to as the "Work").

WHEREAS, Illustrator is a professional illustrator of good standing;

WHEREAS, Client wishes the Illustrator to create certain Work described more fully herein; and

WHEREAS, Illustrator wishes to create such Work.

NOW, THEREFORE, in consideration for the foregoing premises and the mutual covenants hereinafter set forth and other valuable considerations, the parties hereto agree as follows:

1. Description. The Illustrator agrees to create the Work in accordance with the following specifications:

Subject matter _____

Number of illustrations in color _____ Number of illustrations in black and white _____

Size of illustrations _____ Medium for illustrations _____

Other specifications _____

Client purchase order number _____ Job number _____

2. Due Date. The Illustrator agrees to deliver sketches within _____ days after the later of the signing of this Agreement or, if the Client is to provide reference, layouts, or specifications, after the Client has provided same to the Illustrator. Finished art shall be delivered _____ days after the approval of sketches by the Client.

3. Grant of Rights. Upon receipt of full payment, the Illustrator grants to the Client the following rights in the finished art:

For use as _____

For the product or publication named _____

In the following territory _____

For the following time period _____

Other limitations _____

With respect to the usage shown above, the Client shall have ❑ exclusive ❑ nonexclusive rights.

If the finished art is for use as a contribution to a magazine, the grant of rights shall be for first North American serial rights only unless specified to the contrary above.

This grant of rights does not include electronic rights, unless specified to the contrary here _____ in which event the usage restrictions shown above shall be applicable. For purposes of this Agreement, electronic rights are defined as rights in the digitized form of works that can be encoded, stored, and retrieved from such media as computer disks, CD-ROM, computer databases, and network servers.

4. Reservation of Rights. All rights not expressly granted hereunder are reserved to the Illustrator, including but not limited to all rights in sketches, comps, or other preliminary materials.

5. Fee. Client agrees to pay the purchase price of $_____ for the usage rights granted. Client agrees to pay sales tax, if required.

6. Additional Usage. If Client wishes to make any additional uses of the Work, Client agrees to seek permission from the Illustrator and make such payments as are agreed to between the parties at that time.

7. Expenses. Client agrees to reimburse the Illustrator for the following expenses: ❑ Messengers ❑ Models ❑ Props ❑ Travel ❑ Telephone ❑ Other _____.

At the time of signing this Agreement, Client shall pay Illustrator $_____ as a nonrefundable advance against expenses. If the advance exceeds expenses incurred, the credit balance shall be used to reduce the fee payable or, if the fee has been fully paid, shall be reimbursed to Client.

When working with a client you know well, you could send a short-and-sweet, simple working agreement (maybe even incorporating this as part of the proposal). This may be all the contract you need. With all first-time clients, or when taking on big projects, you'll need something more formal and detailed like this Confirmation of Assignment from Business and Legal Forms for Illustrators. *Look for a slightly reworded, but very similar document in* Business and Legal Forms for Graphic Designers, *both by Allworth Press.*

8. **Payment.** Client agrees to pay the Illustrator within thirty (30) days of the date of Illustrator's billing, which shall be dated as of the date of delivery of the finished art. In the event that work is postponed at the request of the Client, the Illustrator shall have the right to bill pro rata for work completed through the date of that request, while reserving all other rights under this Agreement. Overdue payments shall be subject to interest charges of _____ percent monthly.

9. **Advances.** At the time of signing this Agreement, Client shall pay Illustrator _____ percent of the fee as an advance against the total fee. Upon approval of sketches, Client shall pay Illustrator _____ percent of the fee as an advance against the total fee.

10. **Revisions.** The Illustrator shall be given the first opportunity to make any revisions requested by the Client. If the revisions are not due to any fault on the part of the Illustrator, an additional fee shall be charged. If the Illustrator objects to any revisions to be made by the Client, the Illustrator shall have the right to have his or her name removed from the published Work.

11. **Copyright Notice.** Copyright notice in the Illustrator's name ❑ shall ❑ shall not be published with the Work.

12. **Authorship Credit.** Authorship credit in the name of the Illustrator ❑ shall ❑ shall not accompany the Work when it is reproduced. If the finished art is used as a contribution to a magazine or for a book, authorship credit shall be given unless specified to the contrary in the preceding sentence.

13. **Cancellation.** In the event of cancellation by the Client, the following cancellation payment shall be paid by the Client: **(A)** cancellation prior to the finished art being turned in: _____ percent of fee, **(B)** cancellation due to finished art being unsatisfactory: _____ percent of fee, and **(C)** cancellation for any other reason after the finished art is turned in: _____ percent of fee. In the event of cancellation, the Client shall also pay any expenses incurred by the Illustrator and the Illustrator shall own all rights in the Work. The billing upon cancellation shall be payable within thirty (30) days of the Client's notification to stop work or the delivery of the finished art, whichever occurs sooner.

14. **Ownership and Return of Artwork.** The ownership of original artwork, including sketches and any other materials created in the process of making the finished art, shall remain with the Illustrator. All such artwork shall be returned to the Illustrator by bonded messenger, air freight, or registered mail within thirty days of the Client's completing its use of the artwork. The parties agree that the value of the original finished art is $_____.

15. **Permissions and Releases.** The Client agrees to indemnify and hold harmless the Illustrator against any and all claims, costs, and expenses, including attorney's fees, due to materials included in the Work at the request of the Client for which no copyright permission or privacy release was requested or uses that exceed those allowed pursuant to a permission or release.

16. **Arbitration.** All disputes arising under this Agreement shall be submitted to binding arbitration before _____ in the following location _____ and settled in accordance with the rules of the American Arbitration Association. Judgment upon the arbitration award may be entered in any court having jurisdiction thereof. Disputes in which the amount at issue is less than $_____ shall not be subject to this arbitration provision.

17. **Miscellany.** This Agreement shall be binding upon the parties hereto, their heirs, successors, assigns, and personal representatives. This Agreement constitutes the entire understanding between the parties. Its terms can be modified only by an instrument in writing signed by both parties, except that the Client may authorize expenses or revisions orally. A waiver of a breach of any of the provisions of this Agreement shall not be construed as a continuing waiver of other breaches of the same or other provisions hereof. This Agreement shall be governed by the laws of the State of _____.

IN WITNESS WHEREOF, the parties hereto have signed this Agreement as of the date first set forth above.

Illustrator _____   Client _____
                                                    Company Name

                                             By _____
                                                    Authorized Signatory, Title

< Illustrator's Letterhead >

Basic Invoice

Client _____ Date _____

Address _____

Client Purchase Order Number _____ Job Number _____

Assignment Description _____

Fee.. $_____

Expenses................................. $_____

Revisions................................. $_____

Advances................................. ($_____)

Balance.................................... $_____

Sales tax.................................. $_____

Balance due............................ $_____

This Invoice is subject to the terms and conditions set forth in the Confirmation of Assignment dated _____.

The invoice picks up where the agreement leaves off and should be both functional and attractive. This invoice from Business and Legal Forms for Illustrators *presents a good example. No matter how you develop your forms, be sure your terms for payment are clearly printed on them. If you charge interest on overdue balances, you must state this clearly on the invoice.*

< Illustrator's Letterhead >

Invoice

Client _____ Date _____

Address _____

Client Purchase Order Number _____ Job Number _____

                      Fee... $_____

                      Expenses.................................. $_____

                      Revisions.................................. $_____

                      Advances................................. ($_____)

                      Balance.................................... $_____

                      Sales tax.................................. $_____

                      Balance due............................ $_____

This Invoice is subject to the terms and conditions that follow.

1. Description. The Illustrator has created and delivered to Client _____ illustrations for the following project _____.

2. Delivery Date. The finished art was delivered on _____, _____.

3. Grant of Rights. Upon receipt of full payment, Illustrator shall grant to the Client the following rights in the finished art:

For use as _____ For the product or publication named _____

In the following territory _____ For the following time period _____

Other limitations _____

With respect to the usage shown above, the Client shall have ❑ exclusive ❑ nonexclusive rights.

If the finished art is for use as a contribution to a magazine, the grant of rights shall be first North American serial rights only, unless specified to the contrary above.

This grant of rights does not include electronic rights, unless specified to the contrary here_____

in which event the usage restrictions shown above shall be applicable. For purposes of this Agreement, electronic rights are defined as rights in the digitized form of works that can be encoded, stored, and retrieved from such media as computer disks, CD-ROM, computer databases, and network servers.

4. Reservation of Rights. All rights not expressly granted are reserved to the Illustrator, including but not limited to all rights in sketches, comps, or other preliminary materials.

5. Fee. Client shall pay the purchase price of $_____ for the usage rights granted. Client shall also pay sales tax, if required.

6. Additional Usage. If Client wishes to make any additional uses of the Work, Client shall seek permission from the Illustrator and pay an additional fee to be agreed upon.

7. Expenses. If Illustrator incurred reimbursable expenses, a listing of such expenses is attached to this Invoice with copies of supporting documentation. Illustrator has received $_____ as an advance against expenses.

8. Payment. Payment is due to the Illustrator within thirty (30) days of the date of this Invoice, which is dated as of the date of delivery of the finished art. Overdue payments shall be subject to interest charges of _____ percent monthly.

9. Advances. Illustrator received $_____ as an advance against the total fee.

10. Revisions. The Illustrator shall be given the first opportunity to make any revisions requested by the Client. If the revisions are not due to any fault on the part of the Illustrator, an additional fee shall be charged. If the Illustrator objects to any revisions to be made by the Client, the Illustrator shall have the right to have his or her name removed from the published Work.

11. Copyright Notice. Copyright notice in the name of the Illustrator ❑ shall ❑ shall not accompany the Work when it is reproduced.

12. Authorship Credit. Authorship credit in the name of the Illustrator ❑ shall ❑ shall not accompany the Work when it is reproduced. If the finished art is used as a contribution to a magazine or for a book, authorship credit shall be given unless specified to the contrary in the preceding sentence.

13. Cancellation. In the event of cancellation by the Client, the amount charged to the Client as the fee in this Invoice has been computed as follows based on the fee originally agreed upon: **(A)** cancellation prior to the finished art being turned in: ____ percent of fee, **(B)** cancellation due to finished art being unsatisfactory: ____ percent of fee, and **(C)** cancellation for any other reason after the finished art is turned in: ____ percent of fee. In the event of cancellation, the Client shall pay any expenses incurred by the Illustrator and the Illustrator shall own all rights in the Work. The Invoice upon cancellation is payable within thirty (30) days of the Client's notification to stop work or the delivery of the finished art, whichever occurs sooner.

14. Ownership and Return of Artwork. The ownership of original artwork, including sketches and any other materials created in the process of making the finished art, shall remain with the Illustrator. All such artwork shall be returned to the Illustrator by bonded messenger, air freight, or registered mail within thirty (30) days of the Client's completing its use of the artwork. A reasonable value for the original, finished art is $_____.

15. Permissions and Releases. The Client shall indemnify and hold harmless the Illustrator against any and all claims, costs, and expenses, including attorney's fees, due to materials included in the Work at the request of the Client for which no copyright permission or privacy release was requested or uses which exceed the uses allowed pursuant to a permission or release.

16. Arbitration. All disputes shall be submitted to binding arbitration before _____ in the following location _____ and settled in accordance with the rules of the American Arbitration Association. Judgment upon the arbitration award may be entered in any court having jurisdiction thereof. Disputes in which the amount at issue is less than $_____ shall not be subject to this arbitration provision.

17. Miscellany. This Invoice shall be governed by the laws of the State of _____.

Illustrator _____

			ESTIMATE ☐	
		ASSIGNMENT CONFIRMATION ☐		
		INVOICE ☐		
	PAST DUE STATEMENT ☐			

DATE	INVOICE NUMBER	DESCRIPTION	AMOUNT

PLEASE PAY THIS AMOUNT _____

Stephanie Norris
13336 Old Dayton Road
New Lebanon, Ohio 45345
937.687.1075
snorrisus@yahoo.com

Designer Stephanie Norris created this form. When the appropriate box is checked, it can serve as an estimate, assignment confirmation, invoice, or past due statement (never let an unpaid invoice just slide by). The sheet, as suggested by the folks at Sibley/Poteet Design, will have columns for an invoice number, a complete description of the project/item involved, and the amount due.

You can include a printed statement telling the client that any itemized charges are only esti-mates unless the form is designated as an actual invoice. You can also include a blurb that validates the estimate for a set duration (say, 30 days), after which the charges may change.

Whether your forms are designed generically or as separate documents, be sure your terms for payment (including interest on overdue balances) are spelled out and printed clearly.

TITLE / DESCRIPTION OF JOB

COMPANY NAME

PERSON TO CONTACT

E-MAIL CONTACT

COMPANY TELEPHONE ( )

HOME TELEPHONE ( )

ADDRESS

CUSTOMER P.O. NO.

DATE

REQUESTED DELIVERY DATE

CITY ____ STATE ____ ZIP

JOB NO. ____

PREVIOUS JOB NO. ____

☐ ORDER ☐ EST

PRE-PRODUCTION NOTES

MOCK UP
LAYOUT DEADLINE
PRINTING DEADLINE
PRINTER
COPYWRITER
PHOTOGRAPHER
ILLUSTRATOR
OTHER INFO

POST-PRODUCTION NOTES

MARKETING MATERIALS

☐ ADVERTISEMENT SIZE
  ☐ ROUGH LAYOUT ☐ COLOR COMP
  COLORS:
  STOCKS:
  OTHER INFO

☐ DIRECT SIZE
  ☐ ROUGH LAYOUT ☐ COLOR COMP
  COLORS:
  STOCKS:
  OTHER INFO

☐ INVITATION / ANNOUNCEMENT SIZE
  ☐ ROUGH LAYOUT ☐ COLOR COMP
  COLORS:
  STOCKS:
  OTHER INFO

☐ OTHER

☐ OTHER

OUTDOOR GRAPHICS

☐ SIGNAGE DESCRIPTION

☐ BILLBOARD DESCRIPTION

☐ OTHER DESCRIPTION

CORPORATE IDENTITY

☐ LOGO
  ROUGH LAYOUT | COLOR COMPS

☐ LETTERHEAD / ENVELOPE / BUSINESS CARD
  ROUGH LAYOUT | COLOR COMPS

☐ OTHER
  ROUGH LAYOUT | COLOR COMPS
  OTHER INFO

CORPORATE IMAGE

☐ ANNUAL
  NO. OF PAGES SIZE
  ☐ ROUGH LAYOUT ☐ COLOR COMP
  COLORS:
  STOCKS:
  OTHER INFO

☐ PRESENTATION PORTFOLIO KIT SIZE
  ☐ ROUGH LAYOUT ☐ COLOR COMP
  ☐ REQUEST PAPER DUMMY
  COLORS:
  STOCKS:
  OTHER INFO

☐ BROCHURE SIZE
  ☐ ROUGH LAYOUT ☐ COLOR COMP
  COLORS:
  STOCKS:
  OTHER INFO

☐ NEWSLETTER SIZE
  ☐ ROUGH LAYOUT ☐ COLOR COMP
  COLORS:
  STOCKS:
  OTHER INFO

Job sheets, as suggested by Adela Ward Batin, can help you keep projects in order. The reverse side could be a time sheet.

Client _____	Job # _____
Address _____	Date Rec'd _____
_____	Rec'd By _____
Client Contract _____ Phone _____	Due Date _____
Client PO# _____	Ship Via _____
Job Description _____	Shipping Cost _____

Design	_____	$ _____
Copy	_____	$ _____
Computer Time	_____	$ _____
Illustration	_____	$ _____
Photography	_____	$ _____
Production	_____	$ _____
Other	_____	$ _____
Proofreading	1) _____ 2) _____	Revisions

Special Instructions:

Theo Stephan Williams suggests using a variation of this form to track works in progress. Fill out the sheet with the names of those employees or vendors assigned to each stage of the project. Write pertinent notes, facts, and figures by each name.

WEEKLY TIME SHEET

✓	Job #	Client	Description	Miles	Code	M	T	W	TH	F	SAT	SUN
	9779	Maxwell										
				Total								

Code:

M	Meeting Time	R	Revisions
D	Design	RS	Research
L	Layout	MP	Media Plan./Buy
CW	Copywriting	AD	Art Direction
C	Computer Time	CL	Clerical
I	Illustration	PR	Public Relations
P	Production	T	Travel Time
PF	Proofreading	PP	Proposal Prep
		CS	Client Service

Name_____ Date_____ To_____

Keep a weekly or daily time sheet. As suggested by designer Theo Stephan Williams, this form details what you did on each job you worked, when you did it, and how much time you spent. The sheet can make it much easier for you to prepare invoices for clients and to estimate future jobs, as you'll know just how many hours you'll need to finish each phase of any project.

Job #	Date	Client	Description	Due Date	Date Closed	Invoice #	Invoice Date

Theo Stephan Williams suggests using a variation of this job log. The sheet is ordered by job number and covers the major events in a project's life cycle: due date, date the file was closed and stored, and the date the invoice was sent. For another example, see designer Larissa Kisielewska's job log. © Larissa Kisielewska 2001, Optimum Design & Consulting

Date		Paid By	Amount			Sales (Taxable)		Tax Data Sales Tax (@ 8 ¼%)		Total Gross Sales
1991										
Jan	16	Caputo Ink	1000.00							
	21	Maxwell	1082.50			1000.00		82.50		
	24	Cooper Co.	541.25			500.00		41.25		
	28	Scarlet Letters	2200.00							
		Totals	4823.75			1500.00		123.75		4700.00

A simple income journal like this one recommended by accountant Juda Kallus may be all you really need to keep track of your income and the amount of sales tax you must pay.

Business Income and Expenses

3

Owner's Name		Social Security Number	
A. Business/ Professional Activity		B. Business Code (please leave blank)	
C. Business Name or Your Name		D. Employer Identification No.	
E. Business Address		City	State Zip

H. Is this the first year or final year of your business? ☐ Yes ☐ No   If yes, starting date: ending date:

| STATE CODE: | | LEAVE BLANK: | NYC–202—UBT: ☐ Yes ☐ No | Y–203: ☐ Yes ☐ No |

DO YOU HAVE A STUDIO/OFFICE-AT-HOME? ☐ YES ☐ NO IF YES, ENTER HOME-OFFICE EXPENSES (RENT, ELECTRICITY, ETC.) **ON THE OTHER SIDE OF THIS SHEET.**

GROSS INCOME FROM 1099-MISCS AND YOUR RECORDS

DO NOT INCLUDE INTEREST INCOME OR W-2 AMOUNTS!

1. List payers individually or enter total business income	Amt. Recvd. by 12/31
6. Auto lease inclusion	(LEAVE BLANK)
Total	

COST OF GOODS SOLD

COMPLETE ONLY IF YOU SELL MERCHANDISE OR HAVE HIGH DIRECT COSTS

35 Inventory at beginning of year	
36 Purchases	
37 Cost of labor	
38 Materials + supplies	
39 Other costs (Include sales tax paid directly to your state)	
41 Inventory at end of year	
Cost of Sales	

BUSINESS EXPENSES

8 Advertising		- 6 **Co**mputer Expenses (only Supplies + Services)	
10 Auto + Truck Expenses (See Sh.#2–Auto Expenses)		- 7 **Du**es – Professional Associations	
11 Commissions/Agents Fees		- 8 **Ex**hibits / Trade Shows / Conventions	
13 Equipment/Furniture	(SEE OTHER SIDE)	- 9 **Fr**eelancers (See Note* other side)	
14 Employee Benefit	(LEAVE BLANK)	-10 **In**ternet + Paging Service	
15 Business Insurance (Not Medical + Disability)		-11 **La**bs + Photostats	
15a Health Insurance		-12 **Li**notronic Output	
16a Interest – (Mortgage on Business Property)		-13 **Lo**cal Transportation	
16b Interest – Credit Card etc.(Business Portion Only)		-14 **Me**ssengers / Postage / FedEx/UPS	
17 Accounting / Legal / Professional Services		-15 **Mo**ving + Storage (Business Portion Only)	
18 Office Expenses		-16 **Pa**rking + Tolls (Business Portion Only)	
19 Pension / Profit Sharing (Only for Employees)	(LEAVE BLANK)	-17 **Ph**otography	
20a Rent – Machinery + Equipment		-18 **Po**rtfolio Expense	
20b Rent – Studio/Office (Not in Your Home)		-19 **Pri**nting + Copying	
21 Repairs (NOT TO YOUR HOME)		-20 **Pro**ps	
22 Supplies		-21 **Re**search Material	
23 NYC Unincorporated BusinessTax		-22 **Se**minars + Professional Education	
24a Travel + Lodging (Out of Town for Business)		-23 **Sm**all Tools / Equipment ($300 or less each item)	
24b Meals + Entertainment (Enter 100%)		-24 **So**ftware	
25 Utilities + Telephone (Not in Your Home) See back		-25 **Mi**scellaneous	
26 Wages (Only for Employees you issued W-2)	(LEAVE BLANK)	List other business expenses	
27-1 **Au**to Rental – (Business Portion Only)			
-2 **Bank** Charges – (Business Portion Only)			
-3 **Bo**oks + Publications			
-4 **Bu**siness Gift / Gratuities*(See notes on other side)			
-5 **Cl**eaning – Office/Studio (Not in Your Home) See back			

Total Expenses	COS	H/O	Net

Mary Ann Nichols designed these forms with her husband, accountant Juda Kallus. The sheets are fairly detailed lists of items that can be deducted as business expenses, as well as "office-in-home" items on the back of the sheet. These forms and others can be found at www.judakallus.com. © Juda Kallus/Mary Ann Nichols 2001.

Other Business Expenses

PLEASE NOTE: Our line numbers are sometimes a little wacky because we planned them to correspond to our tax software. Missing line numbers are either not relevent or are computation totals that are not needed on this form.

3

30. STUDIO/OFFICE-IN-HOME EXPENSES – 8829

Was area used regulary & exclusively for business? ☐ Yes ☐ No   **NOTE: If answer is "NO" –no deduction is allowed.**

1. Square Feet Used for Business	1.
2. Total Square feet in Home or Apartment	2.
1÷2 = Business Use Percent When Area is Exclusively Used for Business	%

II. HOME EXPENSES

Expenses	Total Paid	Bus.%	Bus. Amt.	Leave Blank	Expenses	Total Paid	Bus.%	Bus. Amt.	Leave Blank
19 Electricity					10 Mortgage Interest				
19 Heating Oil/Gas					11 Real Estate Taxes				
20a Telephone(see**below)	N/A	N/A			17 Insurance				
20b Rent					18 Repairs/Maintenance				
20c Cleaning					Other				

III. OFFICE-IN-HOME DEPRECIATION DO NOT ENTER PRIOR YEARS COSTS IF WE PREPARED YOUR LAST YEAR'S TAX RETURN.

ENTER CURRENT YEAR'S COSTS FIRST	Date Acquired	Business %	Cost	Land Value	(LEAVE BLANK)
40. Home					

13. BUSINESS EQUIPMENT, FURNITURE DO NOT ENTER PRIOR YEARS COSTS IF WE PREPARED YOUR LAST YEAR'S TAX RETURN.

ENTER CURRENT YEAR'S COSTS FIRST. If you are using any equipment/furniture which you acquired in previous years but did not deduct on your tax return, please fill in the information below. Did you sell any property previously deducted in this section? If yes, please attach explanation.

Description of Assets (Each costing $500 or more)	Date Acquired	Business %	Cost	Type (LEAVE BLANK)	Years (LEAVE BLANK)	Method (LEAVE BLANK)

The IRS allows 32.5¢ per business mile in lieu of actual costs, plus business portion of parking, tolls and auto loan interest.

AUTO USED FOR BUSINESS

43 Date Acquired	Cost of Auto (4562)	44a Business Miles	b Commuting Miles (not deductible)	c Personal Miles	Total Miles

45 The IRS would like to know– Is another vehicle available for your personal use? ☐ Yes ☐ No

47a Do you have evidence to support your mileage? ☐ Yes ☐ No   **47b** Is the evidence in writing? ☐ Yes ☐ No

ACTUAL AUTO EXPENSES (OPTIONAL) 4562

Gas, Repairs, Insurance, Interest. on Auto Loan, Registration/License, etc. plus Lease Payments: (Attach copy of Lease Agreement)

Freelance Expenses   The IRS requires you to report on Form 1099–Misc., the Name, Address and Social Security Number of every person to whom you paid $600 or more for commissions or compensation for services rendered to you in the course of your trade or business. A copy of Form 1099 must be submitted to the IRS by February 28th. If you would like us to prepare your 1099s, please call us.

**Phone Expense   The tax law restricts your home telephone deductions. You may not deduct the basic monthly charges. You can deduct costs incurred above the basic monthly charge such as business related long distance calls and the cost of additional features such as call waiting, forwarding, conferencing, speed dialing, etc. that were added for business purposes. Suggestion: Get a second line to be used exclusively for business. All charges including basic charges would be deductible.*

*** Business Gifts*   Limited to $25 per person (not per client), per year.
   Keogh Accounts   See note *** on back of Sheet #1.

Record of Local Transportation & Miscellaneous Expenses

Name _____

Date 200__		From	To	Client/Purpose	Travel Costs	Other Cash Expenses	
Month	Day					Type	Amount
Totals							

Travel expenses that are ordinary and necessary in your trade or business are deductible. For travel expenses that are less than $75 for each occurance, the IRS regulation permits supporting evidence to be in your diary or log, in lieu of a receipt. The diary or log should contain the information requested above.

As suggested by designer Mary Ann Nichols, a record of Local Transportation and Miscellaneous Expenses is a good means of keeping track of trains, buses, and cabs used for business (and don't forget to figure in the use of your own car). © Juda Kallus/Mary Ann Nichols 2001.

Record of Business Meals & Entertainment Expenses

Name _____

Date 200_ (Month Day)	Establishment	Location	Client	Purpose	Amount
				Totals	

Meals and entertainment expenses are deductible if they are ordinary and necessary in conducting your trade or business. These expenses are deductible if a business discussion took place during, before or after the meal or entertainment. For expenses that are less than $75 for each occurance, the IRS regulation permits supporting evidence to be in your diary or log, in lieu of a receipt. The diary or log should contain the information requested above.

As designed by Mary Ann Nichols, a record of Business Meals and Entertainment Expenses is an easy way to keep track of business-related meal and entertainment expenses incurred. According to Nichols, the IRS will accept amounts under $75 for each occurrence without a receipt. © Juda Kallus/Mary Ann Nichols 2001.

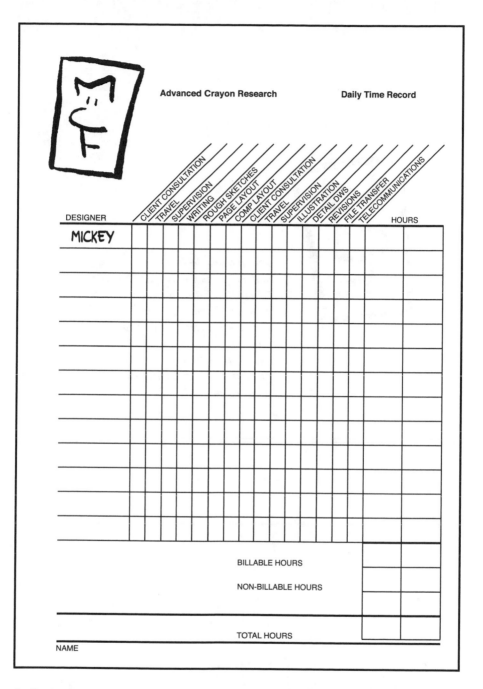

Advanced Crayon Research　　　**Daily Time Record**

DESIGNER	CLIENT CONSULTATION	TRAVEL	SUPERVISION	WRITING	ROUGH SKETCHES	PAGE LAYOUT	COMP LAYOUT	CLIENT CONSULTATION	TRAVEL	SUPERVISION	ILLUSTRATION	DETAIL DWS	REVISIONS	FILE TRANSFER	TELECOMMUNICATIONS	HOURS
MICKEY																

BILLABLE HOURS

NON-BILLABLE HOURS

TOTAL HOURS

NAME

Daily time cards, as suggested by the late Read Viemeister, are an integral part of efficient record keeping. For accounting purposes, record the job number plus activities and time spent. Transfer the time records to a master card for each job.

The author's logo is simple, clean, and has proven to be quite effective. Created recently to reflect a new direction, it was designed to be used in many vehicles, different formats, and various sizes—on business cards, as letterhead, on stationery and business forms, for signage, and a variety of labels.

chapter 8

PRICING YOUR WORK AND GETTING PAID

Sometimes, it's extremely difficult to get clients to tell you precisely how much they want to spend until after you put the proposal in front of them. Then, somehow, they magically know exactly how much they can afford.

—Rex Peteet, Designer

The key is clear communication, fair negotiation, and the written agreement.

—Ellen Shapiro, Designer

Society calls creative folk ARTISTS (in big, bold, capital letters). Artists do what they do for a variety of reasons: personal satisfaction, for public recognition or the respect of their peers, for the sheer fun of it, for posterity or—dare we say it—simply for the bucks. Now, I believe most artists would work without getting paid—for love, as it were—but as BUSINESSPEOPLE (also in big, bold capitals) this would be *ruin*.

Like it or not, designers and illustrators must be businesspeople. So, this chapter deals with pricing your work. We'll discuss how to be adequately compensated for your time by making a proposal, writing contracts and letters of agreement, and collecting your money.

THE PRICE IS RIGHT?

What do you charge when you're just starting out? Your fee will most probably come down to answering these three questions: How much should you charge? How much could you charge? How much do you want to charge?

Think of these questions as the basic rules of thumb. Coming up with a pricing strategy that answers all of these points will help you know how to charge a fair price for your work. For a pricing strategy to succeed, both buyer and seller should demand these three things: a definite price, a fair price, and a competitive price.

How do you arrive at a value for your time that meets all of these criteria? You could charge by the project, knowing how a similar job has been priced out in the past (or by knowing what the competition is charging). Or you can arrive at an hourly fee based on your project expenses and the expenses you incur in the course of doing business.

WHAT TO CHARGE FOR YOUR TIME

You'll remember that in chapter 6, we discussed how to figure out what your break-even point will be. Let's review, in more detail, how to arrive at an hourly rate based on your start-up and variable expenses. Look again at the budget template, and refer to it when calculating what your expenses will be.

High or low, let's assume the following as an example of monthly expenses:

Mortgage/Rent	$ 590
Repairs/Maintenance	30
Licenses/Permits/Taxes	50
Insurance	50
Utilities	150
Materials/Supplies	50
Shipping/Postage	40
Telephone/Fax	115
Travel/Transportation	50
Meals/Entertainment	75
Advertising/Promotion	90
Equipment	125
Accounting/Legal Fees	60

```
Payroll Taxes  . . . . . . . . . . . . . . . . . . . . . . . . . . . . . . . 50
Salary . . . . . . . . . . . . . . . . . . . . . . . . . . . . . . . . . . . 2,420
Total Monthly Operating Costs  . . . . . . . . . . . . . . . . . $ 3,945
Start-up Costs . . . . . . . . . . . . . . . . . . . . . . . . . . . . . $ 3,000
```

Take your monthly total from above and plug it into the following formula:
- ➡ Multiply your monthly operating costs by 12: $3,945 × 12 = $47,340
- ➡ Add start-up costs: $47,340 + $3,000 = $50,340
- ➡ Divide this figure by 52 to get the weekly cost of doing business: $50,340 ÷ 52 = $968.08
- ➡ Divide your weekly total by 5 to get your daily total: $968 ÷ 5 = $193.62
- ➡ Divide daily total by 5 (an average number of billable hours most people can get out of a working day) to get your hourly rate: $193.62 ÷ 5 = $38.72

This represents the absolute minimum you must charge as your hourly rate in order to break even. Remember, this is your break-even point—it doesn't take into account time off for vacation or sick leave, nor does it figure in any kind of a profit margin. However, let's assume that you wanted to realize a $24,000 profit at the end of the year. You can break this annual figure down with the formula given above, and then add it to your hourly rate as follows:
- ➡ Divide $24,000 by 52 to come up with a weekly figure: $24,000 ÷ 52 = $461.54
- ➡ Divide $461.54 by 5 to come up with a daily figure: $461.54 ÷ 5 = $92.31
- ➡ Divide $92.31 by 5 to come up with an hourly rate: $92.31 ÷ 5 = $18.46
- ➡ Add $18.46 to your hourly break-even rate of $38.72 in order to come up with an average hourly billing fee that will give you a comfortable profit margin: $38.72 + $18.46 = $57.18

In order to cover the expenses of doing business and realize a $24,000 profit at the end of the year, you will need to charge, on the average, $57.18 per hour for your time and bill an average of five hours per day. Oh, and by the way, the above figures still don't factor in any vacation or sick time either (hey, I had to give you *some* homework).

CHARGING BY THE PROJECT

You may also want to determine, on a per-project basis, what fee you think you will need to be fairly compensated for the job. Let's assume your client is willing to spend $2,500 for a brochure. First, estimate and deduct production costs. We'll say this comes to a total of $900. After the $900 for production costs has been deducted, you're left with $1,600 as compensation for the labor, or your time on the job. If you divide this by your hourly rate of $57.18, you end up with about twenty-eight hours to spend on this job. In other words, you will need to limit yourself to twenty-eight hours in order to be adequately compensated for your work.

Now, let's go back to what the perceived value of your work is. Is $2,500 a fair price and competitive rate in your area for this type of brochure? This is where your instincts, experience, and assessment of the market value of your work come into play. Research and regard the so-called going rates carefully. If you fees are strictly bargain basement, smart buyers may equate this with poor quality product.

Conversely, inflated pricing will lose you a job just as easily ("You're way too expensive and just not worth it. I can get it cheaper down the street!"). An honest price that reflects market value—whether it's the high or low bid—is always the best. And as Roger Brucker advises, "Sell the price before you send the invoice."

So, your average hourly rate should also factor in what you think the going rate is for different design tasks (the *Graphic Artists Guild Handbook: Pricing and Ethical Guidelines,* distributed by North Light Books, gives rates and billing procedures that are customary for professionals in the graphic arts). A job demanding a lot of production, and very little design or illustration, will yield a lower price (based on perceived value of the expertise going into it) than one requiring the skills of an experienced designer/illustrator and production manager.

When determining what to charge, don't forget that you're a start-up business. Any figures quoted here are just ballparked. The numbers found in the *Graphic Artists Guild Handbook* represent an average that includes studios and agencies that have been in business for years. Factor in your experience and reputation when determining what your fees should be. If you've figured you need to charge $57.18 per hour to cover expenses and turn a profit, you may want to establish a range where you bill *less* per hour for production and clerical time and *more* per hour for design and illustration time. (Creative time, including client meetings and concept development, is generally billed at a rate of about one-third over the fee charged for production). It should also be mentioned that you might want to mark up outsourced services (printing, copywriting, etc.). The ballpark here is 15 to 20 percent.

One final note: When talking to a client about fees and expenses, refer to the project "budget," not "what it will cost" or "the money involved." If they seem reluctant to talk about what they expect to spend, explain to them that it's mutually beneficial to let you know what they've been allocated or are able to afford.

HIGH AND LOW

It's safe to say that at the beginning of your career you won't be commanding the fees of an established studio. Oh, there's nothing to stop you from quoting high prices, but without a proven track record, you're going to be one unhappy (and maybe hungry) camper.

You'll have to price competitively. Sometimes (and probably more often at first), this means lowballing a bid to get a job. I talked to many designers who still use this strategy to get a particularly valuable assignment. This is not a mistake, nor does it reflect the fall of the high and mighty—it's just business. These designers, with years of experience (plus an overflow of clientele and lucrative fees), are looking at the big picture and thinking in the long term. Clients may choose you simply because you're new and a good buy. So, don't think "cheap," think "reasonably priced." Don't say "discounts," say "negotiation."

Low prices are not forever when your work is good and your services are in demand. However, you need to build up a portfolio, and in order to do this, you must initially look at the scope of the assignment rather than the figure on your invoice. You will want to do pro bono work as well. Killer design jobs that yield great-looking samples and/or prestige are excellent self-promotion vehicles and valuable bargaining chips for your design future.

Civic, health, or arts organizations frequently cannot pay very much, but often offer exciting creative opportunities and fabulous exposure. These "little" jobs are also fun and satisfying. Nonpaying only in regard to your pocketbook, pro bono assignments can be stimulating design challenges and wonderful reputation builders. When working with these groups, it's okay to ask about being reimbursed for out-of-pocket expenses or negotiating a trade-off in services. You'll find out more in chapter 9 about the promotional value of pro bono work.

WORKING ON SPEC

XYZ Company has a plum assignment. The art director gives you a buzz to say that they're also considering three other designers around town. Your studio is definitely in the running, but XYZ is asking all concerned to do a spec layout for evaluation.

You may agree to do this little freebie in the obvious hopes that you'll land the account, but most designers will tell you that this is a mistake. I agree. You're working for nothing, with no guarantee that you'll be paid. If the client likes your concept, maybe—just maybe—you'll get the job (and with competition, the odds only get worse).

The Graphic Artists Guild regards spec work as an unethical practice for designers. And obviously, it won't be cost-effective or time-efficient for a busy designer with a new design firm. As designer Bennett Peji says, "Your ideas are your most valuable asset, and working on spec is essentially giving away your design. A designer only does this when he or she feels less experienced, less capable, and simply has the time to do free work."

Your savvy prospects probably won't ask you to work on spec. Those who do will (most likely) understand your diplomatic refusal. Uninitiated (or possibly unscrupulous) clients need to be educated, but still turned down politely.

If you feel you must work on spec, keep your time to a bare minimum. Only submit basic ideas and simple sketches (no finished illustrations, full-blown presentations, or refined comps). Place your copyright notice on all visuals, and date everything. Photocopy all graphics and paperwork. Now, dig up that old rabbit's foot for luck—you may need some!

PREPARING AND PRESENTING A PROPOSAL

Keep in mind that unless you get the job and can bill your client for your time, every written proposal costs you time. Although it's an essential part of doing business, writing a proposal is basically non-revenue-producing work. You'll want to give every pitch your best shot, but don't overdo it—keep your time to a minimum.

Your proposal should say, "This is me. Here's what I have to offer. You're special. I've got a solution to your unique problem. Here's how I can meet your needs."

Your proposal will also be the means by which your clients compare your costs and concepts with that of your competition. It stands to reason, then, that a good proposal is crucial. The components of a well-written proposal should include:

- *Introduction:* This reiterates the sequence of events so far and what you've discussed with your client, "As you remember . . . as we discussed. . . ."
- *Analysis:* This shows that you have listened to what the client has said. You've looked at the problem, studied their market, and investigated the competition. Now, present this research as facts and figures. Tailor your analysis to this individual client's special situation and design needs.
- *Creative Process:* Answers. What makes this job a singular design challenge? How will your concept solve the problem as outlined?
- *Production Process:* How will the bright idea be guided into reality?
- *Fees, Billing, and Timetable:* Be specific, detailed, accurate, and honest.
- *Your Track Record:* Back yourself with a résumé, mission statement, or a statement of the philosophy behind your business. This may provide the final touch in convincing a client that you're the design firm to hire. Don't be afraid to toot your own horn.

Present the proposal in person. One-on-one, face-to-face is the best way to immediately meet the issues and address any questions. After all, a written proposal is merely words and numbers on paper, and your reputation is only a lofty intangible. You, in the flesh, are another matter. A personal presentation shows your commitment to the project, to the *team*, and is a dramatic demonstration of who you are and what you can do. You care enough to be there right from the beginning, and you'll be there all the way. You can solve the problem. You're there to say, "I'm here to give you the answer!"

By that same token, if the proposal must be mailed or delivered, follow up immediately to make sure this valuable package arrived safely, and avail yourself for discussion. Lastly, try to close the sale. Strike while the iron is hot at the end of the personal presentation. If the proposal is mailed, target a confirmation/award date.

ESTIMATING COSTS

Coming up with a budget for a job isn't too difficult once you've determined what tasks need to be done. Assuming that you have an hourly billing rate for the tasks involved, estimate the amount of time needed to perform each task. If you charge $30 per hour for production time and you estimate it will take five hours to do the layout, multiply $30 by five to come up with an estimate of $150 for this part of the job. Use the same task list that served as your scheduling guide, and do this exercise for all tasks involved in your project. Don't forget to figure in charges for your consultation time in meetings with clients, vendors, and other suppliers (you may also want to estimate your time for creating the initial estimate and invoicing afterwards).

An illustration or design job, even a small assignment, is a bit like a ride on the Orient Express for your clients. They have a vague notion of how the train works, but don't really understand how to get to the destination safely, on time, and at the stated fare. They are hoping to get to this destination with personal service and tender care. Now, think of a runaway train going incredibly fast and out of control, arriving who knows where or when or in what condition. The crash of a runaway train is an apt metaphor when you consider that a botched job with an errant budget will lead to the wreck of a business relationship. But the design process can be a splendid trip—an edifying journey for both you and your client (and another feather in the engineer's cap). There should be no unpleasant surprises and no unhappy conclusions. Figuring costs and keeping track of expenses to stay on budget is the way to keep things running smoothly. (See chapter 7 for a sample budget worksheet.)

GET IT IN WRITING

A handshake is a fine token of trust and cooperation, but this gesture provides no real information and is hardly legal proof of any transaction. Once your proposal has been accepted, it's important to establish with your client what the breakdown of expenses (compensation for time and reimbursable costs) on a project will be and how it will be billed.

Both clients and creatives should be well aware of the absolute necessity for some sort of written documentation at the outset of a project. You needn't fear or loathe this paperwork. Not to worry—what you want to write is a short instrument that clearly and simply spells out intent, a documentation of who buys what from whom, for how much, and when payment is due.

The Written Agreement

A confirmation of assignment (also called a confirmation of agreement), contract, or written agreement is a legal promise. It's the document that defines the all-important relationship between you and your client. Common sense tells us to avoid the ambiguity of a spoken exchange and the pitfalls of selective memory. As movie mogul Samuel Goldwyn used to say, "A verbal agreement isn't worth the paper it's printed on."

The wording of any contract should be clean, clear, and complete, and the document should be drafted in contemporary language—archaic Latin buzzwords or bombastic legalese don't validate a thing. Information should be accurate, and language must be explicit, leaving no possibility for inference or assumption.

A simple letter of agreement works for many creatives who delineate their terms and payment schedule on small jobs in this way. A formal contract on a store-bought form is okay, but it may not give you the leeway to customize terms for individual clients or address special situations. This approach may also be too "cookie-cutter" for clients who rightly demand individual attention and may wonder why you, Mr. Big-Time Artist, didn't bother to design your own forms. It's better to go with custom contracts of your basic terms and conditions built off a template and tailored to the client's project. These agreements are easily generated on even the most Spartan computers.

The Elements of a Written Agreement

Your written agreement should clearly define a number of salient points for all concerned, including: the project and scope of assignment, what and when services will be performed, how long it will take to perform these tasks, what it will cost, who pays for what, how and when payment will be made (stating that fees and expenses will be billed on an itemized invoice), responsibilities (what the design firm does and what the client does), what constitutes extra work (corrections, additions, and alterations), how additional work will be compensated, and protections for both parties (rights and copyrights).

You'll find more information on contracts, and a wealth of contract samples, in Tad Crawford's *Business and Legal Forms for Graphic Designers*, *Business and Legal Forms for Illustrators* (both Allworth Press), and the *Graphic Artists Guild Handbook: Pricing and Ethical Guidelines* (distributed by North Light Books).

Letters of Agreement

One way to draft an agreement between yourself and a client is to divide your exchange into two distinct documents: (1) the general contract delineating your working arrangement and (2) the letter of agreement outlining the particulars on a specific job.

Before you draft anything, discuss all particulars and negotiate terms (except price, which you will stipulate in writing). Once you and your client are in accord, send the general contract as a written confirmation of what was discussed. This is an outline of the basic provisions that you and your client have worked out.

Send this general contract at the outset of your relationship, so that redundant paperwork with later assignments is avoided. Then, before you begin work on an assignment, send a letter of agreement for the client to sign and return as a confirmation of the details outlined in your contract. Also, stipulate that additional letters of agreement will cover all work on other projects. Get the document signed, returned, and filed. (Of course, both parties should sign and file individual copies of all paperwork.)

Finally, remember that contracts and written agreements are merely pieces of paper. A signature doesn't ensure performance or payment. What actually makes for a solid deal are the people who sign on the dotted line. And while reaching an agreement is often easier said than done, if you work with honest, ethical, and reasonable folks (like yourself), you should have no problem.

SALES TAX

Many start-up businesses ignore charging (and then actually remitting) sales tax. Let's clarify: You don't pay sales tax; your client does. It is your responsibility to collect sales tax for the state at designated intervals. If the state discovers that you should have collected, but did not, you will be liable for this tax plus penalties. The state will catch up to you, so the best advice is to keep squeaky clean with your state's agency and requirements (and your local tax laws, too).

BILLING PROCEDURES AND PAYMENT SCHEDULES

Being charged by the hour, regardless of whether the rate is fair or the time reasonable, scares most folks half to death. (Remember when the plumber came to fix that pipe in your attic?) But a flat fee allows too much room for abuse of your time, responsibilities, and energies. The client wants to get his money's worth, so you may be asked to jump hoops as a result. Complications play havoc with your schedule, so you underestimate the workload or costs involved. Here's a nice alternative: Estimate or quote the job at a specific price, billed in phases. Detail each phase explicitly, and specify that extra work not covered in the agreement will be charged to the client as an additional expense at your hourly rate. You may also want to bill by completion of phases or consider installments based on a different criterion. The following are some payment schedules to consider:

- ◘ *Payment in Thirds:* Many artists make it a standard practice to ask for one-third of the total fee for a job upon agreement, one-third upon approval of comprehensives or roughs, and the remainder due within thirty days of delivery of the final.
- ◘ *Payment in Halves:* If the job you are working on is larger in scope, you may consider asking for one-half of the fee upon agreement and the rest in scheduled installments or monthly payments.
- ◘ *Payment in Full First:* For smaller jobs, get your fee in cash, up front.

Finally, many designers also recommend giving totals when invoicing clients rather than itemizing the number of hours and their billing rate. Although you should let your clients know up front what you charge for your time, there's no need to raise your clients' curiosity about why they were charged a given rate for a particular task.

Two final points: (1) Make sure your paperwork states that your estimate does *not* include the tax (this will ensure that there are no rude surprises for unknowledgeable buyers) and (2) get yourself a tax-exempt (or resale) certificate so that subcontracted vendors do not charge *you* sales tax.

GETTING YOUR MONEY

New clients can be big risks as well as great opportunities. There's always the chance that any of your customers may be slow to pay or not pay at all. Exercise a bit of caution to save yourself some time, energy, and money. It certainly makes sense to do the following on big jobs, but consider making these policies part of your standard procedure in dealings with all clients. By doing so, you're less likely to get burned (remember: it's your money they are holding).

First off, get everything in writing. Have your client sign all agreements and sign off on any correspondence or documentation.

Be informed. Reach out to the creative and business communities for information about this client. Ask around; consult the Better Business Bureau; visit the Internet. If warranted, get all financial particulars, including the name of a new client's bank, by having him or her fill out a standard credit application (generic forms can be found at your office supply store).

Next, investigate three or four credit references that your client has supplied to you (and again, consult the Better Business Bureau). The size of a savings or checking account is no guarantee that you will ever see that money. Remember, you want to check history, not security. This kind of checking may be unnecessary with a client like Procter and Gamble or *Time* magazine, but do investigate as appropriate. Integrity is not always synonymous with the perceived size of the name or reputation.

Get a personal guarantee of payment from the owner, not the corporation.

Don't finance your client's job. The fees for your professional services don't include outside purchases (called out-of-pocket expenses). Itemize these expenses, and add a service charge to the bill (generally 15 to 20 percent). You can also stipulate that outside purchases such as printing and photography will be billed directly to the client (or request a retainer or advance so that you have cash up front to pay these vendors).

The Fine Art of Not Getting Stiffed

You've stipulated your billing policy in a written agreement with your client. It should state when payment is due for services rendered. Now, you need to bill and receive payment at each stage of the agreed payment schedule before proceeding to the next stage. Before any unpleasantness occurs, make sure all terms of your agreement are perfectly clear. Take a job only when you are certain both parties know when (and how) payment is due.

But what do you do with slow-paying or nonpaying clients? Here are a few words of advice for dealing with deadbeats. (You may label these characters a little more colorfully, if you prefer.) Leonard Bendell, author of *Payment in Full* (Triad Publishing), offers these suggestions for successfully getting what's due:

- ◱ Invoice when work is delivered with the terms "net 30 days."
- ◱ If you're not paid within fourteen days, remind the client with a second statement.

- The bill is overdue if not received within forty days.
- At the forty-day point, ask why you haven't been paid.
- Find out when you can expect payment, or state when you expect payment, but don't threaten.
- Be reasonable, understanding, but resolute. Offer an alternative payment plan (for example, weekly installments over three months).
- Don't harass. There are laws, such as the Fair Debt Collection Practices Act, that govern collection methods.
- Send more letters or make intermittent phone calls until you're paid or the bill is seventy-five days overdue. If the account has not been settled at this point, you could sue in small claims court. As designer Larissa Kisielewska tells us, "Even a certified letter stating intent to file in small claims can often yield results."
- You could hire a collection agency. (However, agencies usually keep about half of what they collect.) Or you may decide to cut your losses if you now feel getting any money from the client is unrealistic.

WHEN PUSH COMES TO SHOVE

Get a lawyer if you have a legal problem, contract questions, or a dispute with a client. I personally know one artist with a law degree, but he is a most definite exception to the rule. Even if you consider yourself to be the Perry Mason of the design world, a little legal advice can only help. Bottom line: While you may be able to negotiate a minor altercation (a small settlement or a small claims court agreement) on your own, get a lawyer for anything that entails a larger legal or economic dispute.

As defined in the *Graphic Artists Guild Handbook*, "small claims courts give access to the legal system while avoiding the usual encumbrance, costs, and lengthy duration of formal courts . . . [the] procedure is streamlined, speedy, and available for a minimal fee. Artists can handle their own cases with a little preparation." If you must go the legal route—and your claim is simple or the sum of money concerned is minor—a small claims procedure is a decidedly easier way to get your day in court. Consult your city's clerk of courts or the Better Business Bureau for more information and guidelines.

On a side note: Membership in the Graphic Artists Guild offers the opportunity to utilize your chapter's grievance committee.

PROFESSIONAL ⬇ VIEWPOINTS

All projects should be broken down into phases. Working and billing in phases ensures that the designer is paid as the job progresses, so that cash flow is steady and so that you don't get stuck if the client cancels the job or changes direction in the middle of the project.

—Ellen Shapiro, Designer

Getting everything down on paper is essential. There has to be a written proposal for every job, large or small. Define exactly what the job is, what your role will be, and the scope of services. A new proposal has to be developed for each project, because no two jobs are alike in purpose and content. Assuming that the fees are in the same ballpark, many clients will make a decision on the quali-

ty of the proposal, how it's written and organized. The proposal is the place to demonstrate your understanding of and your commitment to the project—but it's not the place to develop the project.

—Ellen Shapiro, Designer

Proposals are one way to go. But many designers I know simply submit one-page estimates that are not nearly as detailed (and save a lot of time). I have been doing this very successfully for years. It's way more into numbers and very short on narrative, so it looks rather different. Plus, it always gets faxed, never brought over in person. —Larissa Kisielewska, Designer

Channeling Children's Anger

We build in a concept fee. A concept fee is a way to separate the thinking from the rest of the job. The concept fee has a range, depending on how many designers are involved. If it's one or two designers, obviously, we can afford to do it for much less than if the entire studio is working on it.   —Don Sibley, Designer

I want to continue to find ongoing client relationships. I want to grow in sales, not in size. I'd like to weed out my non-profitable clients, but not my nonprofit clientele.   —Lori Siebert, Designer

You can't charge low prices forever. But if you're smart and you've kept your studio small and your overhead low, you can afford to bid low at the beginning [to establish yourself]. As you get better, have more work to show, and your studio gets larger, you have to let your prices come up accordingly.   —Rex Peteet, Designer

Get a signature on a "job approval" form once a job is done, but before it goes to the client (or printer). Put the approximate invoice price on the form. That, along with the client's signature, will give you an airtight case in a dispute. Get that signature before handing over the job, so you have the leverage.

—Larissa Kisielewska, Designer

chapter 9

MANAGING YOUR NEW STUDIO

Security—that's the problem with freelancing. I was speaking to the wife of one of the most successful illustrators in this business, and I inquired, "How's your husband? Give him my regards." She tells me, "Oh, he's a little worried lately, because he's working on his last job." I asked, "What do you mean, his last job?" And she says, "We don't have anything on the board."

—Simms Taback, Designer, Art Director, and Illustrator

So, you think you're organized? Got it together (if you could only remember where all the elements were)? As I've already mentioned, running your own studio is very much like juggling. Just how many minor chores and major responsibilities can you keep in the air all at once? And make no mistake about it, you're going to be so busy, you may end up dropping a pin or two.

You know all the clichés: You're only one person. There are just so many hours in a day. You'll be wearing a lot of different hats. These homilies are timeworn, but (to throw in another rickety catchphrase) right as rain.

MANAGING YOUR WORK

Managing your business and the projects you bring in is a matter of zeroing in on priorities. It's also a matter of keeping track of people, services, time, and expenses. In order to manage effectively, you will need to get organized, set up systems and procedures, and maintain records and files on all aspects of your business.

You must keep tabs on any project in order to stay on time. Graphic design often involves bringing together many pieces to make a final printed product. Making sure every component of a job is done, and done well, is imperative. As if keeping track of your end of a project isn't enough, you'll also have to watchdog the work being done by support services, such as service bureaus and freelancers.

To keep a deadline and overall turnaround time in mind, break each project down into tasks and minitasks. After identifying each task and minitask, assign an amount of time to each. From there, you should be able to come up with a schedule and a completion date for each task. As each task is completed, record the date, so you'll know exactly when it was done.

Create a job jacket (also called a job folder or job bag) for each project, and place your schedule into the jacket or tack it on the outside. This way, you will know at a glance what tasks still need to be completed on a given job and whether or not the job is on schedule.

Some folks prefer to use a wall chart, blackboard, or bulletin board as a means of tracking the progress of all ongoing projects. Regardless of your preferred method or combination of methods, you'll need to keep track of (and come up with completion dates for) the following components or job phases. They are arranged here in approximate chronology of their completion:

- *Conceptualization and Roughs:* This is where you do your homework. You'll meet with the client, brainstorm, come up with a concept, and obtain the approval to schedule any other components that go into successfully producing the final job.
- *Copy:* Schedule copy with client availability in mind for consultation, brainstorming, and approval.
- *Photography:* Whether scheduling setup or location shots or selecting from client-furnished photography, you should factor in time for reviewing contact sheets and including your client in photo selection. Schedule time for retouching, digital manipulation and enhancement, and cropping and sizing.
- *Illustration:* If you're not the illustrator on this job, provide time for locating suitable talent, as well as plenty of time for roughs, revisions, and final renderings.

- *Typesetting:* Schedule adequate time for copy fitting, proofreading, and revisions.
- *Layout:* Be sure to schedule time for client review, approval, and possible revisions.
- *Color Separations/Film:* Schedule service bureau time if your printer doesn't take responsibility for this. If you're working on any job with a large quantity of four-color work, factor in time for getting bids from several service bureaus.
- *Printing:* Allow time to get quotes from several printers, plus time to review, revise, and obtain client approval on bluelines and color proofs (if your printer handles this). Factor in time to collate, trim, fold, stitch, die-cut, or complete other processes involved in completing the job, in addition to the time for the actual print run and shipping/delivery. And don't forget to schedule press checks (possibly including the client in these checks), if the requirements for the job call for it.

Keeping the Client Posted

Nobody likes surprises. No matter how outstanding your design work may be, you will never be able to build a business if you do not have a reputation for developing good rapport. You'll need to communicate frequently and candidly with your clients and develop an understanding up front of what is required of each of you in order to bring about successful completion of a project. With every job, you have an obligation to let your client know what you will be producing in the way of roughs, comps, when you will be producing them, and when he or she will be involved in the decision-making process. It is also your responsibility to schedule meetings and opportunities for client approval. It's crucial to establish this with your client at the onset of a project, so that you will be able to schedule client approval meetings at different stages of the job.

Some creatives feel it is necessary to develop a history on each of their clients. In addition to names, addresses, phone numbers, and contact records, you may also want to maintain a record of billing procedures, credit and financial information, plus any other information you deem pertinent to the business relationship. Any personal preferences or idiosyncrasies can be kept track of in this file or database—particularly if your past experience with a client's projects has been fraught with a multitude of time-robbing revisions.

And remember, the costs of client revisions seem to increase about tenfold with each stage of production. If it costs $10 to change something on a first rough, it will cost $100 when it is typeset and on your in-house color proof, $1,000 to make the same change in the blueline stage. It's best to make revisions early on and establish a piece you and your client can agree upon at the beginning of a project.

Getting and Staying Organized

It's important to make a list, on a daily basis, of what needs to be done. At the end of the day, you can make a list of tasks for the next day, taking note of tasks that need to be finished. Determine priorities by assigning a numerical value to each task. Make sure you tackle the tasks that have the highest priority on a given day.

Keep track of your ideas and what needs to be done. You can easily remind yourself about any aspect of a project, or about business in general, by recording it in a pocket notebook. Enthralled with everything high-tech? If you can afford it, a PDA (Personal Digital Assistant), such as those made by Palm or Handspring, might be just the ticket. You could also record information on a pocket tape or digital recorder. When you are back in your studio, transfer this information into a larger planning book, or synch up with your computer.

A calendar, diary, or any scheduling log—digital or paper—can help plan, schedule, and keep track of all projects, meetings, and other business-related obligations. You'll find that by maintaining some sort of plan book, you'll be able to keep track of all aspects of your business on a day-to-day basis, so nothing will fall through the cracks.

Job Files

We talked a little about job jackets earlier in this chapter. Your job jacket will serve as storage for all project-related notes and correspondence, as well as scheduling and supplier information. Your job jackets can be organized and stored alphabetically in a file cabinet, while over-sized materials and other project-related art should be stored in flat files.

In addition to categorizing your projects alphabetically by client, assign a number for each project. For example, the Acme logo would be Acme #10001, while Acme's stationery and business cards would be Acme #10002. By assigning each project an identifying number, you can easily keep track of the chronological order of each of Acme's projects. Use these codes, as well, for identifying charges that are to be billed directly to a project.

Designer Roger Brucker of OIA agrees. "OIA employs a job numbering system using the first two letters of the client's first name and last name (or first four letters of a single name), followed by a serial number that is next available," he says. "For example: ACLE-1432. We then use a visual-art filing system tied to that job number. All elements (artwork, electronic files, etc.) are marked with the job number (and once given a number, the element's number does not change) plus date of entry. In this way, all elements can be tracked back to the master job, even when used on subsequent jobs."

MANAGING YOUR MONEY

Running a tab at your local bistro is one thing. Running a business and not keeping tabs on income and expenses is another. Being a free spirit may definitely be a creative boon, but become a button-down banker with your bucks. It's absolutely crucial to know what money is coming in, how much you have at any time, and where it's going. To do otherwise is simply bad business and financial suicide.

In order to keep track of business income and expenses, it's essential to set up separate bank accounts for your business. A good start-up base would include $2,000 to $3,000 in savings, another $2,000 to $3,000 in a checking account with check writing privileges for approximately twenty checks per month, and a company credit card linked to those accounts. Shop around for the best deal from the banks in your area. Regional banks are usually the best for setting up business accounts, as well as applying for loans. They are more likely than larger banks to loan you money and offer the good service that goes with being a "big fish in a small pond." To compare banks, total the fees and interest that each bank would charge on the services above. When you break down the charges for the services you need, it's easy to determine what your best option will be.

Monitoring Expenses and Income

Income, simply stated, is money coming in. Expenses are obviously monies going out. When you balance your expenses against your income, you end up totaling one column and comparing it to the other. This method is very much like balancing a checkbook and is commonly known as the *cash* method of accounting.

The *accrual* method, where expenses are matched to, and directly offset by, the income generated by the jobs they are spent on, may be somewhat impractical for a design or illustration studio (keeping track of watercolor paper, pens, and X-Acto knife blades used on a per-job basis is not feasible). For tax purposes, you can choose either the cash or accrual method, but you must stay with that choice for at least six months. Your accountant can help you choose which method is best for you.

On the freelance or small-business level, bookkeeping (keeping tabs on expenditures and income) may be the only accounting you do, so keep good records. In fact, keeping track of what you're taking in and spending is crucial in order to supply records to your accountant, bank, and the IRS.

Keeping track of your expenses (debits) and income (credits) is easy with a ledger and a disbursement journal. The journal chronologically lists all business exchanges, while the ledger categorizes this information according to IRS classifications for tax-deductible business expenses. In fact, you can order checkbooks that contain their own ledgers or disbursement sheets. And by organizing your expenses into categories that comply with IRS guidelines, you are also complying with the IRS's requirements for a "contemporaneous log of expenses."

Of course, you can go digital with this log—computerize your books! There are a wide variety of good, small, inexpensive financial programs to use on a Macintosh or PC (and the gamut of expensive, high-powered packages, as well). Quickbooks or Peachtree are two programs to consider.

If you're particularly cost-conscious, or the digital approach is too high-tech, a simple, inexpensive check-writing program may be all you need. You can use the classic Dome Book (a "general ledger") or another "one-write" traditional system. Here, checks and journals are aligned sequentially on a pegboard with metal guides. Carbons transfer all numbers and information from checks to journals.

But accountant Kevin Horner at Hammerman, Graf, Hughes, and Co. advises, "Digital technology greatly improves your efficiency and overall bookkeeping. You definitely want to keep your administrative time to a minimum. It may be hard to break the habit of writing checks by hand, but based on my experience with clients, check-writing software will save you much valuable time in the long run. I highly recommend my clients get rid of their one-write checkbooks and general ledger pegboard. Use software—it is a must!"

Organizing Your Financial Records

In addition to a ledger and journal—and above and beyond digital files—you will also need to maintain paper files for keeping track of client invoices, as well as the invoices you receive and pay in the course of doing business. You can keep track of client invoices by setting up three folders, one each for paid, unpaid, and partially paid. When you receive full payment, note the date on your invoice, and transfer it to the "paid" file. If you receive partial payment, note the date on your invoice, and transfer it to the "partially-paid" folder. When you receive the remaining balance, transfer the invoice to the "paid" folder.

You will also need to set up an accounts payable file. This would include all project-related invoices you receive, as well as your business expenses (phone bills, utilities, rent, etc.). One good method of keeping track is to maintain a file for each day of the month, numbered consecutively. When an invoice comes in on the 20th of a given month, put it in the folder marked "20." On the 20th of the following month, before you insert any new invoices for that day, pull the old invoices that you inserted on the 20th of the last month and pay them that day. This method ensures that you pay all invoices on time, but not until payment is due, which as designer Larissa Kisielewska reminds us, maximizes your cash flow in case of unforeseen emergencies.

It's also a good idea to maintain the following records as a supplement to the accounting systems mentioned above: a cash expense log for meals, travel, and entertainment (if there are no receipts or inadequate receipts); an appointment (and business) event diary, as well as a travel log for your car to record business-related mileage and tolls; if you work at home, a method of allocating expenses that are both personal and business (rent or mortgage, utilities, phone, and cleaning). See the form in chapter 7 for templates of these records. If you don't want to manage all this on paper, evaluate buying a PDA for such notation.

Your IRS Obligations

Be sure to put money away periodically to meet your tax obligations. You are required by law to file quarterly returns with the IRS on April 15th, June 15th, September 15th, and January 15th. (These dates may vary by a day or two in any given calendar year.) "Please note," says Larissa Kisielewska, "if you are an incorporated business, you must file and pay on the anniversary of your incorporation."

By the end of the year, 90 percent of the taxes you owe, or 100 percent of what you paid last year, is due. Be sure that you comply with the IRS on this. You may have to pay penalties and interest if you do not file or estimate your taxes accurately.

Don't forget that you will also need to pay Self-Employment Social Security taxes, based on what you (as your own employer) owe. Your old employer used to make these deductions from your paycheck, but as a self-employed designer or illustrator, you are now obligated to pay this tax yourself. This tax is paid annually and filed with your regular tax return on April 15th.

If you are self-employed, anywhere from 25 to 40 percent of every profit dollar should be set aside for taxes. For further information, make an appointment with your accountant to compute your tax liability based on your projected income. Based on this, he or she will be able to prepare your estimated quarterly taxes.

When and if you hire additional designers, understand the ins and outs of payroll taxes for that staff (and know that payroll tax for yourself will also be handled differently). Again, work with your accountant to keep your tax responsibilities on track and in line with all rules and regulations.

When I'm 64 (or 55)

Plan *now* for retirement. Deferred savings plans make good sense for your future. But profit sharing is too complicated, and pension plans are right for higher incomes or larger corporations with a great number of employees. There are alternatives for a small corporation or sole proprietor.

I am not a financial guru (nor do I play one on TV). What follows is merely an introduction to some options, not specific tax advice or financial guidelines. Yes, we live in a great age of information technology. The modern "do-it-yourself, get the job done right" spirit is strong indeed. Maybe you do have the knowledge base and inclination to do your own financial planning. But even the sharpest of my financially-savvy compadres seek out a financial professional for current information and counseling.

Needless to say, the economic climate (and forecast) is always subject to change. But the roller coaster ride of our economy can be well managed by those making a living at this sort of thing. And while the best place for your money will vary at any given time (depending on your age and income at that moment), these folks know ways to minimize taxes and provide for retirement.

IRAs (Individual Retirement Accounts) currently allow you to save up to $2,000 of your annual income in tax-deferred savings. SEP (Simplified Employee Pension) plans allow you to invest more than an IRA permits. Available to any self-employed individual, you can contribute up to 13 percent of your net income. There's a minimum of red tape involved—it's not nearly as complex as defined benefit and contribution plans.

Roth IRAs permit you to contribute up to $2,000, but it's not deductible on your tax return. The advantage here is that all the interest and capital gains are not taxable, *ever*. Regular IRAs are deductible on your personal tax return, but all gains are taxed when you receive distributions from the account. With Roth IRAs, you can withdraw the principal at any time and not get penalized. Plus, Roth IRAs can be used towards a college education, with no penalty for early withdrawal.

Simple IRAs or Simple 401K plans were created in the mid-nineties to help small business employers maintain relatively inexpensive retirement plans for employees Both are fairly similar. An employee can contribute up to $6,000 per year. The employer only has to match 3 percent of salaries one out of every three years. The other two years, the employer only has to match 1 percent of salaries.

Keough, pension, and/or profit sharing plans offer greater tax deductions, but involve more paperwork than the above options. Regardless of whether you are a proprietorship, partnership, or corporation, you can set up a pension plan or Keogh account for your retirement contributions. There are several different types of plans available exclusively to the self-employed:

Money Purchase Pension Plans (MPPPs) allow you to contribute 20 percent, or up to $30,000 a year. When you set up an MPPP, you designate the percentage of your income you'll be putting in each year and stick to that percentage. Profit sharing plans are similar to MPPPs, letting you save up to 13.04 percent, or $30,000 annually. The amount you contribute to this plan can vary from year to year and might make more sense if your income is inconsistent.

Defined benefit plans are based on calculating how much you need to contribute annually in order to receive a specified amount once you retire. With a plan like this, you can contribute any amount of your income, even 100 percent, but because they are costly to set up (an actuary needs to make the calculations), these plans are recommended only for those who have high incomes and are close to retirement.

COVER ME

First of all, it's crucial to have disability income insurance. If you are laid up, you not only lose your salary, but risk losing your business as well. When determining what kind of coverage you should look into, take into consideration all of your personal obligations, such as mortgages and dependents. Shop for the best coverage, rather than the lowest premium.

Look into a noncancellable policy with guaranteed renewal. This will forbid the insurer from terminating your policy or increasing your premium after an initial two-year contestability period has passed. Also, check out policies with a cost-of-living adjustment that will help you keep pace with inflation.

Health care is another expensive, but necessary, evil. Skimp elsewhere if you must, but get the best health plan you can afford. Don't make the mistake of thinking you can go even a day without medical coverage. You never know when lightning may strike, and with the exorbitant cost of hospitalization and health care in general, you don't want to have to pay for medical expenses from your personal funds.

Group insurance rates are frequently lower than those you can obtain as an independent. Many group health-care opportunities are available through professional organizations. However, executive organizations or even your local chamber of commerce can frequently offer better rates than the group insurance that is available through design-affiliated professional organizations.

Some have speculated that this situation exists because insurance companies view those involved in artistic professions as a high-risk group. Like it or not, professionals in the creative arts (including the visual arts) have been excluded in years past from the kinds of preferential rates available to other professional groups.

An alternative source available in some areas are locally based, self-insured funds for printers and those affiliated with the prepress end of the graphic arts industry. An independent insurance agent in your area can usually give you the needed information on group opportunities in the graphic arts industry.

Finding the Best Deal for Your Needs

Of course, if you are in good health, you might even find out from your agent that an independent policy will be a better deal than any group benefits. A new business staffed by a young designer should be able to buy life and disability insurance at reasonable rates. Ensure you will obtain the best rates by bypassing obvious risk factors (don't smoke) and preventing peril (install safety equipment).

Consider a number of alternatives when shopping for the best deal. If you feel your only need is to cover yourself in an emergency, you may want to opt for low-premium payments on a policy with a big deductible. On the other hand, if you have a family to take care of, a Health Maintenance Organization (HMO) can provide for emergencies, as well as offer reduced rates for check-ups and other medical needs.

Should you use different insurance carriers to meet specific needs? This works for many studios, but if you bundle plans (life insurance, disability, and health care) together with one carrier, you'll usually get better rates overall. Shop around for the right agent by checking out recommendations and referrals. Once you've found an insurance carrier, defuse hassles and make sure you are adequately compensated for medical claims by making personal copies of all claim records.

Insurance for Your Business
Investigate these standard areas of coverage when you're starting up:

- ▶ *Valuable Papers:* Compensates for loss of stolen or damaged artwork and files by covering research time, labor, and materials involved. This type of insurance is extremely important when you consider the replacement value of original artwork (digital or otherwise), transparencies, films, and general files.
- ▶ *Property and Liability:* Covers damage to your studio's contents in the event of burglary, robbery, vandalism, or fire and water damage.
- ▶ *Liability:* Covers injury to any nonemployee on you premises.
- ▶ *Business Interruption:* Replaces lost profits if your business is temporarily shut down because of damages to the premises.
- ▶ *Auto Insurance:* If you're using your car for business and let someone else on your staff drive it, you'll need to add them to your policy.
- ▶ *Disability and/or Workman's Compensation:* Covers injuries incurred on the job by anyone employed by you (required in most states).
- ▶ *Computer Equipment:* Additional coverage beyond general contents in the event of damage by such things as fire or vandalism. This might also cover the cost of renting replacement equipment while your equipment is being repaired.

Finally, if you're working out of your home, you'll want to add a rider on your current homeowner's or renter's insurance to cover damage and theft of your studio property.

PUTTING MONEY BACK INTO YOUR STUDIO
Unless you've hit a windfall of profits after operating for a very short period of time and feel the additional business justifies a loan, you'll need to plan for future growth by regularly investing some of the profits of your business in various accounts. You'll want to invest a portion in a liquid account (a passbook savings or

money market, for instance). Although this type of account won't yield a high interest rate, you'll still be getting some return on monies that are just as accessible to you as the cash in your checking account.

From there, divvy up the remainder of your savings into a variety of CD options, stocks, money market accounts, and mutual funds. The best return on any of these investments will vary at any given time, depending on the current economic situation, so shop around and look for the best alternatives to satisfy your short- and long-range goals. Lock in on the best interest rates available for the savings options that fit your unique needs.

HELP . . . I NEED SOMEBODY!

At start-up, odds are you'll be doing it all. Salaries can take a big bite out of your budget, but at some point you may need to hire a staff.

No doubt, you'll know when the time comes what kind of help you most need, but generally, it makes good economic sense to fill an entry or intermediate-level job rather than a more qualified position. Consider the following: As studio principal, you might bill out your time at $100 per hour, but you find yourself spending much of this time answering the phone, filing, and doing other clerical tasks. You'll want to free yourself to do the work that generates the most income. Hire an administrative assistant or get a temp.

Don't hire another full-time designer unless you are sure you can keep that person busy. It's better to cover a temporary crunch by farming some work out to a freelancer than to hire an employee. You'll not only save the costs of the salary, but also the benefits, heavy tax payments, and the furniture and equipment for that person to use.

IS BIG BETTER?

No matter how grandiose your vision or how diminutive your scale, you must maintain high quality in your work—sound advice when you consider that keeping the dollar value of your work up there is the fastest way to get to fat city. High-quality work is best achieved through carefully managing the growth of your business. Businesses that make it past the initial hurdles often come to failure because no provisions were made for growth. Grow too fast, and you may find yourself in debt and scrambling for work. Fail to anticipate the workload, and you might be unable to meet client demands.

There's an old axiom that says, "Be careful what you wish for—you just might get it." Many of the founders of "big" studios I interviewed waxed romantically about the "good old days" when the company was "small"—a less hectic calendar, a daily schedule with more breathing room, nominal travel, simpler management styles and procedures, moderate overhead, intimate assignments—the list goes on and on. More than a few yearned to downsize (or had done so already). Our economy taught life lessons to some who were financially forced to retrench or cut back. Several cautioned that a loss of quality often accompanies rapid or great growth.

Everybody started on a modest scale, many working out of their homes. A number of designers remain situated there, in front of the fireplace, because they prefer a more personal business habitat. Others have endeavored to preserve a warmer, more congenial atmosphere in offices outside the home with loosely-constructed, friendly environments designed to foster an open exchange of ideas as well as hard work. Small potatoes or big cheese, the creatives interviewed for this book are highly regarded for producing superior work and providing superlative service. The size of the operation has little to do with success—it's an individual thing.

LOANS: MAYBE NOW, MAYBE LATER

See chapter 6 for a detailed discussion about loans. But to recap: If you have a good credit history and are of sound character, you may have a good chance of getting a loan after having established yourself in business for two to three years. You might be able to finance a small loan for a piece of equipment after one to two years in business.

Start your studio with a good plan for money management, and then follow through with it consistently in order to improve your chances of getting that loan. If you keep good financial records from the beginning, you'll easily be able to demonstrate to a skeptical banker why you deserve a loan. Here are eleven steps you can take to become an educated loan applicant when you need additional funds:

1. Be realistic. For a freelancer or small businessperson, the odds of getting a bank loan are just not good. Should you be looking elsewhere for that start-up money?
2. Go to your accountant for referrals. He knows you, he knows your business, he knows the banks. Get some advice; even ask him to make introductions and open doors for you.
3. Shop around. Visit three separate banks (or more). Evaluate, and go with your best deal. A small bank may be the best bet, and your local bank is probably your first stop.
4. Lay the groundwork. Build and maintain a loyal relationship (savings and checking accounts) with your bank of choice.
5. Make friends. Build a professional and personal relationship with your banker long before you need a loan.
6. Clean up your house. Reduce your overall debt before you apply for a loan. Establish a solid credit history—repay other loans, and pay them on time.
7. Do your homework. Write a complete business plan. Or, at least, prepare a loan package (there's more on how to prepare a loan package in chapter 6 and below). Have current fiscal statements (plus past financial summaries) ready for inspection. You'll also need to explain why you need the loan. How much do you need? What kind of loan do you want? Be specific, and put it on paper as a proposal. Demonstrate exactly how the money will be used. If you need to make a bona fide presentation with your facts, figures, and visuals, do so.
8. Make it easy. Depending on your cash flow, you could elect to repay this loan as a single payment. Or pay off the loan in chunks or monthly pay-

ments that decrease the principal, with remaining interest computed on the unpaid balance. Most loans these days are simple interest loans, but decline a loan calculated under the so-called "Rule of 78s." This strategy is decidedly unfavorable to the borrower. Stated simply, under the "Rule of 78s," if you pay your loan off early, you'll be hit with a prepayment penalty. It's legal, but a bit underhanded, and most folks don't check their paperwork or fully understand their contract.

9. Evaluate the rates, study the terms, and assess your options. Should you go with a variable rate (which is dictated by the prime lending rate), fixed rate, or semi-fixed rate loan?

 If you go with a variable rate, is there a ceiling on how high that rate can go (and a floor to which it can fall)? If you get a fixed rate, will there be an annual adjustment? Does your lender say, "Well, Art, I'll give you a fixed rate, but I'm going to fix it annually at 5 percent over prime"? Make sure that "prime rate" is established by the Treasury Index.

 You must be comfortable with the structure of the loan—how and when the debt is repaid and conditions of payment. What about the term (the duration) of the loan? What you pay on a monthly basis must fit in with your cash flow. A four-year loan lowers your monthly payments, but ultimately will cost you more in interest. Can you pay off the loan early, or will you be hit with prepayment penalties? Understand your loan agreement completely. Don't look just at the dollar cost of the loan—it really comes down to getting the best rate and terms you can get (and live with).

10. Turn down the extras. You don't need the bank's credit, life, or disability insurance. These options (they're not mandatory) only jack up the end costs of the loan.

11. Go for it. Yes, it is true that little percentage points add up to big bucks, but you can't predict if (or when) interest rates will go up or down. You could lose your best opportunity by waiting until rates are at their lowest point.

You'll need to prepare a loan package before making your presentation to the bank. This formal document should cover the last three years (remember the current quarter, too) and include:

- Company history (keep it to just one page)
- Principals' résumés (again, one page per individual)
- Statement about use of loan (a simple, but specific list of categories and amounts is fine)
- Profit-and-loss statement, including balance sheets and a record of current accounts receivable and payable
- Cash flow statement
- Three-year cash flow projection
- Statement of your terms, pricing, and company policies
- Personal and business tax returns (ask how many years)
- List of equipment

➡ Customer and supplier references (three to five for each)

➡ Personal guarantee

Unfortunately, most lenders will insist you personally guarantee a loan. Neither the tight relationship you've established with your banker nor the heavyweight business you've set up will spare you this considerable risk. If you need the money, you'll just have to bite the bullet. However, you might just look at a personal guarantee as yet another means of showing the bank that you are a good risk.

When applying for a loan, a comprehensive business plan will also be a big plus. (See chapter 4 for a detailed discussion on business plans.)

➡

PROFESSIONAL ⬇ VIEWPOINTS

It's even more important than ever before to make sure your clients are happy. You need them for referrals. In the eighties, if things went wrong, I used to think that I could always pick up the phone and get another client. It wasn't easy then, and it's almost impossible now.

—Ellen Shapiro, Designer

Estimate jobs in a range: "The budget for this job should be in a range of $1,100 to $1,750 per page, depending on changes made by the client as we progress. If we are all careful to catch changes and corrections early, we should come in on the low end of the range."

—Roger Brucker, Designer

A beginner should have an image in mind of what and where he or she would like to be in ten years, and then never waver from that.

—Fred Carlson, Illustrator

Clients are in the position of power. It took me years to learn how to say "no." And I still have trouble sometimes. It took me years to learn how to make sure a job doesn't get out of control because of a client's lack of experience. There are times when you have to be assertive, to say, "It has to be done this way," or "We can't work anymore unless you agree to a higher fee."

—Ellen Shapiro, Designer

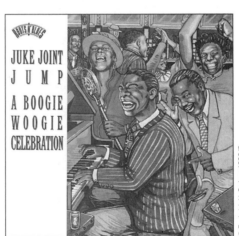

© Frederick H. Carlson 1996/8

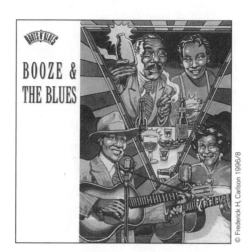

© Frederick H. Carlson 1996/8

I've decided to send art that I really like. If it doesn't sell, fine—I'm still going to do work I like. If I don't get a call, that's all right; I will someday, from some very intelligent art director!   —Ted Pitts, Illustrator

Freelancing requires so much self-discipline. Suddenly, it is up to you to make all these decisions—to get up and get there and to work all day, to not put things off and to not procrastinate. That's the deadliest sin of freelancing: the procrastination bug.

—Mary Grace Eubank, Illustrator

I try to hire dedicated people; we strive to serve our clients to the best of our abilities. By keeping the margin for waste narrow, we can also take on smaller, more unusual and creative projects.

—Jilly Simons, Designer

Serving your current clients is the best way to build a solid business.

—Dan Johnson, Designer

Being articulate is extremely important. You need to be able to walk into a boardroom full of decision-makers who don't know beans about graphic design and be able to explain the job on a level that gets them excited and gains their trust.

—Rex Peteet, Designer

Give them a good, firm handshake, look them in the eyes, and just be yourself. Most of the time your work should sell itself. Answer any questions, but remember you're not a car salesman.

—Bill Mayer, Illustrator

chapter 10

BRINGING IN CLIENTS

Satisfied customers are not loyal; delighted customers are loyal. You wow customers by exceeding their expectations. When they perceive that they have received sacrificial service from you, they are delighted.

—Roger Brucker, Designer and Illustrator

We've talked in earlier chapters about why illustrators and designers are not as business-minded as they should be. Likewise, many of us are not good salespeople either. Perhaps the problem is really one of attitude rather than a lack of ability. Maybe designers fear the image of some high-pressure huckster peddling substandard, unwanted goods. Maybe they hold the mistaken notion that any sales activity is below their creative station.

In truth, sales are the lifeblood of our business, so how do we get past these counterproductive notions? It might help to develop this mindset: You are calling on clients to see if you can help. So think, "How can I help you?" instead of "Do you want to buy?" As designer Ellen Shapiro points out, "As soon as I can, I change the meeting from me selling work to me helping them with their communication problem."

You need to sell. If you're convinced that by doing so you're reduced to pushing snake oil, your business will go nowhere. It's crucial that you believe in what you are doing, and what you are doing is solving problems—a most valuable service and worthwhile endeavor. If you must sell something to make a living, creative solutions make for a wonderful product. Don't you agree? Within this chapter, you'll learn more about how to sell this potent elixir, where to find clients, and how to make effective—no, truly dynamic—presentations. You'll find out how to keep clients hungry for more, so you won't have to go out on a sales hunt with every new job. Let's get busy!

FINDING CLIENTS

Finding clients who need your services is a bit like working with a dating service. You're matchmaking your special abilities with the folks who have the greatest need for them. This sounds simple, but figuring out where to focus your energies involves some thought and planning. It might be best to first break your possibilities down into several business groups in order to isolate where potential business may be. Certain enterprises may be more applicable to designers than to illustrators, but if the shoe fits . . .

Our first category will be business/private enterprise. Here, the possibilities are endless. Is the real estate market booming in your area? Think of ways your skills could be used in creating promotions for realtors trying to sell property. Do you have a flair for restaurant identities and menu design? Now, you get the picture—think about where your skills can best be applied.

Ad agencies/design studios: When you're on your own, you're in a good position to handle the overflow coming from any and all aspects of the business. Possibilities beyond illustration, design, and production include calligraphy or typographic design, storyboarding, art directing, photographic enhancement, manipulation and special effects, and more.

Publishers: Every town has a newspaper, and most cities have at least one publisher of books and magazines. Again, you're in a great position to handle any of the overflow. Find out when the most demanding times are for the publications in your area (is there a magazine that publishes a special issue, requiring more from its in-house art staff in a short period of time?). Contact publishers when you think the production for their peak period is in the planning stages.

Graphic arts supplier: This would include color houses, print shops, and service bureaus. Printers in particular frequently seem to find themselves in need of production skills when a client "dumps" a job on them that was supposedly camera-ready. Even if a printer has his own typesetting and production services, clients will frequently need more design skills than a production staff can supply.

In addition to thinking about where you can market your work, also think about your proficiency level, and match your skills to prospective clients accordingly. If you're just starting out in your career, you'll want to go to quick-print and small shops, rather than your city's largest and most reputable four-color printer. Until you've gained some experience and credibility, your design skills may be better suited to smaller businesses than that multimillion-dollar corporation downtown.

Also, consider your design style and how it matches up with prospective clients. Does the work in your portfolio display an eye for the trendy design that interests a new boutique owner, or is it lean and conservative—more appropriate for a law firm or doctor's office?

Leads

Look for potential business wherever you go. Does your oral surgeon have a hard time explaining surgical procedures to you? Could he use a brochure or handout that explains these procedures? It's getting close to tax time, and your accountant jots her number down on scrap paper because she ran out of business cards. If she's too busy to take care of getting them printed, could you do it for her? Could she increase her business if you cleaned up her image by designing a new card?

Remember, you're not selling a service so much as you're solving communications problems. The professionals you know or do business with all want to improve their visibility and profitability. You may already have the inside line on business possibilities through a former employer. Any situation where you once worked is bound to hold potential. Don't forget, you're already familiar with the work and the work habits of these people, and they see this familiarity as a plus.

Networking

Beyond looking for business potential within your sphere of influence, you should seek specific opportunities for networking that will yield referrals and leads. In addition to providing a good support system, local professional groups can provide splendid opportunities to find some of the most lucrative markets in your area. Possibilities include your regional chapter of the Graphic Artists Guild, the Illustrators' Partnership of America, your city's art directors club, the Society of Illustrators, or AIGA. When you attend meetings, find out for whom other designers are working. Are they swamped? Let them know you're looking for any business they can't handle or any job in which they don't want to get involved.

Don't overlook professional groups affiliated with the communications field or other executive organizations. These people are often looking for support services and frequently are in need of good design skills. Possibilities include local groups for editors, public relations specialists, and ad clubs. Groups like these frequently publish and distribute directories for members and other business professionals as a source of services in the community.

PROMOTE YOURSELF

Self-promotion can take many forms. You can have a Web site, advertise your services in creative directories, and contact prospective clients by phone or by mail (even e-mail). These days, a designer or illustrator will most likely promote both print and digital capabilities.

Yes, we should mention visual presentations, displays, and environmental design. But, by and large, most graphics business consists of paper and electronic communication. So, it makes sense to consider promoting yourself via these avenues as your first order of business. This section (and chapter 11, by the way) will concern itself with marketing your work in print.

Please note, this chapter is primarily geared towards designers (but illustrators will want to read through these pages as well). Chapter 11 targets illustrators (but has useful information for designers, too). See chapter 20 for information about marketing on the Web.

THE SELF-PROMOTION PIECE

The self-promotional mailer is a vehicle many designers depend upon to showcase their work. When the primary purpose of a self-promotional mailer is to dazzle and entice its recipient, creative license knows no boundaries. We've seen bottles of wine and beer with custom labels, fortune cookies with messages enclosed, even hula hoops that have been sent to prospective clients as part of a direct-mail campaign. (And that's just some of the mild stuff.)

More traditional concepts like posters and calendars—if they're really good or useful—may be displayed on a client's wall, doubling your promo's visibility. Clever mailers are frequently passed along ("Look what I got in the mail today. I know you'll appreciate this"). This expands their impact beyond the initial recipient.

If you're looking for inspiration, scope out the glut of annuals and creative directories available. Within these admired pages, you'll view today's most creative and beautifully designed self-promo pieces. *Communication Arts* and *Print* magazines (and most local competitions) include a category for self-promotion. *HOW* magazine has devoted an entire competition to self-promotion, featuring the winners in an annual special issue.

There are almost as many occasions—or excuses, depending on how you look at them—for mailing out self-promotion pieces as there are types of self-promotion vehicles. Seasonal (not necessarily just holiday) greetings, a change of address, acquiring a partner—all these qualify as opportunities for you to showcase your best work in a self-promotion piece.

Since this book is about starting up a studio, we'll concentrate on the importance of direct-mail self-promotion as a means of letting people know you're in business and that you're looking for clients. You want to intrigue a prospective client with a promo piece that demonstrates the high caliber of your work, so you'll want it to be one of the best-designed and well-crafted things you've ever done.

The Capabilities Brochure

The generic self-promotional vehicle known as the capabilities brochure is frequently used by artists for its versatility. A capabilities brochure should provide a tantalizing glimpse of your portfolio by providing a representation of some of your best work. Don't be limited by the concept of a traditional bound-with-a-cover brochure. It can be a single, folded, eleven-by-seventeen-inch sheet, as well as any other size, shape, or format. However, capabilities brochures do have some standard information in common:

- *Client Information:* You'll want to provide a list of the firms you've worked with, making sure to include the ones that have the most prestige and recognition. If you're just starting out, providing a client list may be difficult to do, but if you were a staff designer before going out on your own, you have a right to claim the design and production work for which you were responsible. Check with your former employer to find out if he or she would be opposed to your listing a few of the clients with whom you have worked.

- *Background:* Think of this as your résumé. You'll want to include information about your education and your awards. Include any experience or achievements that will enhance your credibility as a creative professional.

- *Capabilities:* You want to spell out everything you can do and leave no stone unturned. Whether it be handling a major identity program, outdoor advertising, magazine illustration—if ya got it, flaunt it. If you enjoy doing calligraphy by hand or love to create custom typography, if you can provide top-notch copywriting or shoot your own photography, mention it.

- *Your Artistic Philosophy:* Now, do your best to convince prospective clients that your work can be more beneficial to them than any other designer's or illustrator's work.

- *Contact Information:* Don't forget your address, phone number, Web site, and e-mail addresses! This sounds silly, but it happens. Without this most basic info, your promo is essentially useless.

Balancing creative expression with the information prospective clients need about your business is where experience (or the lack of it) comes into play. If you have worked with many high-profile clients, you'll want to play up this credibility. But if you're just starting out, you'll want to demonstrate potential. Your self-promotion piece is the best vehicle you have to show what you can do. In essence, it says, "I got you to notice this direct-mail piece and consider hiring me. I could help you be noticed by your prospective clients."

Trust your gut on balancing the need to demonstrate your creative abilities with the need to communicate your credibility in a clear and concise way. "This credibility," says Roger Brucker, "is established by several vehicles, for instance, examples of what you've done, a description of how you do it, or the testimonies of satisfied or delighted clients."

Direct Mail

We've talked about the capabilities brochure as a vehicle for introducing your studio to prospective clients. The brochure tells anyone and everyone what you and your firm can do. But does it tell Mr. Spacely how you're going to help him sell more sprockets? Does it point out specific benefits to any of your prospective clients? This is where a cover letter, tailored to your prospect, personalizes your mailing and lets you spell out benefits specific to the prospect's needs. For instance, if you want to get a firm's logo and identity business, you'll want to tell the person responsible for making this decision why you're most qualified to do this. Include information about working up an identity for XYZ Corporation and the logo you developed for a local magazine. Include a separate sheet within your capabilities brochure that consists of nothing but printed logo samples. If you've done some homework on what this company needs, mention specifically what you can do to fill the gap.

If you want to multiply the effectiveness of your cover letter, pitch to a market segment, or promote your work to several firms with similar needs, use a generic cover letter and personalize it with the individual's name, address, and company. In the body of the letter, write about concerns common to that particular segment of the market. Be sure to address your contact by name in the salutation.

Mailing Lists

Let's take the example of the logo letter that you composed above. If you obtain a list of new businesses from your local chamber of commerce, you'll have a list of prospective clients to whom you can mail your cover letter and a capabilities brochure. Your mailing list needs will depend on the nature of your skills and who you think will buy your services. You can consult the yellow pages and research directories at your local library and bookstore for leads. Browse creative directories and scan client lists. Special interest publications will often sell their lists, making them available through a broker (who can turn you on to even more list possibilities).

Database software is useful for maintaining and organizing lists. Besides making use of this information in your mailings, you can also use this software to figure out where you're getting your best response.

Another option: CD databases with advanced search engines (such as Phone Search USA or Select Phone) that provide phone numbers and addresses of, for example, all the restaurants (or dentists, or ice cream parlors, or whatever) within twenty miles of your business.

Talent Directories

There are several national talent directories (also called creative directories) that list designers, illustrators, and photographers by service and geography. Major metropolitan regions have talent directories as well. Art directors (especially in agencies and magazine publishing) will browse through these books, studying the photographers' and illustrators' full-page ads. It's very easy for a buyer to spot a look he or she likes, then phone to order the style of their choice.

These types of directories may not be as advantageous an avenue for start-ups, unless you have a particularly unique look or a specialty that someone is likely to buy as a support service (like typographic design or calligraphy). If you're networking with other professionals in your area, you're probably aware of whether or not a local directory is available in your region. If so, determine how useful it is to you in your community. Again, the insights of other designers or illustrators are your inside line to the best opportunities in your area.

Phone Directories

The most overlooked opportunity for visibility may be your local yellow pages, so don't take this avenue for granted. If you're doing business out of your home on a residential line, you may—or may not—be eligible to buy a display ad or qualify for a simple free listing. Check into your phone company's regulations and price structures here.

A listing in your city's business-to-business directory could also be a good opportunity for improving your accessibility, and one that will give you increased credibility as a bona fide business. Again, you will have to have a business line installed in order to qualify. (By the way, these always cost more than residential service.) Finally, don't overlook the yellow pages or the business-to-business phone directory as a source of categorized business listings for making cold calls.

TELEVISION AND RADIO ADVERTISING

You may want to consider local media advertising as another marketing and promotional tool. Radio to sell graphic design? Sure! A sharp, creative radio spot fuels the visuals of the imagination. If done well, your message will definitely get across.

Television time will be pricey, but a good 15- or 30-second spot may be money extremely well spent. You might even consider an announcement on your cable channel's community calendar or a late, late night television spot (when ad rates are dirt cheap).

COLD CALLS

A cold call—person-to-person, by letter or phone—is a contact without request and often without referral. It's essentially selling door-to-door, and as such can be pure frustration. Cold calls are a stellar way to test your tolerance for rejection and for many art directors are a certified nuisance. Persuasive (not obnoxious) salespeople may get decent returns for their troubles, but you may equate cold calls to the flood of those "courtesy calls" you receive just about dinnertime every day—sound like a similar scenario?

If you're intent on this sales tactic, you need to build a list of contacts. Consult the yellow pages. Go to the library or bookstore to research directories and look through publications. Browse the creative directories and scan client lists. Attend trade shows (and read trade publications). Send for annual reports. Join your local ad club. Join a local service club like the Lions or Rotary. Visit the Better Business Bureau and chamber of commerce. Take a stroll through the business district. Talk to your friends and colleagues.

On the Line and in the House

When making calls to art directors (or potential clients), use proper phone etiquette. Identify yourself to the person who takes the call. If you can't get through, leave a detailed, but concise message stating who you are, what you do, and how you think you can help this individual. If you make contact, go through the same identifying process, then clear this person's time by asking, "Do you have a minute to talk?" If the contact is tied up, ask for a specific time when you can call back, and return the call promptly at that time. By doing this, you'll be demonstrating courtesy and prompt follow-up skills.

So you landed that first meeting? Great! You've done your research, right? You have found out all you can about this prospect before the scheduled appointment. You're completely prepared.

Face-to-face, blend the business discussion into a friendly conversation. No hard sell—try a softer approach, avoid the sales pitch. Simply chat to learn more about the prospect and the project. You're just seeking an exchange of information at that point. Show your portfolio. Use an initial get-together to present design solutions that suggest how you can solve the client's communication problems. Observe closely, and keep your ears open. Talk less, listen more. At this point, you're just trying to determine if the potential for doing business exists.

Genially probe for information phrases, such as, "I'm curious about . . . I'd like to know . . . Please elaborate on this . . ." Schmooze a bit with flattery: "Tell me more about your great work at Amalgamated Anagrams. What's it like to be employed with such a hot company? What are some of the thorniest communications problems you've encountered?"

If there is a definite assignment up for grabs, you could say, "I'd like to hear more about your wonderful product and what the firm has done in the past. Can you tell me about this exciting project? Why are you taking this new direction? What'll be tough to explain? What are your goals?"

Once fact-finding about the project is over, you will eventually have to inquire about money. Simple, direct inquiries work well: "What's your budget on something like this?" or, "How much do you want to spend here?"

The client might volley the ball back to your court and inquire what you would charge for such an assignment. Your reply might be, "All clients are not the same. Every job is different. For projects similar to this, I've charged $XXX; this is based on . . . (detail your pricing structure and related particulars)." By the way, certain advisors tell you to give a range between X and Z, while others warn you to never ballpark—always state a firm figure. You'll have to decide what feels and works best for you.

Of course, you will ultimately ask for the prospect's business at some point. Make it easy for both parties with phrases such as, "Great, what if we . . . ? So, where do we go from here? Does this sound doable? Let me run this by you . . . Shall we . . . ?"

COMPETITIONS

Design competitions are a testament to your capabilities and your credibility and are almost always judged by designers who have gained recognition for their own design expertise and won competitions themselves. In addition to recognition from your peers, competition awards attest to the high quality of your work and ultimately justify a high level of compensation for your talent and ability. These awards also look great on the wall of your reception area. They are your "credentials"—easily recognizable as such to anyone who walks into your office and has not yet been exposed to the wonderful samples of your work you are about to show them.

There are competitions sponsored by national magazines; *HOW, Communication Arts, Step-by-Step Graphics*, and *Print* are the best known for this and publish annuals that are highly revered for showcasing the best in the United States. Other prestigious national competitions include the CLIO Awards, the Society of Publication Designers National Awards, and the New York Art Directors Club's annual competition.

You'll also find a wealth of local opportunities through professional organizations (your local ad or art director's club, editor's association, etc.). You're probably already aware of many of them—you know which ones offer the most prestige in your area.

If you enter a competition and find you have a winner, get some mileage out of this piece by entering it in another competition. If it walked away with a gold award at your local art director's club competition, send it off to a national competition. And don't forget publicity. When you win an award, let your clients know about it—especially the client for whom you did the award-winning work. You'll want to notify him personally if this piece has won some recognition. He may want to promote the award within his company and your community, giving you additional exposure.

The best way to "toot your own horn" in a professional manner is to send out a press release to your other clients, local news media, national design magazines, and trade publications (if you feel the prestige of this award is worthy of national recognition).

If you've produced work for a client whose trade has its own competition for design excellence, you'll also want to know if this client has plans to enter anything you've done for him in his industry's competition. Let this individual know that you value the quality of the work you did for him and would appreciate notification of any awards within his industry that the printed piece may garner.

PRO BONO WORK

Donating your design services can be an excellent means of generating publicity. The trade-off you make with the group commissioning the work is your skill in exchange for a credit on the printed piece. You usually have the chance to do your own thing, thus you gain an opportunity to showcase your talents. Local arts and theater groups will frequently offer a talented designer opportunities for high exposure through posters and other promotional vehicles. There's nothing like seeing your work all over town.

Other possibilities for pro bono work include charity fundraisers (walkathons, road races, charity balls). The people who run these events and volunteer their services are often the movers and shakers in your community. They're frequently high-profile types in a good position to circulate your name. And they may be possible sources of future business.

Another advantage to pro bono work is the caliber of the support services at your disposal. Frequently, top-quality printers and color service bureaus will

TEN STEPS TO TELEMARKETING SUCCESS

You should view cold calls as just another avenue for pursuing yet more business. Getting in the door to see your prospect is the initial hurdle, so getting on the horn is your first step. Working the phones (telemarketing) won't be easy street, but may prove to be a path paved with gold (not to mention clichés).

1. First, do your research. Find out all you can about a potential client before you attempt to schedule an appointment. Be completely prepared.

3. Your contact information (name—and spelling of that name—gender, job title, address, and phone extension) must be current and correct. Are you calling the right person? Consult the directories or, if necessary, make a preliminary call to the company switchboard.

4. When you land a meeting, get an exact address and good directions before you get off the phone.

5. Calling back for any of the above info makes you look unprofessional, so get it right the first time.

6. Establish a balance of great confidence, reasonable goals, and realistic expectations. This chemistry will keep you from getting discouraged too fast and quitting too soon.

7. Have patience, perseverance, and a positive attitude.

8. Remember, you are not selling anything with a first phone call. No pressure now, so relax. You just want to get together. Your purpose here is to find out if they have a specific problem you might solve or if there is a general need for problem-solvers like you.

9. Have all your information in front of you (a calendar, appointment book or PDA, client information, a list of clients, and references).

10. If the ball is in your court, suggest a meeting date with alternatives. Be flexible enough to rearrange your schedule, if necessary.

Every call will present a new challenge, so pay attention to both negative reactions and positive replies. Note your responses to all these scenarios. Study (and practice) what does and doesn't work as your telemarketing campaign continues. Don't get easily discouraged. Learn from your rejections, and your calls will succeed—the appointments will come in. And since you'll be spending lots of time on the phone, you'll have plenty of opportunities to develop your communication skills. Now, get out there and make that sale!

donate their services for a charitable event, allowing you to familiarize them with your capabilities. You'll also have a chance to use services and goods that budget-conscious clients may not have afforded you.

And don't forget you may donate your time to the firms offering support services in exchange for collaboration on a promotional piece. Printers and color houses are often looking for good design vehicles to demonstrate their capabilities (always ask if you can get credit for your contribution, and get an agreement that they won't change your design or illustration without your permission).

YOUR PORTFOLIO

Your portfolio speaks volumes for your abilities as a graphic designer or illustrator. If you're unable to present it personally, it should offer as descriptive and as effective a presentation as you would offer if you were there to explain the work yourself.

Be selective about what you include in your portfolio. Young designers and illustrators tend to show their best work, but dilute it with anything they have that's been printed. A dozen pieces of your most representative pieces often are sufficient. Organize the presentation so that your best and most eye-catching pieces are the first ones viewed.

Art directors and others who spend a lot of time viewing portfolios say that the portfolio should be viewed as a design project in itself. Your portfolio demonstrates presentation and packaging capabilities and the intelligent strategy to market a most important concept—you, the *designer* or *illustrator*. Your portfolio should be neat and well crafted. A sloppy appearance, or one that is not unified, will give the impression of an artist who cares little about craftsmanship. If your portfolio is not well organized, it will convey the impression of an illustrator who doesn't think logically.

Experts in portfolio design say that the best way to unify a presentation is to make everything consistent. If you have transparencies, photography, and printed pieces in several different sizes, unify them by matting (or mounting) them consistently so that the color and exterior dimensions are the same. Subtle touches and elegant materials (if you can afford them) give an added touch of quality and often convey the image that you are a success and can afford the best. It might be wise to make this investment if you're trying to impress high-profile clients.

If you must mail portfolio materials to a prospective client, stack matted or mounted print pieces in a custom-made container that fits within a shipping box. This will make for a much neater presentation than pulling some samples out of your portfolio case and dumping them into an envelope.

While designing your portfolio, you may want to consider putting together interchangeable components, so your portfolio can be tailored to a variety of situations. For example, if you were trying to sell your services as a book jacket designer, you would want to include more samples of the work you've done in this area than samples of brochures and annual reports.

The late Read Viemeister, of Vie Design, said that the pieces included should "demonstrate your sketching ability, your rendering talent, as well as design capabilities. A graphic designer should show sketch layouts for proposals, maybe a comprehensive layout with the finished printed piece. This way, a client can see how capably a designer can present concepts before they are committed to print." Viemeister also made a case for explaining how you solved the problem at hand in every project you present. "Be clear about what your responsibilities were—if you handled the overall organization, say so. A lot of customers are not familiar with the design process at all, and they'll want to know the specifics. 'Here's a rough layout of what we did on the XYZ project. Here's the comp, and here's the finished piece.' The client will see this stage and that and get the impression that you know what you're doing every step of the way."

Viemeister then offered these words of caution: "Bits and pieces in a loose-leaf book, wrinkled and folded, don't make it," he commented. "A client will say, 'If you don't value your own work, how are you going to value the work you might do for me?'"

KEEP THE CLIENTS YOU GET

Service—being reliable, on time, returning phone calls promptly, following up, and personally (and personably) ramrodding the job—is the name of the game. Call it every cliché in the book: going the extra mile, handholding, TLC, bending over backwards, doing whatever it takes. Cozy, and oft-used, these homilies are nevertheless (if I dare use one more) right on the money.

Some things you probably know or suspect about dealing with clients include: (1) A prima donna with an I-don't-care-about-you attitude, no matter how good he or she may be, will only generate and keep business for so long. (2) Unless they're masochists, people don't honestly want to work with someone who doesn't care about (or won't take care of) them—would you? (3) Given a choice, a client will prefer the designer known for good work and personal service over the hot, creative Garbo wannabe ("I vant to design alone").

Serve Them Well

Consider the amount of time you've spent in acquiring business—how promoting yourself and cultivating new accounts eats into your billable time. Getting and keeping clients who keep coming back will free you up to bill out more of your time. Clients who keep coming back because you reliably take good care of them are also more likely to do everyone a good turn by passing your name onto those with whom they do business.

THE "BIG" ACCOUNTS

It is entirely possible to keep your studio going with small- to medium-sized accounts. Obviously, your volume of business will have to rise accordingly. However, "big" is relative. Your bread-and-butter account may conceivably be another designer's bargain basement. All things being equal, how many "big" clients should you get? As many as you can handle, of course, but be careful not to put all your eggs in one basket.

You should set a limit on the percentage of income derived from any one client. If your firm stays afloat on the business of one or a few major accounts, it will mean disaster if those accounts pull out for any reason.

SIX TIPS FOR A GOOD PRESENTATION

New York designer Mary Ann Nichols offers these pointers to make a client meeting more productive (and profitable):

1. Do some research. Who are you seeing? What do they do? Who are their clients? What do they need? Can you provide a service they need? If so, tell them how you can benefit them.

2. Look presentable and be courteous. You have only one chance to make a good first impression—use it. Always shake hands, make eye contact, introduce yourself, and be polite.

3. Be confident and listen carefully. Point out your strengths, have a positive attitude, and suggest how your skills can benefit that person. Listen attentively for advice and suggestions.

4. Organize your portfolio. Keep like assignments together—logos with logos, posters with posters, and packaging with packaging. If you have designed a logo and are showing applications of it, keep it together. Don't be redundant—it's not necessary to show the same design in twenty different color combinations.

5. Never apologize for your work. If you are dissatisfied with a piece in your book, take it out or redo it. Never show anything that is not your best. A few excellent pieces are far better to show than many mediocre ones. After all, your goal is to leave a good impression

6. Thank the interviewer and leave your calling card. Always thank the people you have seen for their time and help. Remember to leave behind a copy of your capabilities brochure and a business card or your résumé and a printed sample of your work. This helps the interviewer to remember you and associate you and your work.

Maintain a broad client base for that same reason. If the publishing industry is suffering, you know you're going to be in trouble if all of your business is in this sector. In the event of problems within a particular industry, a troubled economy, or the pullout of a big client, you need to be flexible enough to regroup and work in another arena with a minimum of damage.

PROFESSIONAL ⬇ VIEWPOINTS

Clients want a designer who's going to say, "It's okay, I can help you. I can fix it—I can make it better." And even though you have to jump off a few bridges to make it happen, you try to make it look very easy.   —Dan Johnson, Designer

It has been very important to maintain a relationship with people who are successful and who we enjoy working with. We have grown with most of our clients. Some have moved on to higher positions in other companies, and we have moved up with them.   —Rick Tharp, Designer

Promotions should be done regularly. Some of the very best marketing of all is getting into the important shows, but getting too much exposure can be the kiss of death.   —Ward Schumaker, Illustrator

A designer must set up a situation, through his work or case histories, that says, "I'm the expert—let me do my job." However, it's crucial to get the clients involved, to establish their ownership. Put yourself in your clients' shoes; [try to] see from their standpoint what they are looking for. Never go to the extreme: "Here, take it or leave it." You may sell them on a single project, but if clients don't feel ownership in the process, they won't continue with you.

—Bennett Peji, Designer

© Ward Schumaker 1991

One benefit of having your own business is that you can be entrepreneurial. You can spot an opportunity and try to take advantage of it. For example, in today's paper, there's a story about a new educational program that's being developed and tested. I could tell from the photograph that the developer, a university, needed a designer. I called, and we're taking it from there. —Ellen Shapiro, Designer

Here's an intriguing idea: Call several customers of your target prospect. Ask what they think of the target's visual identity. Now, set up an appointment with your prospect with this teaser: "Would you like to know what your customers think about your visual image?" —Roger Brucker, Designer

It helps if you love your clients. After all, they're putting food on your table. They just bought you that neat outfit or that new car. If you can be genuinely concerned about the well-being of the people you work with, you'll get their love and respect in return. And people like to give work to people they love and respect.
—Mary Thelen, Illustrator

In its most basic form, we have to communicate with each other, and as simple as that sounds, it seems to be where most of the breakdowns occur in this business. Art directors and designers don't communicate with each other. As a group, art directors and designers are not the best communicators. I sometimes question how such noncommunicators have gotten into this business of communication.
—Mike Quon, Designer

chapter 11

HOW DO I GET NOTICED

Promotion involves being something of a character and a personality, which all adds up to being a very visible (and viable) talent in today's field. You must be talented and have a very good product to sell; otherwise, promotion will not deliver.

–Mike Quon, Illustrator and Designer

If you're confident enough about what you do, you have to let your art speak for itself.

–David Catrow, Illustrator

Self-promotion is essential—not just to get work, but also to get the work you want. Pure and simple, self-promotion is tooting your own horn—letting people know who you are, what you do, and reminding them.

I'm a firm advocate of marketing and self-promotion. It will require much organization and discipline, plus a financial investment—and it's worth every ounce of energy, every minute, and every penny you will spend.

Sounds serious, huh? Yes, it is, but also a lot of fun! Self-promotion is a fact of life for the freelancer; with so many good illustrators out there, it's absolutely crucial. New York illustrator (and ex–art director) Peter Spacek has this advice: "Do a large-scale mailing immediately! A full-on attack will spread your name around and will make you an 'entity'—it suddenly gives you 'illustrator' status, even if you've never done a paid job in your life."

SELF-PROMOTION IS ALWAYS WITHIN YOUR BUDGET (NO MATTER WHAT YOUR BUDGET)

We'll discuss marketing on the Web in chapter 19, but for now, let's talk print. Whether you want to use a larger list or do a small, targeted mailing, modest budgets dictate smart decisions. You want your promotional package to be economical, but not look cheap. Of course, color illustration offers a wonderful vehicle to showcase your considerable skills, but good graphics do not have to mean expensive, four-color extravaganzas.

Of course, in the hands of a first-rate printer, well-designed and executed art will always look great. But with our present technology, desktop printing and publishing has soared to new heights. The latest ink-jet printers can produce surprisingly impressive high-resolution prints right in your studio. Higher resolution and faster speed become more economical with every new wave of printers from such makers as Epson, Microtek, Hewlett Packard, and Canon (to name a few).

There are other options, too. A promo reproduced on a high-end photocopier (black-and-white or color) can be even easier on your wallet. Explore the new small-business or home photocopiers, as well. The results are good and getting better (and the costs are reasonable).

PUTTING THE PROGRAM TOGETHER

Any self-promotion requires a battle plan, but limited resources mandate that you do your homework before getting your promotion off the ground. Study your mailing list, and propose a strategy: Determine what you'll be sending (cards, a brochure, flyers—in what combination?), the sequence of events, and when to act. Tally the number of pieces you need (including leftovers for future handouts).

Next, determine the variety and frequency of your anticipated mailing program. To do this, you need to investigate expenses. We'll assume you'll design the piece and set the type, do the layout and any illustration. Pure illustrators might want to work out a swap with a graphic designer doing a similar thing (in other words, offer the designer some illustration in exchange for help with the design).

With your numbers and needs in mind, find a good printer (or locate that quick-print center with the fine photocopier). Obviously, if you're a colorist, you should be advertising in color at some point. If you are not working digitally, or your printer doesn't handle this part of the job, you'll need a good color separator (or, if your budget is tight, a color photocopier).

How does one locate these folks? The first step is to consult the phone book. Also, get recommendations and referrals from anyone who buys print on a regular basis—fellow artists, graphic designers, and any business that advertises. Make appointments to look at samples in general and discuss your job in particular. Find the best work at the best price, and get the show on the road.

Sit down with your contact, and assess exactly what your ideas will cost and what work you can do to defray the end figure. Now, start tailoring that scheme to fit your budget. When faced with cold facts and figures, your whole concept may do a 180-degree turn. Roll with it, and don't be surprised when you come up with a different (and better) plan! Yes, you may have to streamline, but limited finances should only force you to maximize your strategy. Getting the most value for your dollar does not necessarily mean shopping in the bargain basement.

PRESENTING A VISUAL IDENTITY

To present a professional image, give yourself a graphic overhaul. You want to present a unified visual identity. Create a logo to complement a business card, letterhead (stationery imprinted with your name, address, and phone number), plus envelopes.

Choose a clean typeface that works with this visual (creating a standard image) and recycle this combination throughout your paperwork. Illustrator and educator Tom Graham recommends, "If you don't know much about type, keep it simple and clear. I see a lot of young illustrators who are really over the top with type—lots of Gothic black-letter (which has nothing whatsoever to do with their imagery) that is a detriment to their work."

Now, as soon as a potential client sees anything with your name on it, it looks like you mean business. Visualize how good this small, but highly-professional touch makes you look when your correspondence hits that art director's desk.

Oh, yes—preprinted labels (graphically designed around your logo, name, and address) are very handy, but not a vital or immediate priority. Rubber stamps are one creative solution here, or simply be your our own print shop (for short-run custom labeling). Likewise, custom-printed billing looks sharp, but is not a crucial first concern. You can generate invoices right off your ink-jet or laser (with or without the rubber stamp).

COSTS

If you're complaining that this is going to cost some bucks, consider just how polished your competition appears. Establish priorities, and do your makeover in baby steps, if you have to. Use any economical printing means available (as long as you get *good* reproduction), but resolve to present your best face as soon as possible.

Many illustrators budget a certain percentage of their income directly for marketing and self-promotion; a range of 10 to 25 percent is common. Illustrator Roger Demuth jokes that his budget is very clear-cut: "I just spend it until it's gone!"

Estimate a minimum self-promotional program to cost about $2,000 to $4,000 a year. For some, the thought of spending any of these figures will require immediate CPR. Other illustrators will get a good chuckle from this paltry advertising allowance. These are, in my experience, fairly accurate figures, but, of course, those numbers are not written in stone.

It will become fairly obvious that you're going to have to spend a little money to make a little money. Our ballparked numbers take on new meaning when you investigate the cost of advertising in the creative directories. You could buy a somewhat decent used car for the cost of a double-page spread in certain annuals! Conversely, many artists (myself included) have had great response from spartan (with the accent on creative) reminders economically printed or intentionally prepared as rudimentary photocopies (with that accent on alternative or edgy). The trick here is to present trash with class, to look funky and fun. As an occasional contrast to those slick glossy promos, these can be lively and entertaining.

Indianapolis, Indiana illustrator Ned Shaw advises, "Don't ever scrimp on your business, even if you have to borrow money from your granny!" Effective marketing and self-promotion can be a substantial investment, but the returns are phenomenal. Whatever you spend should be considered a good investment in yourself, your business, and your future.

PRIORITIES

Figuring the brochure would generate business—which generates correspondence—I did my brochure first, then the business cards, letterhead, and labels. These elements were initially rather perfunctory. As my marketing program took off, I created and adopted a versatile and preprinted identity system that I used for many years. I later returned to clean and simple (but not very exciting) and eventually gravitated back to a custom logo/label that I adapt to a variety of mailing scenarios and other stationery needs. However, I'm acting as my own print shop on this one. This versatile labeling system is done in Adobe Illustrator; it's all on the computer, and I print out short runs (or hop over to Kinko's) as needed. My relationship with my printer is hardly over, though. When my marketing brainstorms dictate, he's only too happy to do the job.

I have never used preprinted invoices and have always done my billing on my Mac. However, the creative parameters of this most necessary task vary with available time, energy, and inclination. My invoices can be quite short-and-sweet or custom extravaganzas that really finish a job with flare and panache.

The computer, of course, has been an unparalleled asset for all this—from organizing my mailing list/labels and maintaining my correspondence to generating invoices to keeping my accounts and writing this book.

To save time and expense, I design generically. This way, a number of different pieces could be printed simultaneously (thus, economically) using the same elements. You can also cut costs by grouping color separations together.

Here's a basic recipe for successful self-promotion: Send out a brochure to serve as an introduction and to display your initial samples. This mini-portfolio displays one to four examples of your illustration, provides background information, and shows off your style. It should be general enough to cover a lot of territory. You want this mailing to be particularly compelling and to provoke response.

Towards this end, design the initial brochure to contain a self-returnable postage-paid reply card. This is a convenient way to hear from the people on your list. When you get an affirmative return (either over the phone or through the mail), contact and prepare a submission for that particular client. When the reaction is negative, file accordingly.

Follow the brochure with a promo piece on a regular basis—every thirty to ninety days, as your program dictates and your budget allows. There are artists who blitz art directors with one or two mailings every week or two, which is overkill. If done short-term and to a very limited list, this type of self-promotion may encourage some art directors to see what all the fuss is about, but you're probably walking a tightrope.

There are many opinions about how often to send mailings. There is the school of thought that says you should send frequent reminders—a monthly or bimonthly program. Others feel that if you must advertise so much, you are pushing the wrong product. After ninety days, a promo cannot really be termed a "reminder," and a quarterly program is ineffective, because it allows too much lag time. I don't think there's any definitive answer (I myself believe a mailing every forty-five to sixty days is an extremely effective program). What I do know is that a consistent program is the key.

Systematic reminders, in flyer or postcard form, serve as a continual memorandum of who you are and what you do. Flyers are great, and color is lovely; but may not be feasible on a limited budget if used with regularity. Simple, low-cost postcards in black-and-white can do the job famously.

Whatever you send, remember that the bottom line is good design coupled with quality reproduction. In *The Graphic Artist's Guide to Marketing and Self-Promotion*, Sally Prince Davis suggests thinking of your brochure (a pamphlet, booklet, or multifold) as a sixty-second commercial and a flyer (a single sheet, printed on one side) as a thirty-second one. Your postcards thus become the fifteen-second spots.

Don't expect an immediate or overwhelming response to any advertising. Be gratified when it happens, but even if it doesn't, keep the program going. Think "crock pot" rather than "microwave." Sometimes, the client needs to see more; sometimes the brochure makes a quick sale. Either way, the goal is to make sure the markets know you're out there and not let them forget you.

SAMPLES 101

If you don't have any published work to show, give yourself some assignments! Draw a spot for a magazine article, work up a newspaper advertisement, create a greeting card, illustrate a few pages from a favorite book, design next week's *TV Guide* cover, or compile all your hilarious cartoons in one volume. "Published" work is not the litmus test for a bona fide portfolio of samples. If you are intimidated by your lack of credits, the art director will certainly be loath to hire you. Published credits or no, self-confidence combined with strong art in a sample package are the best clues that an artist can produce the dynamic images an art director demands.

Should original work ever be sent as samples? Read my lips: never! As good as the couriers and postal services are, things can be lost or damaged when mailed.

When you send original work as samples, you run the risk of losing valuable art that can never be replaced. Insurance compensation does cover the monetary worth of the art, but the actual piece is gone. Don't take any unnecessary chances with the genuine article—send good quality reproductions, printouts, photocopies, or tear sheets.

Tear sheets are the actual printed pages on which your art appears, "torn" (just a euphemism for careful, clean removal) from the binding of an entire publication. Removing the page makes it handy for a client to review. Rather then forwarding a bulky magazine or book in a mailed submission, send tear sheets. Instead of utilizing the original in a portfolio, include the tear sheet.

MAILING A PORTFOLIO

Mailing an organized sample presentation can be termed "sending a portfolio" of your work (see chapter 12 for an even more detailed look at portfolios). Some art directors will prefer to see an actual binder, and many illustrators send "traveling portfolios" in a variety of presentations. But I would, as I said before, advise against sending the original art.

Keep in mind that many busy creative service buyers don't care to see unsolicited submissions (a sample package, sent cold, without their request). Send a generic brochure with a reply card first; it's far more cost- and time-effective for all concerned. Have you designated markets on which you intend to really concentrate? In this case, initially target your promotional material to these buyers. Choose and design around appropriate imagery, then route the advertising to this selected clientele. Say "hello" with your stunning flyer, but let the art director indicate what to do next. Get the necessary feedback, and then aim portfolios of particular samples at those interested buyers.

Remember—any sample you send should be a representative example of your work. Individualized portfolios will naturally contain kindred illustrations chosen for a certain market or special customer. Save these submissions as the snappy follow-up to a strong introduction.

Less is definitely more. Don't pack your portfolio with everything you've done since the third grade. The number varies with everybody you talk to, but a good range is ten to twenty samples of only your absolute best.

Include a SASE (self-addressed, stamped envelope) to ensure the return of a posted submission.

Knowing What to Send

Request a sample issue of the magazine. Research an agency's recent advertisements. Talk to other illustrators who've worked with this publisher. Go to the card shop and browse. Dig through a month's worth of recent newspapers. Call a secretary or an assistant for some advice before you make that submission to the boss— a friendly insider will probably love being approached as the "person in the know" and can provide invaluable information regarding the company's art direction. You can always cut right to the chase, of course, and simply ask the art director.

Calling All Art Directors!

Should you phone an art director before sending work? A call is okay; a query letter may be better. Cold calls (unsolicited contact) are often frustrating and draining for the artist or annoying for the art director. It isn't necessary to call before sending a promo, and it's a bit redundant to call after *every* reminder (although I know this is done by some folks). Enclosing a reply card with your mailing provides initial directions, so it's not essential to use the telephone here either. While persistence is a crucial factor, art directors don't like to be hounded incessantly. Timely and consistent self-promotion, helped by a lot of sweat equity (and a spot of luck), will get you inside. But not to short-change the telephone, a phone call can work magic in any number of instances.

Certainly use the telephone:

- To "formally introduce yourself." This is a nice lead-in to, "Would you like to see a portfolio?"
- If you have received a positive response (but no assignment) on a reply card. Call to say "hello" and to express the desire to establish a future relationship. See if you can send your portfolio, or at least a few samples, as the follow-up to this introduction.
- When you've received an affirmative return plus a request to forward a portfolio. Great! Call to introduce yourself and to express your delight at the continued opportunity to show more of your work. Send the portfolio right away.
- If you haven't received any response to your mailings. You may want to evaluate your situation through personal contact. Don't badger the client; simply call to update your mailing list. Politely inquire about your mailings, and ask if the prospect wishes to receive further samples. Say something like, "I've been sending my promotional material to you for some time, and I just wanted to personally say "hello." I'm updating my program now—can I keep you on my mailing list? Thanks. Look for something exciting in the mail soon."
- To expedite the response to a mailed submission in limbo: What is happening with that portfolio sent back in March? Don't harangue; say how eager you are to do business, and pleasantly request the status of that submission.

Personal contact has definite benefits. All of a sudden, you're a real person, talking to another real person on the other end of the line. Behind the scrawled signature, beyond print, there's an actual voice and a genuine personality at which the paperwork only hints. A phone call carries a tone of immediate persuasion, while written correspondence may not. Don't hesitate to use the phone; it can be to your distinct advantage.

Simultaneous Nocturnal Submissions

There's no reason to sit and wait for the return of a submission—or even a reaction to that material—before sending it on to another client. Regardless of how prompt the response, you'll find that there'll be way too much lag time between your submission and a buyer's reply to warrant exclusivity.

COMPILING A MAILING LIST

When starting out, personal contacts (if and when you have them) should be a part of that list. However, you'll probably find the number of these clients insufficient for your total mailing needs. Your mailing list needs to be a comprehensive one.

The phone book is a good place to look, but while a great local source, listings won't be complete. The best directory to use to find new clients is the *Artist's and Graphic Designer's Market*, published yearly by Writer's Digest Books. This book is the complete "where and how to sell your graphic art" directory. With over 2,500 listings, it includes contact names and addresses, supplies pay rates and buyers' needs, while detailing submission requirements and tips from the buyers themselves. The yearly edition is available around September.

You can always find the *Artist's and Graphic Designer's Market*, plus other directories, at your local library. You can buy the directories, but many of these volumes are expensive and not readily available. If your budget is currently limited, spend some time in the library's reference section, and bring change for the photocopier.

Just a few words about compiling and maintaining a mailing list: Research, try out, and buy a database application (or a program with an integrated database) to facilitate this task. There are many good programs available: Filemaker Pro, Excel, and AppleWorks, to name a few.

RENTING MAILING LISTS

I would advise investigating a list broker, but only if it's within your ways and means. List brokers are a good source for contacts, but do your homework—the validity and shelf life of mailing lists are at issue for many illustrators and designers. Also, the costs of obtaining these lists vary (list brokers usually charge for a one-time use, and some are more stringent than others).

Obviously, it could get expensive if you're reusing the list, but New York illustrator Kathie Abrams tells us, "If you pick up a list rental with phone numbers, you can make follow-up calls. Once you have contacted an art director, you have 'captured' that name and can mail to her again." Also, make sure to get a printout to keep. If you get only labels, they go out in the mailing, and you won't know whom you mailed to or what their phone number is.

Illustrator Peter Spacek tells us, "You'll be surprised at the places you'll get work from—places you'd never think of sending samples or taking your book." So, consider buying a list from a known list broker; it could pay off.

ARTIST'S REPRESENTATIVES

There are some agents who take full credit for the success of their clients (as if the creatives' talent and skill hardly matter), and there are those artists who feel their agent is every bit the super sales and service force a good rep can be.

Illustrator Roger T. Demuth says, "To get a rep, you almost have to not need one. When your work is salable, you get a rep. They usually want to rep you when you don't need them!" Illustrator Ned Shaw adds, "If a rep is really hot, they only take big money earners. Only work with a rep if they are better at selling than you are."

Illustrator Fred Carlson, in his article, "Marketing Illustration in the National Arena" (published in the Graphic Artist's Guild At-Large chapter newsletter), asks these key questions: "Is the 25 to 30 percent commission worth it in terms of your return on any assignment? Can a third party describe your work with the clarity that you can yourself? Can you trust this third party to receive the check and pass on your 70 to 75 percent at once? And finally, will this third party work as hard in your best interests as you would yourself?"

Can a beginning illustrator get a rep? Realistically, probably not. An untested novice, you're too green—and quite a risky gamble at this early stage of your game. This is not to say that it's absolutely impossible. Some newcomers seem to hit the streets running. Boasting unmistakable ability and oozing fresh technique, they are in the right place at the right time. In our story, Cinderella's creative approach counterbalances her tender experience, and she offers a style ripe for the current needs of a ready marketplace. Agents are always looking for these audacious talents; it's a sweet fairy tale, but is not the industry norm. Do you need a rep? Maybe. Benton Mahan believes that "most people, especially in the beginning, can be their own best agent."

AWARDS ANNUALS

"Another excellent way to get noticed," says illustrator Robert Saunders, "is to submit to the awards annuals. It costs to enter, yes, but figure it into your budget. It's the cheapest advertising going and can establish a fledgling reputation and put you on the fast track if you do it religiously."

Saunders goes on to mention that the best, most cutting-edge art directors are chosen to jury these publications. As this is the audience you want buying your work, the awards annuals thus provide great long-term promotion. "This encourages you to always be the best you can be," he says. "Directory ads offer good exposure, but there's the very real possibility you could spend a mint on the ad and find yourself positioned across the spread from another illustrator's lovingly rendered foot-powder ad . . . yow!"

Awards annuals to enter include: *HOW*'s annual self-promotion competition, the Society of Illustrators, *Communication Arts*, *Print*'s Regional Design Annual, *Graphis*, Society of Publication Designers, The Art Directors Club, and American Illustration. They all have categories for unpublished or self-promotional work. The benefits are real. Says Saunders, "One piece I did that got into *Communication Arts* prompted calls from several national magazines—including a request for samples from the *New Yorker*.

PROFESSIONAL ⬇ VIEWPOINTS

You have to promote yourself. People must see your work. If you don't have an agent, the only way for that to happen is for you to do it yourself.

—Ted Pitts, Illustrator and Art Director

Self-promotion is an absolute necessity, but the form it takes varies. I think beginners haven't yet hammered out what they want to say about the world they see and how they want to say it. Understand that one visit or one reminder may not be enough, and realize that art directors actually have real jobs. They're working full time. Looking at people's portfolios is only part of their job.

—Sam Viviano, Illustrator and Art Director

Put in samples that relate to solving problems. The samples should not make the art buyer ask questions; they should answer questions. The buyer has a set of questions in mind: Are you dependable? Can you work with different size restrictions? Can you solve demanding compositional requirements? Your samples must be positive answers to those questions.

—Fred Carlson, Illustrator

TOM GRAHAM
Illustration & Design

© Tom Graham 2001

© Sam Viviano 2001

Send a letter or promo to the person you want to see. Call in about a week for an appointment. If a gatekeeper says, "What do you want to talk to him about?" just reply, "It's concerning some correspondence we've had." That will normally get you past most gatekeepers.

—Roger Brucker, Designer

Be conscious of your self-promotion all the time. You can't afford to just kick back and say, "Well, I'm busy now, and it's going to continue this way, and I don't have to do too much about it." I think you always have to be aware of how many people are out there doing the same thing.

—Joe Ciardiello, Illustrator

A nice mailer doesn't have to be elaborate. Creativity makes for a memorable promo.

—Dan Johnson, Designer

It's funny how you decide to whom you send your samples. There's the art director who sometimes is a very famous person, who everybody knows and probably gets more mail than he can read. Then, there are all these associate art directors, and you tend to pick out the one with the nicest name, or you send it to all of them.

—Ted Pitts, Illustrator and Art Director

You are looking to connect with those art buyers who are on your wavelength. Not everyone will be, but there is someone for every style and taste. Your goal should be to represent yourself as clearly and attractively as possible, so that you can get a response from other people who think the same way you do. I think it is a neurotic experience to try to be everything to everyone.

—Kathie Abrams, Illustrator

chapter 12

WHAT GOES IN A
PORTFOLIO

The most important thing is the portfolio. You have to have out-standing work—interesting work with a point of view. Some call this a style. Your book must have character and be different and have a strong look, otherwise no one will remember it.

—Simms Taback, Illustrator, Designer, and Art Director

The bottom line is that your portfolio should reflect you.

—Kathie Abrams, Illustrator

A portfolio is a collected display of samples. It's a planned presentation of your work, used to communicate your abilities to a potential client. You do your thing at what's commonly called a portfolio review.

So, what happens during a portfolio review? It's just like a job interview, right? Generally, portfolio reviews are less formal than a job interview, but the game rules don't vary much. Common sense tells us that what counts is self-confidence, a positive attitude, and good personal appearance.

But there are folks who dispute this. According to New York illustrator Robert Zimmerman, "I know for a fact that this is total [expletive deleted]. First, W. Jones Street [name changed by author] and I had appointments the same hour at a financial magazine. Street looked like he had been up for five days straight and was probably wearing clothes borrowed from someone on the Bowery. His portfolio was pure genius. Street got a cover assignment, and I got commissioned to do a spot the size of a Kenyan postage stamp. The guy has since gone on to be a demigod of illustration.

"Second, Kay Dodge-Carr [name changed by the author] and I were on the elevator going up to a large weekly magazine. I was dropping off a job, and she was dropping off her book. She looked like she had been in a fight with a lawn mower. The next week, she was doing full-page illustrations for the magazine, and I was still doing spots no larger than a flattened penny."

Yep, many arty types dress rather (expletive deleted) *casually*. However, it would be irresponsible to insist that an iconoclastic dress code will work in *your* situation, where *you* live. Sure, your mom's not dressing you now, but the bigger picture still says to dress fashionably and neatly.

If you're right-handed, carry your portfolio in your left; be ready to shake hands with the art director without fumbling or shifting the binder. (If you're left-handed, carry your portfolio in your left hand, also.) Eye contact is also a sign of confidence. Look your client square in the face, open your book, and knock some socks off!

A note: I'm a firm believer in the power of an education. But as a freelancer, art directors aren't terribly interested in SAT or GRE scores or your GPA. That dual degree in Rocket Engineering and Basket Weaving is more or less irrelevant when you show your samples. Art buyers aren't too concerned about how a freelancer might interact in a group, nor do they care what you might bring to the organization (or where you see yourself in the organization over the next five years). Likewise, your résumé is important, but not key. Credits and work experience can be hyped—it's the portfolio that counts. As illustrator Ernie Norcia relates, "No one has ever asked me for my credentials as a freelancer. I've only been asked, Can you do it? For how much? "

YOUR PORTFOLIO: QUALITY, NOT QUANTITY

It's only your career we're talking here, so as illustrator Mary Grace Eubank advises, "Invest whatever it takes to represent your work at its very finest. You can look like a million dollars while flaunting credits and scholastic achievements like crazy, but ultimately it is your portfolio that will make—or break—your chances."

Don't sacrifice quality for quantity, and big is not necessarily better. A compact, manageable portfolio makes for an easier, smoother presentation. Bulky binders are heavy and unwieldy. At best, you'll just look clumsy flailing these free weights around the art director's desk. A portfolio review should be a visual workout, not physical exercise for the art director.

Matting each piece is an option (if done with skill), but this may only add weight. Protect your work by mounting your samples. Acetate, polyester, or vinyl sleeves are old school, but tried and true—what else ya got? Think about mounting or laminating loose tear sheets not presented within a sleeve. Lamination adds expense, but looks great and will preserve the life of each piece.

Mounting your work on black looks professional and won't distract from your piece (remember, you're selling the art, not the frame). Some artists mount on white, but I feel a white (even off-white) sheet is too bright and glossy—I want the piece to shine, not the backdrop. However, if your samples are dark and broody, a white backing may provide the proper contrast.

Nothing will disguise mediocre work. Despite the gimmicks, that high-tech binder with space program technology and Technicolor sleeves won't cut it. Substance, not flash, makes the sale.

MAILING PORTFOLIOS

As mentioned in the previous chapter, a "portfolio" is an organized presentation of your illustration, so you'll be mailing this portfolio to prospective clients. You don't have to forward the actual binder containing those irreplaceable originals or rare tear sheets. You will be mailing compiled reproductions, extra tear sheets, or high-quality photocopies.

Look into digitizing your portfolio on a CD. A service bureau can do this for you, or it's easily done right off your desktop. At this writing, CD burners are quite affordable, CD-R (write once/read always) disks dirt cheap, and self-running presentation software readily available.

I imagine there are still some traditionalists who send photography or transparency portfolios (slides are also called transparencies). If you go this route, prepare one sleeve of no more than twenty slides. Label each slide and the sleeve, plus enclose a self-addressed, postage-paid envelope for their safe return.

Whatever your format, and whenever you mail, you'll need to virtually "bulletproof" your submission—you want your package to arrive undamaged, and much can happen during the round trip between postboxes.

Present all samples inside a folder, and sandwich this between two pieces of cardboard, matte board, styrofoam, or foam core. (You should also protect an art assignment under tissue and between two pieces of card, hinged by tape. Label the folder and individual pieces.) Be sure to enclose a cover letter along with your business card. Of course, completely label the outside packaging.

The outer wrap may be a manila or foam-padded envelope, bubble wrap, or even brown wrapping paper. Or you could insert the infrastructure between two additional pieces of cardboard rather than an envelope, to further safeguard the package. Use package-sealing tape (masking tape is frowned upon by the post office and many airfreight services) or reinforced tape, if you're really cautious. On the front of the package, write or stamp "PLEASE DO NOT BEND OR FOLD—ARTWORK ENCLOSED." Include an SASE for its return.

ARRANGING A PORTFOLIO REVIEW

Requesting and scheduling a portfolio review are, of course, two different things. Scheduling hinges on an affirmative answer to that request, and can be done either by letter or telephone. A phone request is informal (even intimate), quick, and right to the point. The written request can be backed by visuals—after all, you're selling product, not patter. Neither method has a definite edge, so take some thought to determine how you want to communicate with the art director.

Some folks are natural writers; their polished letters are powerful and persuasive and not to be ignored. Others prefer the immediate and individual interaction only the telephone provides. As you'll be spending lots of time on the phone and at the keyboard (business generates correspondence and vice versa), you'll have plenty of opportunities to develop your communication skills.

Cold Calls Redux

A cold call, as you'll remember from chapter 10, is a contact without request or referral. It can get you a portfolio review without the preliminary wait involved with written correspondence, but cold calls require time and energy you may not want to expend. Factor in that many art directors consider cold calls a distinct bother, and what do you have?

What you have is essentially door-to-door sales, and perhaps pure frustration. For some illustrators and designers, the very idea of the cold call is unthinkable; others hate them, but still accept making them as a necessary part of business. Many artists view cold calls as just another avenue for pursuing yet more business. It's a sure way to test your tolerance for rejection, but a deft salesperson may get a good return for the trouble.

Drop-Off Policy

There are those busy art directors who will only look at portfolios at specific hours on certain days. These days, more will require that the illustrator leave ("drop off") the "book" (more arty talk for portfolio), then pick it up later at a scheduled date or time. There may be a written reaction—which just might be an impersonal, generic, photocopied form—or possibly a critique or suggestions. You may have no clue regarding the art director's evaluation, and you may have to politely follow-up for a response. If the art director is interested, an appointment is arranged. Yes, you read right: You won't be there. If you feel your portfolio is not strong enough to "speak" for you in your absence, don't show it yet. Take some time, and get that book in shape.

There are those artists who feel that the drop-off saves time and eliminates uninterested prospects. Eventually, you'll face a drop-off policy. It's quite the common practice when making rounds in a larger market.

At some point, you'll have to decide how you feel about leaving your book and the inherent dangers and benefits thereof. Before the portfolio ever leaves your hands, consider how to minimize any risks involved. Expendable samples

SEVEN LAWS OF SUBMITTING WORK THROUGH THE MAIL

1. Submit work to the appropriate person.

2. Send your portfolio when you say you will.

3. Samples must be organized, clean, neatly presented, clearly labeled, focused, and expendable.

4. Write a personal cover letter on your attractive letterhead. Make it brief and friendly—not too proud, not too humble. Include a self-addressed, stamped envelope for the return of the samples. Realize that you won't get your work back immediately—it is being viewed by any number of busy people with hectic schedules.

5. Follow up with a card or phone call. Follow that phone call with another. Remember, with all the hustle and bustle, art directors need your help to connect your name with your artwork. Do not give up, but don't be pushy. When it becomes necessary to inquire about the status of your portfolio, be absolutely courteous.

6. Send new samples frequently. Remind the art director of the valuable contribution you are anxious to make. You want your card on their bulletin board.

7. Build your list of contact names to create more opportunities.

will alleviate the considerable pain of lost originals. A strong binder and sturdy presentation will buffet the blows the portfolio will weather in its travels. Protect the samples, making sure they're securely mounted. Label clearly and completely. Have someone sign for the portfolio before you leave the office. Finally, fight your paranoia. These strangers (doing "who knows what with my precious watercolors") are the same wonderful folks with the choice assignments. A healthy attitude will be awarded by a sigh of relief when the portfolio is safely back in your possession. And guess what? You landed an assignment!

TARGETING A PORTFOLIO

Should you change your portfolio for each type of market you show it to? Many artists, like Mary Grace Eubank, work in concentrated markets. Eubank says that, while she is constantly *updating*, she cannot relate to *changing* her portfolio: "I started doing gift wrap, then went into greeting cards, and from there I went into children's books."

If you have many pieces from which to pick and choose, orient your portfolio to particular markets; a binder with interchangeable sleeves can facilitate this process. At the beginning, you may not have many pieces from various markets. This means a somewhat generic portfolio that addresses a wider client base—not a sampling of divergent styles, but a portfolio that meets a variety of needs.

Although a quirky line style reproduces well and is strong and compelling, the folks at a card company won't relate to a portfolio of black-and-white editorial samples. If you add color or humor (and present card mock ups), the art director can visualize how to use your work. By the same token, greeting cards will not go over at advertisement agencies. The imagery you show must be in the context of an ad (with type) to show how your work meets the agency's needs.

Sometimes, different markets overlap, but people will tend to classify your work. It's a little tough to break barriers and preconceived ideas. The rule of thumb is to always show what's relevant. And just a word about style here: It's best to present a solid, consistent style (especially at the beginning of your career), especially when selling in the national marketplace.

ASSEMBLING A PORTFOLIO

Now, repeat these three words while putting the portfolio together: "Only my best." Generally, small is better, and less is more. Think in the neighborhood of ten to twenty pieces. Focus. Be highly selective. If in doubt about a particular piece, don't use it!

Nothing less than your best work should be in your binder. You're only as strong as your weakest sample. That one inferior piece sandwiched somewhere in the middle of your book will be remembered first—it will detract from the "good stuff" and diminish the impact of the entire portfolio. Don't include anything of which you're not proud. Don't include any style or technique you don't really want to do.

As you develop, so grows your portfolio (we're still talking quality, not quantity). A portfolio should never be stagnant—update it regularly. Samples must be well-protected, but portable and easy to change and examine. Make it simple to carry (with or without handles), of uniform page size, and lightweight. A leather or leatherlike ring binder (open or zippered) enclosing the transparent sleeves offers the simplest answer here.

There is no distinct advantage to either a vertical or horizontal layout, but your portfolio should not be a lazy Susan; make sure the art director isn't swiveling your book—or his head—around from page to page. Have one consistent page orientation throughout. If this proves impossible, group all horizontal pieces in one section and all vertical samples in another. This way, the art director only cranes his neck once.

It's a given that neatness is crucial and that a portfolio must contain crisp, clean samples wrapped in a professional package, all presented with style and taste. A portfolio cannot be a haphazard affair. There should be a planned arrangement and logical progression to the sequence of samples. While good organization is a must, I don't necessarily subscribe to the train of thought that says one must lump all color pieces together (and the same with black-and-white pieces).

The portfolio should be clearly—but tastefully—labeled. No neon lights, just complete identification inside and out. Your work is highly suspect if the presentation shines brighter than your samples.

You can approach the pace and flow of the portfolio in a variety of ways. Chronological (or reverse chronological) organization shows progression and development. Organization by subject matter (for instance, animals, crowd scenes, portraits) works for many artists. You could take a graphic approach and group by technique (such as pen-and-ink followed by watercolors). You might want to organize thematically and demonstrate problem-solving within a specific body of assignments (advertisements, greeting cards, book jackets).

Always start big and end strong. After a trenchant beginning, some portfolios will build to an exciting finish. Many books crest in the middle and slope to a big bang. Others are like a roller coaster ride—with many visual peaks and rests, culminating in a stunning climax.

Labeling Portfolio Pieces

Let your work sell itself. Labels can be used as efficient identifiers or as elements of page design. These compositional devices can be effective if used sparingly and with purpose. A brief description noting the title, client, and project is entirely appropriate. If you must write a note detailing each piece, your samples do not pack the visual wallop needed to carry the portfolio.

NOW SEE CHAPTER 20

You might have read all this and said, "Hey—this section completely ignores the need for an online portfolio." For some, sending a portfolio through the mails harks back to the age of the dinosaurs. For others, doing the rounds with a physical portfolio is very archaic. Indeed, Seattle-based illustrator Mark Monlux says, "I haven't done it in YEARS. However, I get a request every week asking me for my Web site, and I inform people constantly of the site. Its layout and presentation is equally as important as a portfolio and is seen by far, far more people."

Not so fast. I coached Little League, and I'm one of those folks who understand the practicality of hitting all the important bases. You will find our entire chapter 20 devoted to Web stuff, so you're covered either way. Now, go back and touch third base.

PROFESSIONAL ⬇ VIEWPOINTS

Young people coming out of school show everything—students are so eager to prove they're talented, they put in too much. Show a portfolio with some consistency. Make it the very best you have, but be highly discriminating.

—Reynold Ruffins, Illustrator, Designer, and Art Director

If I had listened to everyone when I was first looking for a job, I would have taken every piece out—so I decided to go by my own instincts.   —Elwood Smith, Illustrator

My first portfolio contained some illustrations on colocystectomy! And I had some funny chalk drawings that I'd created: creatures with one foot and horns out of the forehead and things like that—light, children's book sort of things. It showed some drawing style, and I thought that was the most important thing.

The portfolio case I had was something I'd gotten when I was in high school, one of those tie jobs. It was a black thing, about two by three feet with a little flap that you'd tuck in to keep your artwork from spilling all over the sidewalk and shoestrings that you'd tie on the three remaining sides that weren't hinged. And it was completely destroyed. It was just all frayed and torn—I had used it as backing when cutting with my X-acto knife. I realized that I had to do something about this portfolio.

I decided to build my own case the night before a portfolio review. It looked like a coffin for a flounder, big and bulky. I put all my junk in there—my pictures of gallbladders, brains, and livers—and took it in. Some art directors would just look at it and laugh. I'm sure as soon as I left they said, "What a dork! He comes in here with a wooden box, showing us gallbladders . . . but he sure can draw!" At least, I hope that's what they said.

—David Catrow, Illustrator

© David Catrow 2001

You'll need a portfolio that reflects your strong suit, and for this you have to know yourself. Are you linear? Are you tonal? Do you paint? Do you do pen-and-ink? Concentrate on whatever it is you enjoy, but stay aware of what the art directors are buying.
—Chris Spollen, Illustrator

Make sure every piece in your portfolio is as good as it can be—no halfway-accomplished tasks.
—Fred Carlson, Illustrator

First, realize that people are going to say things that you don't like. You have to develop a pretty thick skin to go out there and deal with people. (But) if you enjoy what you're doing and you're drawing for yourself, then it really doesn't matter what people think.
—David Catrow, Illustrator

Show one style. It will confuse art directors if they see a different style on every page in your book. Everybody is pretty much a specialist; it's better if they see one direction.
—Joe Ciardiello, Illustrator

Your book may need to be changed for different markets, but the portfolio itself should stay out of the way of your art. If it quietly and efficiently showcases your work, it's doing its job.
—Kathie Abrams, Illustrator

Your book is an important reflection on how your work will be perceived by art buyers, art directors, or creative directors. It must be uniformly presented, look professional, and be clean. Try to put in only excellent artwork. The number of pieces is not as important as quality.
—Bill Mayer, Illustrator

chapter 13

THE MAGAZINE
MARKET

I think there's only one market in which to begin. That's to do editorial work for magazines. Magazines are looking for beginners, they're on the cutting edge of new stuff, they're interested in what the art schools are turning out.

—Simms Taback, Illustrator, Designer, and Art Director

How many different types of magazines are there? For many illustrators, there are only two types of magazines: those that take your work and those that don't. The point here is that the magazine market is wide open and diverse, but there are some basic categories.

Look for magazines in the following categories (the categories are real, the following titles are all fictional): local and regional publications (for example, *Ohio Every Second, Yellow Springs Today!*), trade journals (*Velcro World, Industrial Strength*), general audience or consumer periodicals (*American Laughstyles*), special interest magazines (*Spelunking Gerbil, Contemporary Antiques, Starting to Stop*), and in-house or company organs (*Inside This Company*).

Every publication is directed to a particular reader, therefore, different magazines require different kinds of artwork. You won't find bizarre illustration in the *Saturday Evening Post*; it wouldn't mesh with the conservative audience.

Every magazine has its own editorial tone and visual tenor. The editor and art director make sure that graphics and text work together and that the flavor of the magazine is consistent throughout.

When a certain story lends itself to a particular treatment, the art director goes to the artist who best fits the bill. Some publications (children's magazines, for instance) take a wider range of work. At any magazine, every art director tries to match an artist's approach with the story and style dictated.

WHAT MAGAZINES NEED

Copy, photography, and illustration share the pages of any periodical. Magazines want illustrators, designers, photographers, stylists (hair, food, fashion), model makers, prop builders, production artists, calligraphers, cartoonists, copywriters, and editors.

Magazines look for illustrators who can do four-color or black-and-white illustration. They want both digital and traditional illustrators. And like any client needing a freelancer, magazines will want professionals with good rendering skills, plus a fine line, color, and design sense. All magazines require skilled artists. If your skills are weak, the magazine doesn't need you. You do see some artists with a very minimal delivery, but in this case, it's a stylistic manner.

Be aware that magazines work on very tight schedules. You will often be asked to turn a job around within a few days, and sometimes overnight. Illustrator Robert Zimmerman cautions, "If you work in a style that requires a great deal of detail, or simply requires considerable time to create, then the magazine market probably isn't for you. You do not want to offer a style you won't be able to deliver at the highest quality, in the time given."

Many magazines (for example, consumer or both special and general interest publications) lean towards a conceptual approach (your strong suit, right?). Some publications (such as regional and trade magazines) are journalistic in nature. While some conceptual work may be used, they mostly solicit photorealism to record events as they happen.

RESEARCHING THE MARKET

How do you find out if a magazine accepts freelance artwork? Call the people you would be working with—the editor, art director, or art staff—and simply ask.

Glance through a sample issue; check the credits within the magazine, and see if the work is done by staffers or contributors. Check the masthead; all magazines list those vital folks who create the periodical.

Discreetly jot down information about a new publication at the newsstand. You can take a moment to clear this with the clerk or owner beforehand. Introduce yourself, state your purpose, and express your thanks. But remember, this is not the public library. However, you shouldn't have any trouble in any bookstore where browsing is welcome and accepted.

And speaking of which, listings of magazines can be found at most libraries. Consult the following: *Artist's and Graphic Designer's Market, Writer's Market, Magazine Industry Marketplace,* the *Standard Periodical Directory,* the *Gebbie Press All-in-One Directory,* the *Gale Directory of Publications, Ulrich's International Periodicals Directory,* and the "Red Book" (the Standard Rate and Data Service [SRDS] listings of ad agencies, businesses, and publishing personnel). Use the creative directories. Most artists include a client roster in their advertising. While you'll have to research contacts and addresses, you'll cull a long catalog of potential customers from these lists.

Here are some magazines that cover the magazine industry: the *Artist's Magazine, Folio, Print, Confetti,* and *Magazine Design and Production.* Look also at *Upper and Lower Case, Print, Step-by-Step Graphics, HOW, Graphis, Advertising Age, AdWeek, Art Product News, Art Direction,* and *Communication Arts.*

FINDING THE LOOK

A magazine must establish a consistent, distinctive look. Its style—the "tone" of the magazine—should be evident as soon as you glance at the cover.

Send for a sample or go to the library and look at all the recent issues available. Study the illustrations a magazine uses, look at editorial content, think about the subject matter. Is the magazine conservative or progressive? Hip or traditional? Is it politically left or right? Does it specialize in hard-hitting exposes or typically feature stories on food, travel, or fashion? Are the visuals appropriate? Are art and photography conceptual or realistic?

Compare any two magazines (*Life* to *Rolling Stone,* for example), and you should instantly get an impression of what these periodicals are all about. If you don't, the magazine is in trouble, because it's not directly addressing its target audience.

EDITOR OR ART DIRECTOR?

Generally, send your submission to the art director. Most magazines have an art director (plus, if they're big enough, maybe an associate art director and/or assistant art director). Some do not. In these cases, the editor or publisher—often one and the same person—reviews art submissions.

Art director Steve Miller gives this important piece of advice: "Never send a portfolio unless you have return postage guaranteed. If you want your material returned, pay for it. If you don't want the stuff back, fine. Leave it up to the art director. She or he can either put it in the 'tickler' file or drop it in a round file [the waste can]." Illustrator Robert Saunders follows up. He says, "Never send a returnable portfolio unsolicited, though. No A.D. [art director] wants the burden. These days, it's often sufficient that an A.D. can access your Web site. It's quicker and easier, with no liability on the A.D. to return anything. Portfolios are still used, but increasingly less and less."

Do your homework, and establish the appropriate contact at the magazine. Don't forward a portfolio unless you have a specific name or know the correct department accepting submissions. One phone call should do the trick, but if you cannot come up with a name (perhaps the position or its occupant are in transition), label your promo "ATTENTION: ART DIRECTOR" (or "ART DEPART-MENT" or "ART BUYER"). At the outset, this is okay, but not highly recom-mended. When you want to establish or maintain personal correspondence with the magazine, make it a point to get the name of the art buyer as soon as possible.

BEST MAGAZINES FOR BEGINNERS

Which type of magazine would be good to start with? Think about the magazines you enjoy most. Browse the library and the newsstand. Look at all you can, then dream a little—visualize where you'd like to be, with whom you'd love to work.

Some feel there is no "best" place for the beginner to start, that all the mar-kets are good—if you're good, why not start right at the top? But trying to start your freelance career at *Time* will probably be like kissing the business end of a shark—good luck!

Others recommend a conservative gambit. Start with local newspapers, work your way up to lesser-known magazines, and eventually to larger or more-presti-gious publications. Begin with small staffs, operations where you won't get lost or mired in the red tape of the big companies. Work at the modest periodicals, accept the low fees to get published credits, and gradually climb the ladder to the heady atmosphere of "the big time."

CULTIVATE A VARIETY

Don't limit your submissions to one type of magazine, or worse yet, one magazine only. Submit to as many magazines as you have a mind to, as many as you can. Freelancing is a numbers game—your livelihood depends on the total drawings you sell. In all likelihood, one client or type of client won't support or sustain your business. Your style must meet the needs of a variety of magazines if you're to succeed in the magazine market.

There's no reason to wait for the return of a submission or a reaction to your material. Regardless of how prompt the response, remember that there's too much lag time between your submission and a buyer's reply to warrant exclusivity

Simultaneous Submissions

You can send the same illustrations to several magazines at the same time. Your initial advertising should be somewhat general in scope. You'd have to be prolific—not to mention incredibly rich—to send a different promo to every ven-dor on your list! Follow-ups and portfolios should be targeted to specific clients, but the same illustrations can be sent to several magazines at the same time.

Be aware of audience overlap, however. While wonderfully silly, is that funny drawing of Mother Goose what the art director of *Field and Stream* really wants? Make sure any illustration sent to a variety of magazines will meet the needs of all those buyers.

GOING POSTAL

Because art directors are busy people, receiving samples through the mail can be an efficient use of their time. I say *can* be, because many art directors are inundated with submissions, and they obviously have other things to do besides looking at portfolios (like, umm, art direct the magazine, for instance).

But what about the artist's time, energy, and finances? Magazines probably see more people through the mail simply because it's much cheaper and easier to send samples than to visit the office.

Say the periodical is in Cincinnati, and you're in Indianapolis. You have to drop everything and drive two-and-a-half hours to get there and again to get home. You have no guarantee that you're going to get a job out of all this. When you weigh the costs and risks of doing business through the mail, there is no comparison.

On Commission

Advertise with completed samples, but generally, don't try to sell finished, unsolicited illustration through the mails. Consumer and special-interest publications invariably commission artwork for specific assignments. However, some magazines (literary magazines, for example) will often buy existing art, because they allow artwork to stand on its own. And then, there is stock.

STICK A STOCK IN IT

The idea of second rights sales is hardly new, and illustrators have been offering subsequent reproduction rights for ages. But recently, few issues have churned up as much raging controversy as selling stock illustration and royalty-free images.

Why? As Roger Brucker says, "There is no right way to do the wrong thing," and stock is a multilayered onion to peel. It's one thing to sell stock on your own—to, shall we say, control your creative destiny. The allure of quick, big bucks is always just that—a lure. And understand that any stock sale (especially cheaper stock images) or royalty-free package ultimately puts you in direct competition with your commissioned work and fees.

Know that the contract provided by a stock house may not be particularly artist-friendly. Who receives the creative credit for your work? Are there lowball prices for art, but high commissions for the stock house (which mean negligible returns for you)? Is there a clause in the paperwork that forbids you to sell stock elsewhere (even images not under contract)? Does this exclusive clause indenture you to the company for five years? Say you fail to withdraw your stuff by a stated deadline, is there an automatic rollover clause that begins another five-year term? Who controls the sale and communication about the transaction? Are you involved in client contact, pricing, contracts, and usage?

If you are thinking about selling stock—on your own, with your agent, or through a stock house—bone up (more homework)! Read more about it, and go out on the Web. First stops: Visit the Graphic Artists Guild (*www.gag.org*), the ispot (*www.theispot.com*), and Illustrators' Partnership of America (*www.illustratorspartnership.com*) Web sites. Educate yourself about this important issue.

PROFESSIONAL ⬇ VIEWPOINTS

I never send a piece unless I know my prospect's name, the correct spelling of that name (important), and—very importantly—that the prospect is still employed there. Because my promo—assuming it even reaches someone—is seen in context with those of my competition, anything less just sends a message that I didn't know or care enough to find out about my prospective client. Do mailings the same way you would do an assignment: with thoroughness and attention to detail. Leave nothing to chance.

—Robert Saunders, Illustrator

You must think of this as a business and that your artwork is the product. Always answer the problem that the art director set out for you to answer. Deadlines are very important. Someone can live with a piece of art that is not quite perfect, but they can't live with a blank page in a magazine.

—Ben Mahan, Illustrator

Magazines and newspapers are markets that will give you a lot of freedom to do conceptual and maybe experimental work. The budgets are much lower, but you will get some good exposure in these publications.

—Bill Mayer, Illustrator

Present your portfolio in a professional manner when approaching magazine markets. Avoid work that looks too obviously like a class project. Avoid work that looks experimental for the sake of being

© Chris Spollen 2001

experimental. Stick to good work geared to the type of client to whom you're showing your book. It's always better to have fewer pieces that are really good than a ton of boring pages. Even if it's only a handful of great material, it's better than a giant, mediocre portfolio.

—Joe Ciardiello, Illustrator

The best advice anyone ever gave me was this: An art director, looking over my sketches, asked me, "Why do you think I called you to do this job? I called you for what you do." —Laura Cornell, Illustrator

I'm drawing for me. I think people see that and know I'm enjoying it. It looks like you waved the magic wand, and your feelings that day came out on the paper. When you draw for yourself, this comes across as something very nice, indeed.

—David Catrow, Illustrator

Address the needs of your marketplace. Accept the fact that you won't get the big money or high-profile work (*Time*, *Esquire*, etc.) right away. Get exposure, but more importantly, explore your media and the way you see the world.

—Sam Viviano, Illustrator and Art Director

chapter 14

SELLING TO NEWSPAPERS

I take the philosophy that you have to draw every day. And you have to put that pressure on yourself to draw on demand, because a client isn't going to come up to you and say, "Here, I want you to draw this when the urge really strikes you."

—David Catrow, Illustrator

While content is certainly the wild card, the basic format of a newspaper doesn't really vary much from one to another. In that the primary function of a newspaper is to report news, even the *New York Times* and the *National Enquirer* are still editorial sisters under the skin.

You will find neighborhood newsletters, local and regional newspapers (such as the *Dayton Daily News*), big-city newspapers with a national circulation (like the *Times*), newspapers with a national scope (*U.S.A. Today*), tabloids (the *Enquirer*), plus general or special interest newspapers (*Funny Times*, for instance).

Within the pages of any newspaper, different types of artwork are required. Freelance illustrator (and Art Director for the *Dayton Daily News*) Ted Pitts tells us that a beginner wanting to freelance to newspapers can be a specialist.

Illustrator Robert Zimmerman agrees. "Art directors at newspapers are extremely busy people who are working on very tight deadlines," he says. "They do not want to be guessing at what they will get as a final illustration style. The people that get the most work in newspapers deliver a specific style of illustration. With so many illustrators available, art directors can pick the person whose style best suits the assignment. This might be technical, map work, humorous, or caricature. Whatever it is you do best, that is what you should offer."

SKILLS FOR NEWSPAPERS

As copy, photography, and art share the pages of the newspaper, one can certainly find a freelance gig as an illustrator, designer, photographer, or writer. You could also work as a production artist (however, this position is usually a staff job) or calligrapher. Newspapers also look for artists to create informational graphics—maps, charts, and diagrams—as well as researchers to develop these projects.

It could once be argued that black-and-white illustrations were the bread and butter of newspaper illustration, but thanks to the influence of *USA Today* and the computer, color has exploded in the industry.

FREELANCE VERSUS STAFF

A staff illustrator's position is highly coveted, and competition is stiff. A better title for the job is probably "staff artist," with a job description most likely encompassing page design and the creation of said informational graphics.

There just aren't that many staff positions for illustrators at newspapers. Throw in the economics of hiring a full-time staff person as opposed to a freelancer and your chances are better as an independent.

Who's Your Daddy?

Let's take this opportunity to discuss another difference between staff artists and freelancers. A factor critical to your long-term career survival is the issue of who owns usage rights, or copyright, to your work. We mention copyright and stock elsewhere in this book, but this chapter is a perfect place to continue the string. Illustrator Robert Saunders reminds us that staff artists at newspapers, as employees, generally relinquish all rights and authorship to their work. "Upon completion," Saunders says, "these illustrations become part of the paper's own image archive, from which the newspaper can then license your work without attribution, forever and however it wants."

Play out the scenario yourself: The archive grows and merges with other archives (it's happening in the real world even as I write these words). Eventually, we see the creation of a stock image resource that's large and widely promoted. From here? "Your full-time employment becomes expendable," says Saunders. "You find yourself out there competing against your own stock work in a dwindling buyer's market."

In our current business climate, freelance illustrators are increasingly "asked" to sign contracts demanding all rights before being given a newspaper assignment. You can refuse a bad deal. You can court other art buyers—even other newspapers—who offer fair terms. These buyers are out there, just as there are others who offer lousy contracts. Says Saunders, "Retaining, or at least receiving fair market compensation for the copyright to your own work, is critical to your profiting from the investment of time, energy, and love you've put into your craft."

Aww, Rights Now

As mentioned above, there are newspapers offering freelance contracts stipulating illustrators (as well as photographers and writers) give up all past, present, and future rights to work done for that newspaper as a condition of freelance employment. Understandably, contributors are balking and refusing to sign such lopsided, unreasonable agreements (the provisions of which may endure many decades after a creator's death). Your fellow creators are fighting the good fight through organized protests and letter-writing campaigns; there are court cases pending as I write these words, so stay tuned. Better yet, educate yourself, and join in to help the cause.

I have said this before, but it always bears repeating: Read your contracts carefully. Know what you are being asked to sign. Stand up for your rights. Fair value for fair work is always the goal.

CALL TO QUERY

Newspapers may not use freelance illustration for fast-breaking, hard news stories—the staff illustrator may get the call when a deadline is extremely tight. But another side of that coin is that late-breaking jobs *are* assigned to those freelancers with a reputation for dispatching short turnarounds in this high-pressure market.

The section most open to freelance work is the op-ed page. Features or magazine sections that are planned well in advance of publication are also freelance possibilities. Here, you are dealing with events, trends, and ideas.

To find out if a newspaper accepts freelance work, call the art director, or art staff, and ask. Consult the *Editor and Publisher's Yearbook* (and the weekly magazine *Editor and Publisher*).

NAME THAT TONE

Compare two newspapers (the *Washington Post* and the *New York Daily News*, for instance) to contrast those qualities that make each publication unique and individual.

Determine a newspaper's philosophical content and political position. Analyze and evaluate subject matter while examining writing style(s). Then, study all illustration and photography. Is the art conceptual or straightforward? Do visuals and copy mesh to better convey the point of the story? Do you agree with the editorial stance? In your evaluation, does the artwork succeed?

Illustrator Tom Graham says, "I think it is important to objectively analyze the look a newspaper is currently printing. Chances are, they will not stray far afield from that look. If what they are currently printing really turns you on, and you feel you would fit right in, maybe even do it better, then proceed."

ART DIRECTOR VERSUS EDITOR

Do you send samples to the editor or the art director? As a general rule of thumb, I'd send to the art director, unless instructed otherwise.

It's okay to submit samples to the editor. The editor or publisher—frequently one and the same person—often reviews art submissions. Some newspapers, especially smaller ones, may not have an art director. Maybe administrative responsibilities are shared or rotated amongst staff members, or the chief artist acts as art director. Perhaps the features editor is the freelance coordinator. Many papers have an assistant managing editor for graphics or designate an illustration buyer.

Establish the appropriate contact at the newspaper by doing your homework. As said before, don't forward a portfolio unless you have a specific name or know the correct department accepting submissions.

START LOCALLY

What newspapers would be good to start with? Begin with a community newsletter, then work your way up to the local newspaper and beyond. Begin with small-staffed operations. Work at these modest publications, accept the low fees for published credits and experience, and gradually climb the ladder. It also does not hurt to do a few "freebies" to get on track, as long as these loss leaders are not with highly-capitalized, major-market newspapers. Understand and make sure there is a measurable benefit from giving away your work.

Simultaneous Submissions

Don't submit to one newspaper at a time—there's no reason to wait for the return of a submission or a reaction to your material. If there's only one newspaper in town, it may or may not buy freelance, so local options may be limited

Commission or Submission

Newspapers generally commission artwork for a specific article. News breaks fast, and current events are exactly that. A mailed submission will probably not be timely for a newspaper. If the paper uses freelance work, the art director will certainly want to spend money on art that fits the copy—not "comes close" or "might work with some imagination."

Promote yourself by sending copies (not originals) of your finished artworks. Don't hope or expect the editor to bend the news around your samples.

DIRECTORIES OF NEWSPAPERS

Listings of newspapers can be found in the *Editor and Publisher's Yearbook*. Also consult *Working Press of the Nation*, the *Gale Directory of Publications*, the *Artist's and Graphic Designer's Market*, and the *Writer's Market*. Read the *Columbia Journalism Review*, *Editor and Publisher*, and the *Washington Journalism Review*.

ORGANIZATIONS

Your local ad club is a good place to start (and do go to regional trade associations events, too). Join the Graphic Artist's Guild. Look into the Society of Newspaper Design, the National Cartoonists Society, the Association of American Editorial Cartoonists, the Society of Illustrators, and the Illustrators' Partnership of America (IPA).

PROFESSIONAL ⬇ VIEWPOINTS

Do you send samples to the editor or the art director? As a general rule of thumb, I'd send to the art director, unless instructed otherwise—although I think the op-ed page might be the one exception to that rule. I did a lot of assignments for the op-ed page of the *Boston Globe* years ago, and it was the op-ed editor to whom I first pitched my work (and later, dealt with exclusively). —Robert Saunders, Illustrator

Just today, I pointed out to [fellow *Dayton Daily News* staff illustrator] Randy Palmer a blurb in our *CoxNet* newsletter. It was advertising to other Cox newspapers a special tabloid Cox has put together culled from the archives—complete with a big ol' Randy illustration from a few years ago on the cover! He knew nothing about it. His first reaction was, "Hey, they can't do that!" Then, after realizing Cox owned his artwork, he said, "Well, I guess they can, but I hope they give me credit." —M. B. Hopkins, Illustrator

You have to be someone who is easy to work with. Nobody wants to work with a prima donna or someone who's difficult. —Ben Mahan, Illustrator

© Mark Monlux 1997

I used to have a hard time getting promised printed samples from my clients. Then, I altered my contract to stipulate that I would receive twenty copies within thirty days of printing, or the client would owe me an additional $100 and the samples. Now, my closet is overflowing with samples.

—Mark Monlux, Illustrator

You have to convince an art director that she needs you. Your best shot is to start small. Little idea-oriented concepts that translate into quarter-page, half-page illustrations will get you a foot in the door. Try to get tear sheets as soon as possible (and always negotiate for extra tear sheets to mail out to the people you've already seen).

—Chris Spollen, Illustrator

chapter 15

WORKING WITH ADVERTISING AGENCIES

I worked for a large advertising art studio for twenty-five years. The last year or two there, I knew I wanted to go out on my own. I took a business class and aimed at going into business for myself. After preparing myself for a year or so, I announced that I was freelancing. The studio I worked for asked if I would still work for them, so the transition was fairly easy; and since my employer had encouraged me to meet and deal with clients, I was a known commodity to area art buyers.

—Paul Melia, Illustrator

You may well ask, what does an advertising agency do? That depends upon the agency, of course, because no two agencies are alike. In general, advertising agencies solve marketing problems by communicating what the client wants (and needs) his market to know. To do this, ad agencies develop printed matter, audio, and audiovisual work from concept to finished product.

So, is ad all there is? Well, no—they create copy and appropriate graphics for ads in magazines and newspapers, produce radio and television commercials, conceive billboards and direct-mail campaigns, and create interactive, multimedia, and Web site presentations. Most produce literature, sales brochures, and other such collateral material. You'll find the larger agencies doing market research and public relations as well.

ADVERTISING AGENCIES VERSUS PUBLIC RELATIONS FIRMS

What's the difference between an ad agency and a public relations firm? Public relations firms assist clients by increasing public awareness of their clients' existence, presenting a new image, or even polishing a tarnished reputation.

PR firms attempt to keep clients in the limelight with published stories, newspaper articles, television spots and interviews, lectures, book signings, or autograph sessions. They'll even create media events and publicity stunts. The high profile created by a PR firm helps position a client favorably in his or her particular market, works to counteract negative publicity, or establishes a new direction for that client.

Public relations firms produce "indirect advertising," and assignments from PR firms do parallel those of ad agencies. Since the full-time staff usually concentrates on marketing research and consulting with clients, PR firms often use freelance artists, writers, or graphic designers. Public relations firms are good places to get work, because they generally don't have art departments and would be more likely to use freelancers. In addition, PR firms can be a direct network to ad agencies or design studios.

SKILLS NEEDED

Agencies use freelancers for illustration of all types in all media. They employ designers, writers, photographers, and model builders. If an agency doesn't have someone in-house with the necessary abilities, a freelancer gets the nod. Small agencies might regularly require a great deal of freelance help. Big agencies may use freelancers only when staff are on leave or when they have an overflow of work.

Good freelancers often fulfill design and production needs, but you might find that the "fun stuff" stays in-house, while the tedious "grunt work" goes to the independent contractors. And in our recent business climate, illustrators have lost a large market share to photographers (due to a current preference for reality-based imagery).

The larger agencies might employ only one or two skilled illustrators. As these folks usually double as art directors or designers, this is where you, that talented masked artist with the silver portfolio, ride in.

FULL-SERVICE AGENCY

A full-service agency is a multimedia agency working in broadcast, print, and with online/Internet accounts. As the term implies, they do it all—from newspaper ads to TV campaigns and audiovisuals, sales literature to direct mail, public relations to market research. A majority of agencies make this claim, but few perform equally well in all areas.

WHEN FREELANCERS ARE NEEDED

In a large city, many agencies rely on good freelance help. In a regular-sized town, not only are independent contractors called when a "special look" is needed, but when the regular staff is on vacation, sick leave, maternity leave, or if the agency gets a temporary overflow of work.

For instance, around the Christmas holidays, an agency with many retail clients may be inundated with work. Freelancers may be called in to help through this busy season. As soon as the holidays pass, work levels revert to normal, and freelancers are no longer needed.

FINDING SUITABLE AGENCIES

Knowing what a particular agency does and who its clients are takes some digging. First, network. Check out the Internet—this is an enormous resource for finding suitable agencies. Phone the chamber of commerce and Better Business Bureau for information about local agencies. Talk to your colleagues, check with printers, and touch base with businesses that advertise. Ask around. Get as much background information about the local advertising scene as you can. The next step is to call the agencies yourself.

You don't even have to ask for the art director initially. Talk to the receptionist. If he or she doesn't have the answers you need, you'll be directed to someone who does. Simply ask, "What are your specialties? Can or do you use freelancers? In what capacity?"

Remember the three virtues in selling your art: Be persistent, be polite, be positive. If your communication skills are professional, you shouldn't have any problems. You'll find people in this field to be friendly and helpful. Illustrator Robert Zimmerman agrees and says, "I would suggest a fourth virtue (even though this truism doesn't contain the letter *p*): Do consistent, excellent work." He's right. Without good stuff, persistence may be deemed annoying, politeness only gets you in and out the door, and being positive won't compensate for quality.

Schedule a portfolio review. While you're there, ask to see the agency's book. It's a legitimate request; I don't think the art director will balk at showing the piece that snagged all those awards last year.

Introduce yourself around town, and see what the different agencies are doing. Then make up your own mind. Some decisions are made for you. You work in pen and ink; the Jones Agency, which produces television commercials, probably won't require your services. Of course, Smith Studios next door specializes in printed material and needs an artist of your talents.

But remember, someone at the agency—usually the creative director or art director—will determine whether or not your talents suit *their* needs. Make sure they're aware of your talents.

THEY'RE SPECIAL

What does an advertising agency mean when it says, "We specialize"—for instance, "We specialize in food and pharmaceuticals"? What this says is that the agency's accounts bracket the food industry—from fast food restaurants, food manufacturers, grocery retailers, and wholesalers—to pharmaceutically oriented clients.

Can you supply five visual metaphors for the effects of stress on decision-making ASAP? Are you adept at rendering chocolate and chocolate products (don't laugh—those illustrators who can are especially prized!)?

Food and pharmaceuticals are just two lucrative facets of the advertising game. Even if you don't particularly enjoy illustrating chuck roast, carrots, or a bottle of antacid, chances are you can find an agency to utilize your forte. Of course, you'll need to be familiar with related terminology and visuals, as well as the particular marketing needs and tactics of these clients.

YOU'RE SPECIAL

Something to consider is whether you should specialize in a certain product area. Use common sense. You know best where your strengths lie. Stay busy, but enjoy what you're doing.

Some agencies find a comfortable niche and stay there, believing that specialized experience allows them to create better work. This can be true, but there is a danger of falling into a rut. This also holds true for the freelancer. Don't limit yourself. More flexibility means a wide variety of assignments; greater assignments mean better money. Keep all available doors open; only specialize if you freelance in a big city that has more than enough work to support your specialty. Flexibility and variety will allow you to gather pollen from a wider range of flowers.

KNOWING THE MARKET

To tell if ad agencies work with freelancers (or know when they need one) is simple: Ask them. Show your book, then market and promote yourself like crazy. It might depend on the size of the agency (a large agency doesn't use as many freelancers as a small one). Again, if you have referrals, get some background information. If you don't, you'll only find out by making some inquiries yourself.

Obviously, you won't know when they need a freelancer until *they* do. Designer Theo Stephan Williams says, "A common rule of thumb is, don't call them, they'll call you! Once you've shown your portfolio to the agency, they have a good idea of your capabilities. Drop the art director a short note of thanks after that first meeting. Share your interest in producing work for the agency. Don't grovel or give them starving-artist war stories. Act successful, even if you did have to walk twelve miles to the bus stop in a driving Sahara dust storm. Everybody likes working with a winner, not someone who is unsure of themselves!"

There's at least one art director at an agency. Big agencies often have a number of art directors, who may answer to the creative director.

Whom to talk to? One phone call, and you'll know for sure. Ask the receptionist who the art buyer may be. Michael Wooley, over at Weber, Geiger, and Kalat, in Dayton, Ohio, recommends, "The more people who know you and your abilities, the better. The first person to try is the creative director, but also contact art directors, artists, copy chiefs, and copywriters."

Should you work for as many agencies as possible, or should you try to get as much work as you can from one or two agencies? You must get work where you can, depending on the size of your town and the temperament of the advertising community. It would not be wise to do an assignment for one agency, then go directly to the competition and create work of the exact same stripe. Don't expect the first agency to welcome you with open arms afterwards.

There is some paranoia between agencies. Agency A may wonder if you shared marketing strategies with Agency B. Ask yourself if there is a conflict of interest between two rival accounts. You may never have to deal with this situation, but be aware that it does exist.

WAYS TO BREAK IN

Agencies use a lot of layout comps (comprehensive sketches of an ad or concept) during client presentations or when pitching an idea to prospective buyers. If you can do a good comp, this would be an apt way to break into the market. Use your layout skills to pave the way for future illustration.

If you can, get referrals from people you know in the field who might have agency contacts. Ask them if you can drop their name while making your sales calls: "Hello, my name is so-and-so, and I received your name from so-and-so as a possible contact. I'd like to set up an appointment to show my portfolio." Be sure to make the appointment at the agency's convenience.

If you're new in town, join organizations that are frequented by local art directors and creative individuals. There's an ad club in just about every town. Consult the chamber of commerce regarding the names of these associations, meeting places, and times.

Put your self-promotion and marketing plan into action. Establish contacts, and then don't let them forget you. Send a thank-you note after your initial appointment, and follow up with frequent reminders. Call occasionally—stay in touch!

APPROPRIATE SAMPLES

If you've been doing greeting cards, but want to do some advertising work, I wouldn't mix apples and oranges. Ad agency art directors won't be interested in your card samples as greeting cards, per se. You won't be writing copy, so your cutesy puns are only good for a quick snicker as they turn the page. Those marvelously fuzzy bunnies won't sell refrigerators or sports cars, and those risqué cartoons would never fly in the newspaper!

But perhaps you feel that your card imagery is indeed pertinent for this demanding market. The move to make is to show how your greeting card material can be developed as a full-blown ad (in context with type). This will then demonstrate that your work meets the real needs of an agency's clients.

LOCAL TALENT

In advertising, time is of the essence. Local talent may be preferred, especially if you're needed on a regular basis or to meet tight deadlines. But, as Robert Zimmerman points out, "Today, agencies are looking for an exact visual fit for their client. They don't give a hoot where the illustrator lives."

As an agency's freelance assignments develop very quickly, art directors soon get to know who's good, who's dedicated, who's reliable, and who's available—location may not be an issue.

BUYOUTS AND WORK-FOR-HIRE

"Buyout," illustrator Robert Saunders notes, "is a term that buyers might use when they approach you, but that the illustrator should decline to use. Instead, state the sale as a package or bundle of specific usage rights that are carefully defined." There is no true industry consensus about the definition of the term, only confusion. "Some buyers think it includes original art," Saunders elaborates. "Others think it means exclusive usage. Still others believe it includes the entire copyright forever and could care less about the original art." This is why the term needs to be defined specifically and include the precise usage rights the client wants to buy.

"Buyouts" are frequently requested in advertising and greeting-card work. In a buyout, the client, instead of you, will control the fruit of your vision and energies; the client determines how, when, where, and how often your illustration can be used. If the original art is acquired as part of a buyout, you've forfeited any rights of ownership. There is no subsequent compensation for the continued printed use of your image, and you'll have no say in the fate of the actual piece. The buyer owns all reproduction rights and can exploit her property as she sees fit.

Obviously, it's better for the artist to sell limited rights only. Evaluate what the client truly needs, and base negotiations on this determination. Original art, if sold, should be a separate transaction. When you create artwork, your ownership of the physical work is immediately established along with the ownership of rights. Buyer or seller should not assume that the sale of rights and originals is a package deal.

If you can't negotiate out of a buyout, and the client insists on owning all rights despite your best efforts to sell only the rights that are needed, you can:

- ◪ Say "no thank you," and be prepared to walk away from a bad deal.
- ◪ Accept a trade-off, if you can live with it and if it's to your advantage for the future. Is it a good credit to have or a great vehicle for your work? Will it be a dynamite portfolio piece? Is it an entry into a new market?
- ◪ Make it worth your while. A good rule of thumb to remember is that the more you sell, the higher the sale should be. Price accordingly and with prejudice.

The artist should also be aware of the circumstance known as "work made-for-hire." In a nutshell—*and in the eyes of the copyright law*—the illustrator laboring under a work-for-hire contract effectively becomes an employee without any employee benefits. As the creative's "employer," the client owns the work and controls the copyright. This is unfair at best, but perfectly legal; the work-for-hire provision robs artists of their just due and is definitely a worst-case scenario.

This is the real world, however, and if your baby is down to her last diaper just when you're offered a work-for-hire contract, you may understandably be tempted to accept. I would never preach to, or condemn, those artists who accept these deals. Don't rally behind the cause if you can't reasonably justify the principle. Just know what you're getting into, and accept the consequences of your decision in the light of your situation.

For practical consultation regarding standards and practices, *The Graphic Artists Guild Handbook of Pricing and Ethical Guidelines* should be on every artist's bookshelf. Also consult Tad Crawford's *Legal Guide for the Visual Artist, Business and Legal Forms for Illustrators* and *Business and Legal Forms for Graphic Designers*. If you can find a copy of the now-out-of-print *The Artist's Friendly Legal Guide* (North Light Books), it's worth purchasing.

ORGANIZATIONS

On a national level, the Graphic Artists Guild has chapters across the country. Also look into membership with the Illustrators' Partnership of America (IPA). Most large cities have local chapters of the National Advertising Federation, the American Marketing Association, or the American Institute of Graphic Arts (AIGA), and many cities of modest size have an advertising club, art center, or art forum.

I learned that agency art directors have a different attitude than greeting card art directors. They are more aggressive and less tolerant. Because they work with much tighter deadlines, they're under an entirely different kind of stress. I would come to them with a portfolio full of greeting-card and original illustrations, and they'd say, "You have beautiful work, but how could we use it? We need to see these illustrations in the context of an ad, with type." At the time, I thought, "What's wrong with these doodahs? They're art directors; it's their job to visualize how a particular style would fit into their work." But their suggestion to put my illustrations into an ad format was one of the best pieces of advice I ever got, and it was free. —Mary Thelen, Illustrator

Every time you do an illustration, your ego is on the line. It's part of you; it's something you created. When it's rejected, it's really difficult to keep in mind that it's not you, it's that piece of art that's being rejected. You develop confidence, but in the beginning, it's very difficult. I, myself, had a hard time with that.

—Mary Grace Eubank, Illustrator

When I taught illustration at Carnegie-Mellon University several years ago, a student requested a meeting. "I just showed one of my illustrations [for an advertising assignment] to my friend over in the Fine Arts department," she sniffed somewhat tearfully. "Do you know what she said? She told me that I'd be illustrating cat food boxes for the rest of my life!" After I stopped roaring and wiped my eyes, I told my student that next time she sees her "friend," she might indeed be illustrating cat food boxes, but her "friend" will undoubtedly be eating the cat food. —Ilene Lederer, Illustrator

Demonstrate your creative process. You have to convey to the art director a consistency of ideas and techniques—your style. The art director wants to pigeonhole you; make it easy for him. If I had it to do over again, I would probably emphasize consistency of a particular technique. —Chris Spollen, Illustrator

chapter 16

SELLING TO BOOK PUBLISHERS

Young people getting into the field should be aware that often, solving a particular graphic problem still requires artistic lateral thinking, not the point-and-click direct mentality that comes from computer programs. Yes, technology has been a boon to the freelancer, but don't let yourself be trained by the computer; let your own educational and life experiences lead you forward. You have to be there to know your subject.

—Fred Carlson, Illustrator

The book market offers the freelancer a rich and rewarding arena in which to practice the craft. To begin, let's discuss the difference between trade books, textbooks, and mass-market books. A library reference book will define trade books as "books intended for the general public, and marketed through bookstores and to libraries, as distinct from textbooks, subscription books, etc." A textbook is "a book used for the study of a particular subject; a manual of instruction."

Textbooks are educational materials, sold directly to educational institutions. Trade books are sold at retail and appeal to a select audience. They can be scholarly works or professional titles, special-interest books, instructional manuals, biographies, serious fiction, larger-format books, cookbooks, and juveniles (often, but not necessarily, with a teaching motive).

Mass-market books are sold at newsstands or bookstores and other retail outlets; they're produced in high volume at less cost (to hopefully generate big sales). These books are more commercial-looking and created to appeal to a large audience. Mysteries, spy novels, gothics, fantasy and science fiction, historical and modern romance novels all fall into the mass-market category. Mass-market books normally pay higher fees, because of larger print runs.

IN THE HOUSE

A publishing organization, with its various imprints and/or divisions, is called a "house." Several different companies may be found under the central umbrella of a publishing house. For example, take the fictional house of Caputo and Sons, Inc. This Pittsburgh company, in business since 1955, owns a number of imprints; these subsidiaries publish a wide variety of books covering a broad spectrum of topics.

Each of Caputo's imprints has its own distinct list and appeals to a particular audience. Maxwell Cooper Books, one of its imprints, is an Ohio company specializing in children's and cartoon books. Another imprint, Garner Publishing (based in Kentucky) features spiritual nonfiction. Yet another, Rice Press, publishes cookbooks.

HOUSE HUNTING

How do you find what type of books a house publishes? By that same token, how do you locate those publishers that best suit your talents? Haunt the library and the bookstore. Call a publisher, and request a catalog. Look for work you like— chances are, if you like their work, they'll like yours. Locate an address on a first or last page, dig up a phone number to get the art director's name, and mail him or her your promotional pieces.

If your information is sketchy, refer to directories such as the *Literary Market Place*, *Writer's Market*, *Short Story and Novel Writer's Market*, *Poet's Market* or *Artist's and Graphic Designer's Market* to get names, addresses, and phone numbers.

You can also check out all the major and minor companies at once by attending the BookExpoAmerica conference. It's held in May, at a different location every year; for further information, visit their Web site at *www.bookexpo.reedexpo.com*.

What is the best way to break into this market? Let's assume you've looked at books. You've done your research—patronized the library and the bookstores, browsed the newsstand, visited schools, and attended trade exhibits. You've studied covers, interior layouts, internal illustrations, and technical drawings. You've analyzed book design—compared trade books and textbooks, children's books and adult titles, plus examined the mass-market paperbacks. You've located addresses, names, and phone numbers and are ready to mail your promotional pieces.

What to send? Forward the art director samples of your work to keep on file. Best are printed pieces pertaining to your strength—art directors want to work with specialists. Enclose a cover letter with the sample package, or make sure an initial brochure highlights your work history. Publishing credits add credibility, and parallel experience is a plus (any work that even remotely resembles publishing responsibilities can only help). Follow up with a phone call at some point shortly thereafter. Ask if they'd like to see more samples, or suggest a portfolio review.

It breaks down to this: Determine where you fit in, then go for it. Get your marketing and self-promotion in gear, and fine-tune your book. Buy a spiffy interview outfit, and polish your in-person routine. Work the phones and the mail, and then hit the road!

BOOKED SOLID: FREELANCE POSSIBILITIES

Publishers use freelancers for illustration (on jackets and covers, as well as the interior), design, in production and technical areas (such as interior layouts for book dummies), as photographers, stylists, and model makers.

Other than books, what do publishers produce that might need freelance help? Publishers need freelancers to create ads, direct mail, and promotional pieces. Freelancers will also work on newsletters, brochures, catalogs, and point-of-purchase displays. Many book publishers also produce activities (coloring books, for instance), educational aids (flash cards), games, and posters that provide educational opportunities.

You'll find that most publishers use freelance help, especially the larger houses. The easiest way to verify this is to call an art director and ask.

WORKING THROUGH THE MAIL

Book publishers are open to mailed submissions, and it's probably easier to work long distance with a publisher than with other illustration markets. Most publishers are quite used to working through the mail. Usually, deadlines are reasonable to generous in book publishing, and book projects are typically extended affairs—rarely rushed into, seldom rushed through.

Mailed submissions are viewed as the initial phase of the process. Matching the right illustrator with the right project is done thoughtfully and over time, so a mailed submission dovetails right into the work schedule of an extremely careful, but exceedingly busy art director.

JOBS FOR DESIGNERS

There is not a large market in all cities for book designers, but it does exist. However, it might be a bit more difficult to freelance as a book designer, because publishers may prefer their designers to be local, if not in-house. When they look out of town, the house hires freelancers from the big publishing centers (New York, Boston, and Chicago). These cities employ a lot of book designers, and those folks work with all the major publishers in those areas.

Why? Any designer can design covers, but the interior is a specialized area that requires specific training (often on-the-job). A design studio may create a cover, but it will usually be the specialist—the book designer—who designs the interior. However, a house usually finds it preferable to hire one book designer to do both cover and interior.

To introduce yourself, send samples of pages where typography is a crucial design element, and present this portfolio to appropriate art directors or editors. Obviously, print samples will be best. Bright ideas and enthusiasm will be appreciated, but knowledge and experience are what the publisher needs and demands.

A designer—one with a good education (let's say a B.F.A. with a graphic design concentration)—qualifies to be a book designer at an entry level. Publishers will only use freelancers in book design if they have a lot of experience. You may only be able to learn book design by working on staff at a publishing house; otherwise, your design work may be limited to covers.

COLLABORATION

So, you have a writer friend who wants you to illustrate her book and then submit it to a publisher for consideration. Sorry to say, this isn't the way it's usually done; you're probably just wasting your time. One should never say never, but this isn't the way a potential book is usually welcomed. Suggest that your friend submit the story to the editorial division, while you concentrate on the art department.

Publishers prefer to arrange the marriage, so to speak, unless you are both author and artist. Some writers have the clout to demand a certain illustrator, but most publishers will match up a manuscript with their artist of choice. The in-house design process is crucial to a book's final look and ultimate success, so few books are submitted or accepted as a *fait accompli*, in finished form.

If you're the writer and illustrator, your book should be submitted as a book dummy. A book dummy is, as the *Graphic Artists Guild Pricing and Ethical Guidelines* defines it, "a book, brochure, or catalog idea in a roughly drawn form, usually made up to contain the proper number of pages and used as a reference for positioning and pagination."

A smart dummy (sorry, I couldn't resist) should be accompanied by the manuscript, and one or two samples of the finished art—not the originals, however. If you're an illustrator hoping to land a book project, submit a portfolio that best showcases your style and that will, with luck and some market study, meet the publisher's needs.

SAMPLES

What type of samples should you send to book publishers? As with any portfolio sent through the mail, send nonreturnable samples for the files or "expendable" samples you can afford to lose, such as a photocopied book dummy, reproductions, tearsheets, transparencies, high quality black-and-white or color photocopies, or a digital sampler. No matter what is sent, you could also direct the recipient to your Web site for more.

Samples should be both black-and-white (line and/or gradated tone) and color. A portfolio sent to a book publisher must obviously convey style and technique, and your work should be a close fit to that of the publisher. A house specializing in technical manuals would simply toss out children's illustration, for example, so keep your samples relevant.

Demonstrate solid character development and interaction. Let's see a main character in a variety of moods and emotions, from different angles, in various positions. Show this central figure with others: one-on-one, in small group shots, and in large crowd scenes. Vary environments—intimate surroundings, wide-open spaces, diverse weather conditions, in a variety of climates.

Think story: Highlight your ability to juggle subject matter, orchestrate action, and communicate a sequence of events. Show that you understand composition and the crucial relationship between type and visuals.

Send appropriate samples. You won't find many little duckies on the covers of murder mysteries or three-headed Martian brain munchers in the children's book *Mr. Clumsy's Workshop*. If you're writing the story, include a rough book dummy. If you don't have printed pieces, write your own or redesign for existing tales, then do book covers and page illustrations for these.

Remember that book publishers don't ask much—only that it's absolutely clear that you know how to design and illustrate a book. No sweat, right?

WHOM TO CONTACT

Hmm . . . editor or art director? Research, research, research. Study the directories. If you can't find the person's name, make lots of calls, and ask questions. Find out who accepts submissions, and ask specifically for that person's name, title (editor, submissions editor, art director?) and department.

The editor probably has more control than the art director. But art directors may be more supportive of your cause, and dealing with them (if they like your work) may be easier. In general, send an art submission to the art director. If you are writing the story, too, send your package to an appropriate editor.

LOCAL FIRST?

I always feel it is best to start locally, so you can have that person-to-person contact, but it's neither completely necessary nor mandatory. Although unlikely, there may not be a publisher in your area.

Art director Debbie Kokoruda says, "Publishers may try new or inexperienced people, because their accessibility is the trade-off. If you are soliciting your work to publishers all over the country, it should be because you offer a lot of experience unavailable to the publisher. It's more difficult to work with out-of-towners, but it certainly is common practice in publishing."

DIRECTORIES, ORGANIZATIONS, TRADE MAGAZINES

The Literary Market Place (LMP), Artist's and Graphic Designer's Market, and *Writer's Market* are excellent sources. Also consult the *Publisher's Directory, Short Story and Novel Writer's Market, Children's Writer's Marketplace* and *Children's Writer's and Illustrator's Market*. Write to the Children's Book Council to receive its list of publishers, which includes names of art directors and editors.

Organizations you may want to join would be the Graphic Artists Guild, the Illustrators' Partnership of America (IPA) and the American Institute of Graphic Arts (AIGA). The Guild and the AIGA boast local chapters and a national membership (the AIGA also hosts an annual book show). Look into the Society of Children's Book Writers and Illustrators, plus the Chicago Book Clinic and Book Builders West (which also have annual seminars and a book show). In the Boston/New England area, there is the Bookbinders' Guild and the Boston Globe book fair. Again, write to the Children's Book Council. Check out your local art director's club.

One popular magazine covering publishing is *Publisher's Weekly*. Also read *Writer's Digest, Print, Communication Arts, HOW, Step-by-Step Graphics*, and *Graphis*.

PROFESSIONAL ⬇ VIEWPOINTS

Your work should be unique and original above all. The way you think and draw is something that will set you apart from all of the thousands of other illustrators. Stop looking at other people's work, and just draw the way you draw, and your work will be completely unlike anyone else's.

—Bill Mayer, Illustrator

Those artists more gifted in communication seem to go a lot further along. Those with people skills seem to get a boost to their career that goes beyond talent.

—Mike Quon, Illustrator and Designer

Maintain quality in all jobs. Always work towards the next plateau, and dedicate 100 percent of your ability to every job. Don't compromise—encourage quality in yourself and your clients. Push yourself to go beyond what the assignment requires.

—Fred Carlson, Illustrator

Work-for-hire, of course, is one of the stickiest areas for an illustrator to tread. I always stress to my students that work-for-hire means giving up authorship of the

work, where a buyout, at least, does not. This usually drives the point home pretty well, especially when they learn that, legally, the client can claim they are the creator of the piece the illustrator just poured their blood, sweat, and tears into.

—Matt McElligott, Illustrator

chapter 17

THE GREETING CARD MARKET

After graduation, I got a job in an office and hated it. I don't know what possessed me, but I printed up sixteen postcards. And I did it all the wrong way—the paper was bad, the printer wasn't right—I had no idea what I was doing. But I knew that anything would be better than working in an office.

—Jennifer Berman, Illustrator

Let me begin with a point of clarification here: In the greeting card industry, a design is essentially the same as an illustration. A design is the idea (or concept), and the illustration is the finished product. The term "design" refers to the visual element that accompanies the editorial (the copy) on a card. This artwork may be used for a single purpose—a select card, one page, or an individual spread in a booklet or calendar. The design may be a basic character study, a particular scene, or a still life. It could be an abstract composition, a simple pattern or border, or perhaps a concept composed entirely of calligraphy or type.

Any medium can be used for a card design. You'll find designs done digitally, prepared in pen or pencil, water media (including acrylics and gouache), cut paper/fabric collage, and embroidery. A design can also be paper or clay construction or hand-tinted photography. It could even be executed entirely in what is termed "finishes"—gold leaf, die cuts, embossing, etc.

How does a greeting card company choose the cards it will publish? A card company targets production to selected markets, such as the young and trendy in specialty shops or the generally middle-class shoppers at the drugstore. Keeping a deliberate finger on the pulse of current popular culture, card and paper-product companies do extensive market research to determine what categories of cards the public wants to send. Premarket testing determines which visual styles and messages the buying public prefers.

WHAT TYPES OF CARDS ARE THERE?

Basically, card companies produce two types: occasion cards for standard holidays and established events (birthdays, graduation, anniversaries, friendship, sympathy) and non-occasion or everyday cards.

Within these two primary lines, look for these general categories: traditional (an established, long-accepted, and rather realistic approach), studio (contemporary and sophisticated, with biting wit), humorous (also funny, but usually simpler and not as caustic, leaning toward the cartoon), romantic (hearts and flowers, decidedly sentimental), juvenile (appealing to children), cute (adorable characters in charming situations), stylish (a modern and chic look), and alternative.

What Are Alternative Cards?

For a company to sell more products, their cards must reflect contemporary subject matter and topics of special interest to the card buyer. Current trends and the changing lifestyles of American consumers over the last decades dictated the development of a new genre that stretched the parameters and attacked the old taboos: the alternative card.

Almost every company now markets so-called alternative cards, so it's safe to say that the label is somewhat inoperative. Thanks to the alternative card phenomenon, it's not unusual to see cards dealing with left- (and right-) wing politics, women's rights, divorce, remarriage and the extended family, the singles scene, or alternative sexual preferences. There are cards for dieting, congratulations on your promotion, pet death, technophobia, high (or low) finance, and coping with everything from poor service to retirement. If the subject is relevant and current, chances are, you'll now find a card addressing the situation.

You'll still find the "warm and fuzzy" cards, carrying cuddly copy or bubbly messages, but today's product lines approach subject matter with new sensibilities. Modern cards also act as small doses of psychotherapy, delivering sensitive counseling or gentle expressions of advice, support, and concern. But, look out—cards these days are also rife with sly wit, biting sarcasm, and decidedly offbeat (even downright strange) humor. They may make you blush, and you'll read language previously found only in graffiti.

SUITABLE ART

The greeting (often called the sentiment) in a card defines the art and, of course, vice versa. Different art styles are preferred for different types of cards. Think of Gary Larsen's *The Far Side* done by Norman Rockwell, and you'll easily get the point.

A card company must consider its entire card line when choosing what to publish. The aim is to achieve an overall stylistic balance, both visual and editorial, throughout the product line. Visually, you will find a range from the highly traditional to the very hip and a great variety of art styles and media.

The trendiest, most avant-garde or ultrasophisticated modes may not be incorporated into a product line, however. Subject matter (for example, unicorns or teddy bears), a particular style (say, a minimal drawing approach), or fresh technique (like digital caricature) must prove to be more than a fad to be considered for the line. Greeting card art directors and designers often look to the fashion and interior-design markets to gauge the success of an available look or theme, or even of a color palette.

It is argued that only small card companies can afford to be on the cutting edge of new trends. A smaller card line means shorter lead times in preparing product. This translates to a much slighter financial risk should a fad prove short-lived. Because of this advantage, these small mavericks set the pace for the industry at large.

MANY HAPPY RETURNS—RESEARCHING CARDS

How can you research what type of cards a company produces? First, visit the company's Web site (if available) to get an initial overview of its product. Your next stop will be the local card and gift marts. Go to every shop you see (some franchises carry one company exclusively, but most stores carry lines from many different companies). Spend lots of time at the card racks researching the type of cards each company offers. Buy the cards you like best and that seem closely related to your own style. Check logos, and get a feel for which companies put out the kind of cards that most appeal to you.

If you're not buying today (or didn't record pertinent info from the Web site), jot down company data while browsing—but always clear it with the clerk or owner at some point. You won't have any trouble if you just introduce yourself, state your purpose, and express a small bit of thanks. Oh, yes—bring a pad and pencil—don't borrow envelopes for notepaper!

If you can't find a particular company's wares online or at the stores, call and ask where to find its cards in your area. You could also e-mail, fax, or write to the company's creative department. When writing, use your letterhead, and enclose a business card, so the company has reasonable assurance you're not a spy for the competition.

To research virtually all the greeting card companies at once, attend the New York Stationery Show, held in May at the Jacob Javits Convention Center. Here, you can interview and show your portfolio, market and promote your work, network, and examine every aspect of every company—all at one time, under one roof.

OTHER PAPER PRODUCTS

Most greeting card companies also produce other paper products, such as note cards, stationery, party goods, and gift wrap. For example, Bean Greetings (a hypothetical company) must offer their card shops a complete line of paper products and be able to fill all the product space in the shop. If Bean only makes cards, the stores they service will have to buy other merchandise from the competition, who we'll call Arden Designs. If Arden also produces cards, they will be more likely to snatch a larger share of the card-shop trade.

While freelancers may not be used as frequently on these other paper product lines (as with greeting cards), there are companies that specialize in stationery and note cards, gift wrap, or party goods. These may be better outlets for your art.

While hardly worth the paper they are printed on (that's a joke, kid), eCards (electronic greeting cards) are a booming product line for many card companies, and the need for artists and animators to create them is growing exponentially. (BlueMountain.com and Amazon.com are two of the biggest buyers of eCards.)

USING FREELANCE HELP

Generally, small companies use more freelancers, because their output can't support an ample or full-time art staff. But many small companies are one-person operations. There are also complaints that small companies don't pay as well and may not pay promptly.

Large companies use fewer freelancers, because they have extensive in-house art staffs. If your style is notably unique, you may get the nod for a particular job, but you could indeed be viewed as the proverbial "little fish in the big pond." When you work with the giants, size does not always equate with job opportunities or harmonious relationships, and the red tape can be particularly frustrating.

The medium-size competitor is probably your most dependable and reliable source. Since they're slugging it out with the big kids in certain product areas, these mid-range companies have busy staffs. They actively welcome and court outside help—card designs are always changing and the demand for new art, plus the desire for a variety of looks, is often more than the in-house staff can handle.

The greeting card industry has a voracious appetite for bright ideas and innovative styles. According to the Greeting Card Association in Washington D.C., greeting card publishing is the largest user of creative talent next to advertising, and freelancers are considered the fresh air that keeps the card industry breathing.

One way to gauge the size and dependability of a card company is by reading their listing in the annual *Artist's and Graphic Designer's Market* (North Light Books*)*. Card companies that don't have a listing here are not likely to need much freelance help.

Another simple way is to contact the company. Check out the Web site (it's quite common to list job opportunities and guidelines online). Send an e-mail (or call the personnel office or creative department), and ask directly: "Do you use freelancers? To whom do I send my samples? Would you please send artist's guidelines for submission?"

SAMPLES

Send work that demonstrates your excellent drawing ability, a good color and design sense, plus the superior technique you've honed to perfection. Send imagery appropriate to cards and to this particular company (and you've determined this by exhaustive research, right?). If the chemistry is right, the only inappropriate samples are those irrelevant to this field. Let's say you do an airbrush look, which is often used in greeting cards. If all your airbrush samples are illustrations of engines and machinery, don't expect many assignments from a greeting card company. If your art style, wit, and personality are suited to greeting card work, it shouldn't be a big chore to determine which of your samples are appropriate to send.

Print samples are a plus. You could also send a CD sampler, transparencies, tear sheets, or color photocopies (again—don't send the originals). A few cards are done in black-and-white, so black-and-white samples are okay for showing line work, but you really need to present color! Samples of layouts are not really helpful, unless you're applying for a position in the production art department (a crucial part of any card company, by the way).

Busy art directors need to get a sense of your style and skill. They don't have a lot of time to view portfolios, read e-mail, chat on the phone, or see to returning samples sent without sufficient return postage. Don't make the unreasonable request that the card company insure the return package.

Often, copies are made for the files, but it's best to send samples that the art director can keep. If you're worried about the security of your submission, copyright your stuff.

Another option is to send a nondisclosure agreement, as long as the company you're sending samples to is willing to sign it. Always be thorough about protecting your work—don't, for instance, send an entire line of cards without knowing where the company you're submitting to stands on nondisclosure agreements. If they flat-out refuse to sign them, you might want to reconsider sending that unsolicited submission.

If you want your samples back, say so, and include an SASE. Make sure you follow through with periodic updates.

THE VERSE IS YET TO COME

Should you write verse on your initial samples? Remember, you are a visual artist. Art directors do not necessarily buy copy; editors do not necessarily buy art. Verse or copy on artwork is not de rigueur, unless you're also selling yourself as a word-smith. If you are talented with text and wish to be considered as a writer, make this clear in your cover letter, and include verse suggestions with your package. Humorous copy ideas can be submitted in the form of a card dummy with rough illustration, if the visual is part of the joke. Serious copy is submitted without illustration.

COMMISSIONED DESIGNS

Card companies are open to mailed submissions, but marketing your concepts can be a very tough sell (and because ideas themselves are *not* copyrightable, marketing your hot concepts alone is not prudent).

Card companies, rather than buying over the transom, usually commission designs. Company policies may vary, of course, so check with each. Each company has an individual philosophy and program, every studio has its own way of doing things, so don't create finished art and try to sell it for publication

You may have a great concept for a card, but that doesn't mean it will fit the requirements of the product lines currently being assigned. Actively pursue the commission work, and continue to develop and present your designs; this will be the fruitful path to success without undue heartache. Once you've established a track record with a certain studio, it's a different story. The company might solicit submissions and may even offer a contract guaranteeing a certain minimum purchase.

SELLING ALL RIGHTS

Should you sell all rights to your design or negotiate for royalties? According to Ms. Marty Roelandt, an experienced greeting card art director, it's not uncommon for card companies to purchase all rights to designs. Card designs are invariably done quickly and in volume. They have little marketability in other areas, and you can't usually sell an old design to another company. Unless you have a unique character, concept, a hot look, or a style that is well known, expect companies to want to buy your card designs outright.

What about royalties? Keep in mind that royalties on a single design could add up to less than an outright sale. A line of cards (or products utilizing your imagery) is another story. If the control of your artistic vision (in either scenario) is justifiably a hot button for you (and it should be), selling all rights is certainly not *your* best deal.

As illustrator Ilene Lederer tells us, "In the greeting card industry where so many images are continually produced, it is very difficult to consistently follow up on what royalties are due, especially if you are working with a small company, which may or may not maintain diligent records. Large companies often have formal accounting procedures, and they will send regular statements. Nevertheless, I prefer to get paid a fair-use price up front whenever possible."

"The early stages of courtship," as illustrator Marti McGinnis labels beginning negotiations, is a good place to determine just what kind of rights the greeting card company expects. "In gentler times, it was no problem for illustrators to retain the copyrights to their work," she says. "But with the explosion of corporate giants and global marketing on the Internet, it's getting increasingly common for large and small companies alike to demand 'all rights throughout the universe.'"

No, she's not making this up. Don't be a space cadet, however; fully understand this little licensing moonwalk. "If you're willing to grant a package of (literally universal) rights," says McGinnis, "make them pay for 'em! What's that you say? You don't mind seeing your creation become the next hottest fashion trend (like it did for the Pets.com sock puppet)? Okay . . . sign off on all rights for whatever it is they're paying you per 'illustration' (maybe $200, $500, $1000), and watch them—not you—rake in all the licensing royalties!

"If they won't give you extra money, then at least make your own demand: that *your* signature be a part of the design, so at least your name gets out there every time they use your creation.

"Another thing about art directors: No matter how wonderful they are (and you will work with plenty of great people), the paperwork will be issued by the company lawyers protecting corporate interests. The people who hand you these anti-artist documents often have no idea as to what it is they're asking you to sign off on (after all, they've signed off all their rights as employees). They may not—or will not—be ready to comprehend your concerns for your rights as a freelance artist."

A good contract is an artist-friendly contract. Educate yourself as to what this means (and means to your career). Refer to previous chapters in this book to begin your contracts homework (listen up: There is reading and writing involved, and there *will* be a test when you negotiate your next contract). Read Caryn Leland's *Licensing Art and Design* for great, practical information and an extended discussion on this subject. The single best thing you can do for your business education is to become a member of the Graphic Artists Guild. Blast off to the Guild Web site (*www.gag.org*), and check it all out.

CARD FORMAT

At one time, the vertical card had more "rack appeal," because the vertical format best displays captions clearly. But with modern display cases, layout is now simply a matter of company preference. Consult individual artist's guidelines for this information.

Most designs are still vertical, but you will see horizontals. Don't worry too much about sending things in a card format, unless you have printed samples of cards done for other clients. If you've got the right look for the line, an art director will direct you on the specifics when you get an assignment.

If you have decided to send mock-ups, they should be designed with the caption in mind. No matter what the format, this top third is important and must look particularly attractive. Design around that part of the card, which will show in the display.

One Size Fits All?

There is no standard for the industry. Submission guidelines will instruct you as to that company's size specifications and requirements. In general, it will be in proportions similar to a five-by-seven-inch format.

THE SERIES

A series of cards within a consistent theme is called a "card promotion." With a promotion, a company must devote a larger share of its new designs to a single, specific look. Marketing a series is risky to the greeting card company putting many of its eggs in your one basket, so it's not always desirable. If your card promotion is your initial approach to a company, you may not get very far.

A company's entire product line—for instance, single counter cards, promotions, the number of designs in each caption category (birthday, anniversary, etc.), and other myriad decisions—is all determined by management and marketing. Except in small operations, where two or three people run the whole show, the creative staff is never totally in control.

Staff art directors and line planners give out the assignments and are well paid to develop ideas for promotions and other products. It may be difficult for you, a raw unknown, to usurp their function.

A fruitful (and, hopefully, long) business relationship with any company begins when you receive and complete your first assignments. Show that you're competent, dependable, and a pleasure to work with, and the company will be open to your bright ideas. If you're reliable and your work is good, if you can add your own special touch to your assignments without being heavily directed, the art directors and line planners may look to you for new product concepts.

Okay, you're convinced you've developed an absolutely killer idea for a promotion. If you have faith in your concept, don't sit on it. Keep in mind that you buck the odds, but full speed ahead—submit your brainstorm, or mention it in a submission for future consideration.

TRENDS

To research greeting card trends, look at fashion, home decoration and furnishings, and advertising in general. When the research gets tough, the researchers go shopping. You can obviously go online, but to truly study current design, graphics, color, and pattern, you must visit the ultimate consumer-testing laboratory, otherwise known as the shopping mall.

You must be alert to what's happening around you—in your neighborhood and across the globe. So, here's more fun homework: Watch television and read (for news and entertainment, business and pleasure; especially read women's magazines, since the target market for cards is female, 18 to 40 years old). Play at the toy store. Listen to the radio, and go to the movies (even observe popular celebrities). Talk to friends and family about feelings and values important to them. As mentioned before, for an overview of what's new and hot in the industry, go to the National Stationery Show in New York City. Other gift shows are held in other cities around the country, too.

Bottom line: Keep your eyes on popular culture and your mind open; the information is all around you.

PROFESSIONAL ⬇ VIEWPOINTS

Keep your eyes open to the creative possibilities. It's so true, from Robert Crumb, who chronicles the reality right out his window, to late-night comedians Jay Leno and David Letterman—whose single best source from which they get their material is: the daily news. —Robert Saunders, Illustrator

In March of 1999, the German greeting card dude Archie Perleberg flew me and about twenty-five other artists and designers from around the globe to a remote paradise island in the South Seas (Pearl Island, Davoa, Philippines) at his expense to design new cards for his handmade line, "Perleberg."

After it was ascertained that we were not be being sold into indentured servitude, I, and the rest of this fascinating collective, set about designing greeting cards by the beaches of this actual fantasy island for three weeks. Here's what I learned from the industry expert: The greeting cards that sell the best for Hallmark are the ones with the words "You're Special." I am not making that up. Any of it. Here's what I learned from the whole experience: Open-minded freelance creatives can have fabulous experiences!

The guy (Archie Perleberg) eventually picked twelve of my designs and marketed them as "Marti's Happy World!"

—Marti McGinnis, Illustrator

© Mary Thelen 2001

© McGinnis 2001

There are certain events you cannot miss, and one of them is the New York Stationery Show. There, you can meet reps who sell to specific geographic areas. They sell the cards for you. A rep gets you the orders, and you fill the orders. My reps are my national sales fleet.
—Jennifer Berman, Illustrator

You need to keep your mind open just wide enough to let the interesting stuff in. Don't worry about what is trendy or hot; follow your intuition for the solution of each project.
—Ilene Lederer, Illustrator

You may be really good at greeting cards, but don't limit yourself to just that. Learn how to do a second or third specialty. And don't sit around waiting for things to happen. Be active and aggressive, and make things happen for you. Take advantage of every opportunity.
—Randy Glasbergen, Illustrator and Cartoonist

It's important to research what art directors want to see. It saves you work and lets you know where you should put the extra effort.
—Mary Thelen, Illustrator

You can do much better in the humorous greeting card market if you're able to write funny ideas as well as illustrate them. A good writer is harder to find than a good artist. If you're both, you'll be doubly valuable to any freelance editor, especially among smaller card companies that don't have a large writing staff (and actually, even the large card companies don't have "large" writing staffs). As a freelancer, if you can write and draw your cards, you'll get a double paycheck . . . one for the idea and one for the art. This could also lead to a whole line of your cards, especially if your work has a distinctive personality.
—Randy Glasbergen, Illustrator and Cartoonist

chapter 18

WORKING WITH ART AND DESIGN STUDIOS

Sell yourself.

—David Goodman, Design Consultant

What is the difference between an art studio and a design studio? An art studio generates just that—art, usually in the form of illustration. It's hardly written in stone, but designers generally aren't illustrators, and illustrators generally aren't designers.

If you're an illustrator, and you're not working on staff somewhere, you are more than likely a *freelance illustrator*. As far as I can tell, the days of the dedicated art studio (the pure illustration shop staffed only by illustrators) are behind us. Murphy's Law says that I'll be proved wrong just by writing those words, but I believe you'll find this to be a fairly accurate statement.

Design studios still flourish, however. A design studio, as we discussed in chapter 3, concentrates on visual communications that might utilize illustration and photography. The design studio conceptualizes a piece, designs it, then buys the art and photography elsewhere, if necessary.

WHAT A CONCEPT!

Many design studios like to see the way you "conceptualize." "Conceptualizing" is having the vision to see—and show—a sparkling diamond in chunks of raw coal. An interview can, and a portfolio review should, reveal how you nurture and develop inspiration.

Most likely, you'll be showing thumbnails or roughs. Maybe it will be the complete transition of a particular assignment, from the germ of an idea through the initial thumbnails, rough sketches, comprehensive layouts, and printed piece.

SKILLS NEEDED

In general, the freelance skills needed by a design studio are speed, intelligence, technical skill, and a unique perspective combined with a fresh approach. Design studios (and any art studios still out there) will demand solid layout capabilities, exceptional computer savvy, good marker rendering, plus, of course, excellent design and production skills. Drawing and painting prowess, a fine color sense, plus an advanced technical repertoire will also be your calling cards.

As an illustrator, your portfolio must boast finished, high-quality illustration skills. A range of styles and techniques will be welcomed, whatever your specialty—realism; cartoon, cute, or whimsical illustration; flat color graphics; hand lettering or digital type design; collage, photography, or three-dimensional work—whatever gets the job done.

WHAT'S SO SPECIAL?

Some design studios specialize in certain types of work, while other studios are known for their versatility. Whether they specialize or not may actually depend on their clients' needs and demands.

In an article for *Graphic Arts Monthly*, designer Marjorie Spiegelman states that, "Graphic designers work on various scales, from letterheads and business cards to enormous, architectural, three-dimensional graphics, and everything in between. We design marketing brochures, corporate identities, packaging—virtually anything that involves visual communication.

"Some designers specialize by product (annual reports), others by method (desktop publishing). Others are most remarkable for a certain style (Peter Max in the 1960s). Our design firm's specialty is neither a style nor particular product, but the way we solve problems."

SELL, SELL, SELL

How do you present yourself to a design studio? At the beginning of the chapter, I quoted design consultant David Goodman, who advises you to first sell *yourself*.

How to do this? The job begins with making the other person comfortable. Project a feeling of well-being, and the prospect will feel good about you. Next, observe closely and listen carefully. Talk less, listen more. When asked, "What do you do?" answer with a layered response: "I'm an illustrator. I've worked for clients like (so-and-so)." The key is to make meaningful contact. Remember: You are not selling anything at a first meeting; rather, you are attempting to make a good impression and generate interest.

At this point, illustrator Tom Graham says, "A good question to ask an art director is, 'What are you working on?' or 'Working on anything interesting?' Chances are, they'll love to talk about their latest project, maybe ask what you think. This takes the focus off you for a bit. My experience early on was, I was nervous and talked too much."

Now, according to Goodman, comes the moment of truth: the exchange of business cards (which, Goodman maintains, says more about you than the words printed on it). Why? The business card is perhaps the first—or last—visual impression you make. It is the lowest common denominator of design or illustration between two parties, easily carried (in a wallet or pocket), mounted (on a bulletin board) or stored (in a rolodex). It's a little bit of you—and your art—that can go a long way.

To sum up, it's not so much where you are on the ladder, but how you communicate where you want to be. As Goodman says, "Selling is a person-to-person activity."

LOCAL TALENT

Do design studios work primarily with local talent? For the most part, yes. Local talent will usually be preferred if freelance work is needed on a regular basis or to meet tight deadlines.

Aesthetically, I wouldn't limit myself to only regional design studios, and I wouldn't pigeonhole my business locally. Obviously, if you're just starting out, it makes more sense to work one-on-one with local studios, but certainly keep your eyes peeled beyond your city limits. Once you've established yourself, it will be easier to go national.

BEST INTRODUCTION

The best way to introduce yourself would be to think of your introduction as a one-two punch. First, grab their attention with an eye-catching mailer. These initial samples get you in the door. Now, show that fabulous portfolio, and display your effective communication skills.

What if you get a positive response to your brochure, but can't appear in person? Direct the interested party to your Web site and/or send a portfolio. This is easy for you and more convenient for a busy art director.

If you're mailing, prepare no more than twenty images (and enclose a SASE for a safe return). Include recent tear sheets, if you have them. A CD sampler can also be very effective. Be sure to follow the package with a phone call (or enclose a self-addressed, stamped reply card) confirming receipt of your work. Try to set up appointments to meet all those nice folks who simply adore your work.

Contacts may tell you that they don't require freelance help right now and don't know when they might. Don't be discouraged. Remember those three cardinal virtues: be polite, be persistent, be positive. Just say something like, "I do understand, but I would greatly appreciate the opportunity. If I could show you my work, you can keep me in mind should anything come up."

Emphasize that you'd truly enjoy meeting them, and ask for just a moment of their time. If you still strike out, wait for another inning; try again at a later date.

BREAKING (IN) AND ENTERING

What's the easiest way to break into this market? Designer Dan Johnson says, "This is not the right question, *because there is no easy way*. What is the *best* way? A lot of hard work. There's no substitute for knocking on doors, sending mailers, making telephone calls, and being very persistent (within reason). You have to be there when the work is there; you cannot create the work. There has to be a need, and you have to fill this need.

"There are always several people who can do that, beside yourself. So, you have to be in front of the contact's mind, or you have to be there at the right time. Now, factor in talent, speed, and competitive pricing; these are some of the best ways to break into this market."

STUDIO STYLE

How do you research the style preferred by a design studio? A good studio won't have one style or use only one kind of illustration. The type of illustration needed is based on the client's needs. However, you may be asked to generate imagery with a certain "look."

As illustrator Jay Montgomery advises, "If the company has one, go to its Web site to see the type of work presented. This will also give you a general idea of the projects the company has done in the past."

DIRECTORIES, ORGANIZATIONS, AND MAGAZINES

Looking for design studios? Ask the chamber of commerce or call the local Better Business Bureau. Try your regional business-to-business yellow pages. Check the members' directory of your town's ad club. Consult the membership directory of the American Institute of Graphic Arts (AIGA).

Organizations you can join to get to know more designers? How about the Graphic Artists Guild, the Society of Publication Designers. Look into the City and Regional Magazine Association (CRMA), the Society of Photographers and

Artist Representatives Inc. (SPAR), the Society of Typographic Arts (STA), and your local art directors club. You might also want to contact local universities.

Magazines focused on design? Read *Print, HOW, Step-by-Step Graphics, Communication Arts, Graphis, Advertising Age, AdWeek,* and *Graphic Design: USA.*

➡️

PROFESSIONAL ⬇ VIEWPOINTS

There's an old Herb Lubalin story: An art director brings his work home to show his mother. He says, "Look Ma, look what I did." The mother says, "Herbie, what did you do? Did you make the picture?" He says, "No, Ma, I didn't make the picture." She says, "Did you make the type?" He says, "No, Ma, I didn't make the type." She says, "Did you do the writing?" He says, "No, Ma, I didn't do the writing." She says, "Well, what did you do, Herbie?" That's what an art director is!

—Simms Taback, Art Director, Designer, and Illustrator

I've always felt that, as a freelance illustrator, I have a responsibility to the profession as a whole. I know that sounds kind of preachy, but I assure you, it's self-motivated as well. For many clients, I'm their first experience with an illustrator, and I represent the field at large, at least to them, at that moment in time. If I accept bad terms for a contract, or underbid, or treat the client poorly, I'm affecting everyone else's ability to succeed. And somewhere out there, there's someone else representing me. What goes around, comes around.

—Matt McElligott, Illustrator

© Simms Taback 1997

Be careful! The first time I ever worked for an agency out of Canada, I had a hard time negotiating a fee. We finally settled on a "dollar" amount that, while not great, was satisfactory to do the job. When I was all done and sent them the invoice, the art director informed he had been negotiating in Canadian dollars! What I got was about 60¢ on the dollar! I had no idea that Canadians even had dollars up there! I just hit myself over the head with a sturdy mallet and never made the same mistake again.

—Robert Zimmerman, Illustrator

chapter 19

SELLING TO SMALL BUSINESSES

Many people don't seem to realize that a good designer can, with the right information, design just about anything. It's your skill at defining a problem—and your ability to creatively solve it—that you're really selling, not just your ability to put together a book, brochure, or whatever.

–Vicki Vandeventer, Designer

Illustrators or designers just starting out may find the old axiom "less is more" an appropriate business metaphor. One might think established businesses would be the best bet, but that keyword *established* does not necessarily translate into more opportunities or creative freedom. Indeed, your fresh, bold ideas may find a very happy home with small businesses.

WHAT TYPE OF FREELANCE HELP DO SMALL BUSINESSES NEED?

Many folks consider working with small businesses to be bargain basement, low-budget, "clip art"-type grunt work. We can be more creative and industrious than that, can't we?

Design for a small business could be creating a logo for a business card or drawing the illustration for an upcoming newspaper ad. You may design and paint bold graphics for the office interior or use that logo for the shop's exterior sign. Perhaps while adapting both logo and ad illustration for a direct mailer, you'll be working up a new drawing for a postcard reminder at the same time.

How about interior signage? Pricing and sales change regularly, and the store owner's hand lettering just won't cut it. Besides, he loves your funny characters from the ad and wants you to incorporate them into the store displays!

A VARIETY OF SMALL BUSINESSES

Small businesses are not just the little hardware store down the block. All small businesses have visual needs, from simple stationery or business cards to advertising, promotion, display, and signage. Perhaps you've noticed a business that doesn't have a graphic profile—that might be a good place to start. Maybe it never crossed the proprietor's mind to use print vehicles to get his message across.

The wise small-businessperson knows that good graphics sell products. A storeowner may carefully watch expenditures, but is conscious of the fact that successful shops probably got that way through advertising.

With the business on a limited budget, the owner most likely has no art background and will certainly not have your design sense or technical expertise. Smart enough to know what's needed, but with no idea how to get it together, the small-businessperson turns to you for quality, affordable graphics.

A small shop owner's graphics may not justify employing an agency, but your hometown sensibilities are a big plus to land such accounts. As local talent, you're able to meet tight deadlines and will understand the needs of your buying community.

The same thing applies for neighborhood newsletters, town newspapers, and city or regional magazines. Often, these publications will only work with regional talent, because these artists are neighbors who understand the issues and current events that affect the local population.

The public television station, the university, a deli, even your dentist—any small or local business with print demands, and that's every business that advertises or generates correspondence—can use freelance help.

And don't forget the kind of community networking that can result from working in your "hometown." A shoe store employs you to do customer caricatures as a buyer's incentive. One happy customer, a restaurant manager, loves the gimmick and asks you to roam his bistro weekend evenings. A patron enjoys your work so much, she hires you to do a party and commissions a birthday portrait as well.

These small businesses are only your first stops. Good assignments are where you find them, and the path to a wealth of opportunities begins in your own backyard.

INTRODUCING YOURSELF

How do you find out if a local business needs freelance artwork? The best way is to simply introduce yourself by publicizing your services. Yes, marketing and self-promotion again! Your local campaign is important. You have the decided advantage and incentive of knowing the home turf, so take a direct and aggressive approach.

"Aggressive" does not mean obnoxious or overbearing; it means a keen and concerted effort. Mail your brochure, and follow with a phone call about a week later. You're literally in the neighborhood, so don't let the contact go cold. Ask for the store owner or manager.

Introduce yourself, make sure the brochure arrived, and tell this person you'll be making the rounds on a certain day, at a certain time. Ask if it would be okay to drop in and schmooze, perhaps show some samples, too.

You're obviously after an affirmative response, but even if there's no job and you get a positive reaction, go to talk and gather information. Bring your portfolio, but forget the big sales pitch. Lay the groundwork for your continued promotion. Chances are, when there is a need, they'll remember that person with the pleasant smile and beautiful art work. If they ask not to be bothered, believe them. These are busy people, so don't pester. Say, "Perhaps another time, if this is inconvenient?" or "May I keep you on my mailing list and call again for a future appointment?"

Chatting up the main avenue of the business district will probably take no more time than your usual stroll when shopping. It could be the most lucrative window shopping you ever do.

Who to contact at a small business? The store owner or manager is your best bet. A sales clerk, while receptive, won't have the authority to commission your work. However, as the sales staff have the ear of the storeowner, they could be allies to your cause. If the boss is presently unavailable, begin with the clerk, and make a date to return.

FINDING NEW BUSINESSES

How do you find out when a new business is about to open? New construction or reconstruction is an obvious tip off. Keep your eyes open, wade through the dust, and make inquiries. The chamber of commerce should be able to supply you with a list of new businesses in your area. Business trade publications in most markets publish corporate announcements; business magazines on a local level like to welcome new businesses to that market. New businesses about to open often issue press releases to the local media; watch for that. Check the newspaper for grand opening announcements or lists of incorporations.

SAMPLES

The small-businessperson is interested in how you can help the store, so your samples will have to generally relate to the business environment.

Illustrator Fred Carlson says, "I've found that, while some clients buy style and some markets buy subject matter, they're probably more subject-matter-oriented. Small businesses buy subject matter that relates to what they're doing. The visual should be easy to reproduce. You can't present an extremely complicated image with a lot of half-tone variations to a small-business owner; he's not going to spend the money to print those kinds of things.

"Small businesses have fairly simple print needs and relatively small budgets for print, so show artwork that fits in with lower budgets."

AWWW, GO ART DIRECT YOURSELF

Small businesses generally don't have an art director. This means that you may have to not only create the artwork, but also get it printed. Don't pass up an opportunity to work with a printer, because it just means more work (grumble, grumble). If you're worried about the finished product or merely want to further your graphics education, it's to your advantage to see the job through to the end. Why not factor added responsibilities into your bid and have a fun learning experience at the same time?

As Carlson says, "You may very well be asked, 'You can do the drawing, but can you do the production and design and get it printed?' This falls in your lap sometimes, because the buyer isn't that sophisticated about the division of labor in the graphic arts, so he might just assume that you, as an illustrator, would know all these other things. What you should say is, "Sure, I can do all those extra things—it will cost you, but I'm certainly willing to do it.'

"If you maintain this relationship with certain local clients, it keeps the checks coming. The more you specialize, the less chance of a relationship with a small business. They're going to have the most basic needs, and if you can service those basic needs, you're going to do all right."

And Art Direct Your Mama, Too

But I don't want to give the wrong impression. Knowing how to get a piece effectively printed is *not* merely a matter of putting in a little extra quality time at the printer's. As Matt McElligott says, "A knowledge of inks, separations, dot gain, line screens, film, etc. all contributes to getting a piece done right. A good graphic designer understands this and has probably put in years learning the ropes. For some illustrators, there may be a point where it makes sense to say, 'I'm an illustrator. I understand my limitations, and if you want the piece done right, let's call in a graphic designer to handle the print end. It might cost a little more, but the results will be worth it.' In the long run, this is certainly preferable to delivering a bad print job back to the client."

LOCALS PREFERRED

Are small businesses open to freelancers who don't live nearby? Realistically, you don't have to live down the block from the store to service a small-business account. However, if your distance from any theater of operation inhibits the job hunt or delays completion of an assignment, location can be a liability.

Maybe you know several local businesses that assign their work to design studios. Does this mean they wouldn't need any freelance illustration help? Not necessarily. A design studio will probably handle all aspects of a particular job, but this shouldn't discourage you from showing your work to a small-business owner, as the studio usually farms out the illustration end of the project. The owner may encourage the studio to use you. Find out about that same design studio, and show them your work or mail samples; it will certainly help your chances. If the studio doesn't have an exclusive arrangement with the store, you may want to approach the owner regarding other graphic needs around the establishment.

NAMING NAMES

There are sources other than the yellow pages for names of local businesses. The chamber of commerce and the Better Business Bureau are your best bets here—and join your local art directors club.

PRINTERS

Do printers need freelance help? Not really. By and large, if a small business goes to a printer to get the complete job done, the outcome is probably going to be very simple. Printers are not going to want to spend a lot of money on a creative solution, so they tend to price out low and zoom through the aesthetics. Chances are, they'll probably use somebody on staff.

But printers often practice self-promotion and frequently barter services with illustrators. You may be asked to illustrate a catchy promotion piece, trading your fee for free tear sheets and good publicity. Certainly, getting your work printed as a sample selection on a slick promo is good advertising for both you and the printer.

THE SMALL (BUSINESS) PRINT

Prior to accepting an assignment for a small business, please remember to do your homework and follow these caveats:

- ◘ Take good notes.
- ◘ Ask incisive questions.
- ◘ Know (and be ready to discuss) your rates.
- ◘ Evaluate how the client's needs compare to your own.
- ◘ Be up front and clear about terms.
- ◘ Don't be afraid to ask for what you really need to do the assignment; Don't be pressured into cutting the deal on the spot.
- ◘ Get written documentation at the beginning of a job (or do the paperwork from your end).
- ◘ If need be, minimize risk by asking for payments at various points of completion.
- ◘ Approach all negotiations with open eyes and mind.
- ◘ Remember that negotiation is a learning process.

◘

PROFESSIONAL ⬇ VIEWPOINTS

Displaying your work in small venues like a coffeehouse can get your name around the immediate area. Years ago, I approached the owner of a local coffee establishment (right around the corner from my studio, where I went every day for my latte) about the possibility of displaying my work, accompanied by a short bio and business cards. He went for it, customers loved it, and since I patronized the bar daily, I interacted with the regulars, got numerous inquiries, and widened my networks. I even sent out announcements about the show to prospects.

—Robert Saunders, Illustrator

Be prepared to do a lot of educating when dealing with small business owners!

—Marti McGinnis, Illustrator

Style has everything to do with this vision—the way you analyze what you see and the way you put that down on paper. For the beginning professional, every single job should be an enormous learning experience. Make this personal growth a career-long goal.

—Sam Viviano, Illustrator and Art Director

© Robert Saunders

© Robert Saunders

When working with small businesses, especially newsletters, one challenge is convincing them that your rates are fair and reasonable. Before they found your Web page, these clients were probably using public-domain clip art that came with their computer. How you convince them is an individual matter, depending on your style of work, the temperament of the client, and other pricing examples you can point to on the Internet.

—Randy Glasbergen, Illustrator

Working with small local businesses has been a real education for me, providing opportunities to sharpen both creative and business skills. But owners of small businesses are often naïve when it comes to advertising their goods and services. While they admit to their dependence on designers and illustrators to enhance their "look," they may not have a reasonable budget to work with, nor have any understanding of the creative process. It may take great patience to develop a relationship with such a client, but once convinced of your value to them, such clients will, in time, allow you great creative freedom and may end up being an important link in the network of your future.

—Ilene Winn-Lederer, Illustrator

Whatever you can do to get your foot in the door is a step in the right direction. I think it's best to build up experience at a local level. Work with people who are right near you. You can go back and forth; there's a give-and-take there.

—Roger DeMuth, Illustrator

237

chapter 20

MARKETING ON THE WEB

It is vital to get a Web site up of your work. Send out mailers to all
your clients telling them about it. But this is not enough. Buy into a
commercial Web site as well. It's not costly—about $600 a year for
twelve images. When clients go to this heavily-advertised site and
look up your work, they'll be automatically linked to your custom
page, giving you that much more exposure.

—Chris Spollen, Illustrator

The business is very different now. We should look to the future as being full of possibilities. As traditional uses for illustration disappear, the Internet and new technology will create new outlets for images.

—Joe Ciardiello, Illustrator

The twenty-first century is really here, and it *is* a brave new world out there. The rise of the Internet has created an unparalleled marketing and promotional opportunity for illustrators and designers. As illustrator and cartoonist Randy Glasbergen says, "The Internet has had a very positive impact on my career and revolutionized the way I do business. I've had my work published in America for more than twenty-five years, but the Internet has brought my work to a much larger, and more profitable global market, with many international clients.

"Before getting online in 1995, I did the traditional promo things, like postcard mailings and talent directories, with varying success. Soon after I put my work online, I started getting more inquiries in a week than I used to get in a whole year. I'm busier than I've ever been, and I haven't mailed out a promo card or taken out a directory ad in more than four years."

This writer feels that, at this juncture, it's *all* important. While I do see the handwriting on the wall (on the Web is probably a better metaphor), it's not prudent to advise you to scrap your print campaign or store your actual portfolio. But do read on, and begin to evaluate what will be your process and marketing program.

SURF'S UP!

So, what do you have to offer? What makes you *the* designer or illustrator to call? How do you get this across to your prospects? These are the basic marketing and promotion challenges you face working in any venue, and the answers determine the state of your business, regardless of where you market.

For better or worse, freelancing is a salesperson's job. That's neither a celebration nor an indictment, but merely a fact. You cannot freelance successfully with a casual or lazy attitude, and you must approach your Web endeavors with the same work ethic.

To understand what e-marketing entails, we must first do some intensive surfing. I'm not talking about getting your feet wet in the waters off Malibu (although, if you're in a position to do so, jump right in). But I am suggesting that you window shop with a vengeance.

Cruise the vast cornucopia of commercial, informational, entertainment, and individual sites. A simple Yahoo! or Google topic or "keyword" search will get you there. (For instance, if you're looking for freelance illustrators, type in "illustration.") Now, there's a bit of homework! Take notes, study, and review what these destinations offer (and what they don't).

Also, participate in or simply audit discussion forums related to design and illustration (and a variety of general chat rooms, bulletin boards, and newsgroups as well). The Graphic Artists Guild Web site (*www.gag.org*) and the ispot (*www.the-*

ispot.com) are the places to start. There, you'll get a good feel of who's out there doing what you do and the pertinent hot-button issues that may affect your marketing.

CONTACT SPORT

Make sure that all your resource info for your team (names, street addresses, phone numbers, and e-mail addresses) is readily available.

Obviously, know the name and access phone number of your ISP (Internet service provider). As Internet traffic gets heavy, store any alternate ISP access numbers, should you run into a busy signal. Know who hosts your site. Is it your ISP or another company posting your Web site on its server?

Don't go it alone—have a technical support company or individual in place. Stay in touch with the designer of your site. Maybe you even have a buddy who knows this stuff. Make sure the names and phone numbers of this support team are at your fingertips. Know your ISP's technical support number, and jot down the name of the tech who was particularly helpful getting you out of that jam last month.

Know how and where to contact your accountant, employees, or partners, during business hours and at home. And if you fill credit card orders, keep account numbers, billing, and contact information at hand.

TO (WEB) MARKET WE WILL GO

Marketing on the Web can bring in plenty of publishing and advertising clients, but it will also expose your work to many people who are buying art for the first time—people who haven't had access to this type of work in the past.

Randy Glasbergen points out that Web marketing is not the same as selling to print clients. "On the Web, now and again, you're likely to be working with people who are not publishing or advertising art directors. You're going to encounter independent entrepreneurs, small-businesspeople, corporate folks, etc.—people who like your work, have a need for art, but have little or no experience working with creative talent.

"That means you'll have to justify your $500 fee to somebody who's been using free clip art for years. It means you may do a project for a client who runs a trucking company and is all new to this sort of thing. These clients will have no idea what terms like CMYK or TIFF mean. It means you may need a little more patience with some clients, and they may need a little more handholding."

Illustrator and designer Peter Zale suggests that you should "build the site with some kind of personal touch. Even include some work in other media (your writing, for instance) or something to give the site some resonance, a certain aesthetic, or sense of drama."

"It's smart to change something every week or two," he adds, "whether it's samples or whatever. Sure, it's basically a portfolio, but try to entice prospective clients to come back. Fresh content is always good on the Web."

"Another nice idea," says Zale, "is to use your site simultaneously for some sort of community good, whatever that may be. I think sites that promote and establish a complete global or civic identity stand out for their own sake, and it gives the visitor a warmer experience. It's important to try to make the site an experience beyond the work itself."

THE NAME GAME AND BEYOND

This section is not legal advice. You'll need to author your own definitive legal guide to Web design, so do thorough research and seek all necessary counsel beforehand. However, let's share some information.

First, make sure your company name, logo, and site design are uniquely yours (and if this means carrying out a trademark and copyright search, do so). Writing in the Graphic Artists *Guild News*, lawyer Andrew Berger advises you to exercise caution and care when designing for the Web. Berger states, "If you choose the wrong domain name, post material that infringes another's trademark, or link to pirated material," you may be headed for litigation.

Your domain name must be catchy, unique, and noninfringing. This will be difficult at best, but crucial. Work up a list of possible names, and then check your list of options with a domain name registrar. Do a search to see what's registered (or warehoused), available, or similar. Berger says to keep the following guidelines in mind:

- Don't choose a domain name that is the same or confusingly similar to a famous or distinctive trademark.
- If your domain name is also your name, you may be able to use it, even though it is the same as another's famous mark. However, there may be some legal conditions attached.

Don't risk copyright infringement. Get authorization for any copyrighted resource that is not in the public domain or justified as "fair use." Do your complete homework here, as these designations are not cut and dry.

Likewise, place your copyright notice(s) prominently on your site (and actually register your work). And hey—it wouldn't be overkill to place that copyright notice on every page and/or with every piece of art.

Do you need permission to link to a site? If so, get it.

Who owns your Web design? Berger says you do, unless such design is classified "work-for-hire." As we've mentioned before, "work-for-hire" occurs when you create a design as (1) an employee in the course of your employment, or (2) as a freelancer transferring copyright through a signed contract specifying the design as a work-for-hire.

THE PLAN (DREAMS, GOALS, AND BUSINESS PLANS)

Remember the business plan we discussed in chapter 4? No surprise here, it certainly applies to your Web marketing system. What are your goals? How do you intend to accomplish all this and fulfill the necessary tasks? What's your timetable, and what are your strategies for the future?

Good questions still, and just as crucial for any success on the Web. The business plan—don't leave (your) homepage without it.

WORLD WIDE PORTFOLIO: THE MONLUX HIERARCHY

Having a Web site is as necessary in today's market as a portfolio. And just like your physical portfolio, your "virtual book" requires as much care and thought. "A poorly-structured Web site will reflect just as badly on you as a poorly-arranged portfolio," says Seattle illustrator Mark Monlux. He tells us that several of the same rules apply and offers five caveats that take an Internet twist.

Know your target audience

A basic marketing truism, but the Internet gives it a different spin. Is your target audience Mac- or PC-based? "It's important to know that font size will vary between platforms," states Monlux. "Does your target audience prefer the Netscape browser to Internet Explorer? Different formatting software will have features that will be available on one or the other. Constructing a uniform Web site to cover all your bases is nearly impossible. So, do your research ahead of time."

Be cutting-edge

"You might hesitate to create the most cutting-edge Web site using the latest technology, because you fear your target audience's browsers are not up to the task," Monlux says. "Place that argument aside. By the time you devise an inter-active format, create templates, prep the art, then finally compose and post your site, the technology you used in your original plans will be rapidly going out of date—best to strike while that new-fangled digital iron is hot."

Understand that Web sites are organic

Be prepared to constantly upgrade your Web site. Based on practical experi-ence, Monlux says that a fresh look every year will keep your site from stagnating. You want your target audience to say, "I recognize his style." You don't want them thinking, "It's all the same old stuff." A Web site should be full of life—and all living things change and grow. Rapidly-developing technology dictates that your showcase must be just as fluid.

Hire professional help

You will be inclined to tackle a Web site on your own, and yes, it is a chal-lenge similar to those you face every day. But, unless you are actively construct-ing Web sites on a daily basis, Monlux advises you to hire out. "Let a pro work with you to produce the best effect available," he says. "Hey, portfolio consultants are hired all the time. This is the same, just on the techie side of things. If you are one of those professionals who consider themselves a Renaissance man (due to budget constraints if nothing else), at least consider working with a tech to soften the high learning curve. Even a simple tip—such as how to embed text into your code to help browsers locate your site more easily—can be acquired by a simple consultation."

Use other sites to increase your exposure

Take advantage of the multitude of Web sites that allow you to post portfolios on them for free or for pay. According to Monlux, "There are tons of these sites, and they will increase your exposure on the Internet. Most of these sites have a preformatted structure, so that each artist is represented equally. Once there, you should still have your own primary Web site to which you can direct traffic."

WHO'S MINDING THE STORE?

Marketing on the Web means you are establishing a "cybershop." You set up a Web site and find someone to maintain (in other words, "host") it 24/7 on a computer system called a "Web server."

Your electronic "storefront" exists in the same virtual space as your physical studio, and just like a brick-and-mortar shop, this store could sell products (T-shirts, mugs, mouse pads, etc.) with your designs. (Note: There are also many services that will set up a store for you and pay you a percentage on sales.) Or your site offers services, education, or information. Your site may act as your portfolio or be your personal art gallery. Perhaps it is simply your creative steam valve or the wellspring of your art theory.

Greg Holden, author of *Starting an Online Business for Dummies*, tells us that two of the most important factors determining a Web site's success are where it's hosted and how it's designed. Says Holden, " A Web hosting service is the online world's equivalent of a landlord. You need to find a hosting service that will make your online business available to your prospective customers."

Potential clients can get to your site in any number of ways. Include your URL on your business cards, letterhead, brochures, invoices, etc. Prospects may find you through search engines, such as Yahoo!, Lycos, or Alta Vista. You may be listed on commercial or not-for-profit links pages. Maybe you do print advertising. You can advertise in (or offer your own) electronic magazines (e-zines). You could take out a classified ad in an online publication or advertise on another site. You can utilize a traditional or electronic mail list (although unsolicited e-mail is generally frowned upon). Perhaps a personal or corporate recommendation on a related Web site sends a client your way. You might be the beneficiary of a rave editorial review. You may benefit from good word of mouth—somebody somewhere simply says to "check this out." You can sell your work or products through an online auction house (such as eBay).

Illustrator Jay Montgomery tells us, "Many illustrators create their first Web site as just another portfolio for art directors, thinking that they will not get work [directly] from it. I have actually received assignments off my Web site from people finding me through search engines and listings with free directories."

But take care. "Obviously, the illustrator needs to be extra vigilant here," Montgomery adds. "I mainly get jobs from other young 'Web savvy' individuals or companies. And it's just like any call from a sourcebook—take all the precautions you would with a new client."

Last but not least, if you are selling directly off the site, what's your accounting method? As mentioned previously, this will either be cash-basis or accrual-basis. Determine how you record sales/income, and keep *good* records. Note amount received, form of payment, monies owed on account, date, name, address, phone numbers, e-mail addresses, and goods sold and/or services provided. Do you need to charge sales tax in your customer's state?

WEB SIGHTS

What should be included on a Web site? Here's a nuts-and-bolts list of basic ingredients:

- ➡ Company name and logo (duh!)
- ➡ Contact information and ways to get feedback: maybe a response form or guest book, definitely an e-mail link
- ➡ Philosophy or mission statement, plus information about you; perhaps a FAQ (frequently asked questions) page
- ➡ Consistent and understandable titles for all pages on your site and links to get to those pages
- ➡ Sample works or portfolio
- ➡ Existing clients/shows/galleries
- ➡ Any reviews of and/or articles about your work; include client endorsements and testimonials
- ➡ Copyright notice, legal disclaimers and notices, other legal information, and privacy statements
- ➡ If you are selling directly off the Web site, an order form, and customer service, payment, and shipping info
- ➡ META tags, which are embedded HTML instructions that enable search engines (like Excite) to track, catalog, and display information about your site
- ➡ A links page to other related sites (somewhat optional)

IT'S A SMALL WORLD AFTER ALL

Something to consider: It is called the "worldwide" Web, so you may want to bone up on *global* marketing. If you are selling off your site, your homework for tonight is to investigate how to get paid from an overseas client or customer. What is the proper procedure to do a wire transfer? How do you handle an international credit card purchase?

You'll want to look into working with online payment services like PayPal (for domestic and international sales). Know exchange rates and conversions, and understand the value of a dollar to your foreign client. You may need to field the issue of sending hardcopy art overseas, and you might have to tap into online translation services for foreign-language e-mail.

ONWARD (THE END NOTES)

We've reached the end of the chapter (and our book), but once you turn this page and close the cover, you're just beginning the exciting journey down your freelance path. I know this sounds vaguely like we're on the road to Oz, but that's essentially what the book has been about—there's no place like home (and business).

And the business of illustration and design is indeed changing. This chapter alone is proof of that—the Web (let alone the explosive potential of marketing over the Internet) was only science fiction when I wrote the earlier version of *Starting Your Career as a Freelance Illustrator or Designer*. I hope this book has helped to make sense of the adjustments and to dope out what's ahead. But more importantly, *you* will be an agent of change, and certainly the catalyst for your personal, creative, and professional growth. As illustrator Robin Jareaux tells you, "Take your deadlines seriously, but be lighthearted about everything else. It's a privilege to be an illustrator or a designer. You'll find freedom, variety, and constant opportunity to learn. Every manuscript you read, every concept you develop, makes you mentally richer. Every contract you negotiate makes you wiser. You are bringing color and light to the world, so work hard—but enjoy the adventure."

Good advice. Let me leave you with these last thoughts: Be proactive, make learning your lifelong practice, show up, and join in. Do this, and I expect great things for you and your career. Let me know how it's going—I'm hooked.

PROFESSIONAL ⬇ VIEWPOINTS

Most likely, you are selling yourself to Web and print designers. Your site has to appeal to the most design-conscience clients: designers. If your site does not function properly, has missing links, is hard to navigate, or looks like an illustrator created it, they're just a click away from going to your competitor's site.

—Jay Montgomery, Illustrator

I looked on the Internet to find opera and theater companies to send my work to and found comprehensive listings of companies nationwide, with links to individual sites and even specific artistic and publicity directors with their e-mail addresses.

—Robert Saunders, Illustrator

When I was doing straight freelancing, the Web was in its infancy. One thing I did was to perceive a niche and try to fill it. This sounds intuitively obvious, but it's not as easy to do. I perfected my

approach to become Peter Zale Para-dezign. Like a paralegal, I stepped in and assisted designers in finishing projects, whether it required design, illustration, or production.

—Peter Zale, Illustrator

Don't think you have to design and create your Web site all by yourself. If you are an illustrator, and not necessarily a Web designer, get help from a colleague or friend that does Web design full time. If you have the money, go to a design firm, and pay to get it professionally done.

—Jay Montgomery, Illustrator

My Web site is the best self-promotion I've ever done. My content changes daily, so visitors come back again and again for a fresh look. I've gotten more assignment work from my Web site than I ever got doing mailings or using the sourcebooks. My Web page has brought me jobs from huge companies like Hewlett-Packard and

Johnson and Johnson, as well as good-paying jobs from small businesses, such as a Hebrew translation service and a pizza restaurant in Greece.

—Randy Glasbergen, Illustrator and Cartoonist

This is a very uncertain time in the illustration field, and my advice to anyone entering the field is: Develop computer skills, even if you work traditionally. Think more entrepreneurial. Find outlets for self-generated projects. Consider self-publishing. Learn about design and the use of type. Learn how to create animation. And last, but certainly not least, **KEEP DRAWING.** —Joe Ciardiello, Illustrator

RESOURCES

I list only a sprinkling of Web site addresses in the actual text. I'd rather make it a one-stop shop for you; so let me point (and click) you to the Atlanta chapter of the Graphic Artists Guild—*www.atlanta.gag.org*. Here, you will find an extensive and comprehensive list of links that will keep you surfing way, way past your bedtime.

The following is just a small list of books you may find helpful on your way up the freelance ladder. There are always more; but these offer a good starting point.

- ➡ *Graphic Artists Guild Pricing and Ethical Guidelines, 10th edition or current*, by Graphic Artists Guild et al. (Cincinnati: North Light Books, 2001). The bible for arty types.
- ➡ *Artist's and Graphic Designer's Market*, by Mary Cox (Cincinnati: Writer's Digest Books, 2001). Your mailing list starts right here.
- ➡ *Business and Legal Forms for Graphic Designers*, by Tad Crawford and Eva Doman Bruck (New York: Allworth Press, 2000) and *Business and Legal Forms for Illustrators*, by Tad Crawford (New York: Allworth Press, 2000). The job's not over 'til the paperwork is done.
- ➡ *Creative Jolt*, by Robin Landa, Rose Gonnella, and Denise M. Anderson (Cincinnati: North Light Books, 2000). Nicely done—jumpstart yer art 101.
- ➡ *The Education of an Illustrator*, by Steven Heller and Marshall Arisman (New York: Allworth Press, 2000) and *The Education of a Graphic Designer*, by Steven Heller (New York: Allworth Press, 1998). Interesting, pertinent stuff, particularly the syllabi samplers.
- ➡ Just about anything in the *Visual Quickstart* Guides, *WOW!* Series, and *Real World* series of computer-related texts (Berkeley: Peachpit Press, annual series). For digital designers and illustrators of all shapes and sizes.
- ➡ Two of the most useful magazines in your library will be *Step-By-Step Digital Design*—formerly *Step-by-Step Electronic Design*—and *Step-by-Step Graphics* (both Peoria: Step-by-Step Publishing, monthly series).
- ➡ *Putting Your Small Business on the Web*, by Maria Langer (Berkeley: Peachpit Press, 2000)
- ➡ *Self-Promotion Online*, by Ilse Benun (Cincinnati: F & W Publications, Inc., 2000)
- ➡ *Starting an Online Business for Dummies*, by Greg Holden (Foster City: IDG Books Worldwide, Inc., 2000). Gotta Web site, gotta read 'em.

INDEX

Books from Allworth Press

Careers by Design *by Roz Goldfarb* (paperback, 6 × 9, 256 pages, $19.95)

Business and Legal Forms for Graphic Designers, Revised Edition with CD-ROM *by Tad Crawford and Eva Doman Bruck* (paperback, 8½ × 11, 240 pages, $24.95)

Digital Design Practices, Third Edition *by Liane Sebastian* (paperback, 6¾ × 9⅞, 416 pages, $29.95)

The Graphic Designer's Guide to Pricing, Estimating and Budgeting, Revised Edition *by Theo Stephen Williams* (paperback, 6⅞ × 9⅞, 208 pages, $19.95)

AIGA Professional Practices in Graphic Design *edited by Tad Crawford* (paperback, 6⅞ × 9⅞, 320 pages, $24.95)

Selling Graphic Design, Second Edition *by Don Sparkman* (paperback, 6 × 9, 256 pages, $19.95)

Licensing Art and Design, Revised Edition *by Caryn R. Leland* (paperback, 6 × 9, 128 pages, $16.95)

The Education of an e-Designer *edited by Steven Heller* (paperback, 6¾ × 9⅞, 352 pages, $21.95)

Legal Guide for the Visual Artist, Fourth Edition *by Tad Crawford* (paperback, 8½ × 11, 272 pages, $19.95)

The Business of Being an Artist, Third Edition *by Daniel Grant* (paperback, 6 × 9, 352 pages, $19.95)

Graphic Design History *edited by Steven Heller and Georgette Balance* (paperback, 6 × 9, 352 pages, $21.95)

Education of an Illustrator *edited by Steven Heller and Marshall Arisman* (paperback, 6¾ × 9¾, 288 pages, $19.95)

Education of a Graphic Designer *edited by Steven Heller* (paperback, 6¾ × 9¾, 288 pages, $18.95)

The Advertising Law Guide *by Lee Wilson* (paperback, 6 × 9, 272 pages, $19.95)

Please write to request our free catalog. To order by credit card, call 1-800-491-2808 or send a check or money order to Allworth Press, 10 East 23rd Street, Suite 510, New York, NY 10010. Include $5 for shipping and handling for the first book ordered and $1 for each additional book. Ten dollars plus $1 for each additional book if ordering from Canada. New York State residents must add sales tax.

To see our complete catalog on the World Wide Web, or to order online, you can find us at *www.allworth.com*.